Anthropology of the Old Testament

HANS WALTER WOLFF

Anthropology of the
Old Testament

FORTRESS PRESS
PHILADELPHIA

Translated by Margaret Kohl from the German *Anthropologie des Alten Testaments,* Christian Kaiser Verlag, Munich, 1973

First paperback edition 1981

Library of Congress Cataloging in Publication Data

The Library of Congress Cataloged the First Printing of this title as Follows:

Wolff, Hans Walter.
    Anthropology of the Old Testament / Hans Walter
Wolff ; [translated by Margaret Kohl from the German].—
Philadelphia : Fortress Press, c1974.

    Rev. translation of Anthropologie des Alten Testaments.
    Bibliography: p.
    Includes indexes.
    ISBN 0-8006-0298-6 :
    ISBN 0-8006-1500-X (pbk.) :
    1. Man (Theology)—Biblical teaching. 2. Bible. O.T.—Criticism,
interpretation, etc.   I. Title.
BS1199.M2W6413   1974   233   74-21591
                                                                                    MARC

9114B81   Printed in the United States of America   1-1500

CONTENTS

PREFACE

This book has grown up in the last decade – and what a stirring up men have undergone during that time!

The work began in Mainz, with a seminar on the basic anthropological concepts, to which Werner H. Schmidt made an important contribution. A lecture delivered in Heidelberg during the summer semester of 1971 led to the present outline, Gerhard von Rad – then in the last semester of his life – encouraging me to publish a work of this kind. The reader owes far more to my conversations with that unforgettable teacher than the bibliographical references can give any idea of. Lectures in South and North America in the spring of 1972, as well as various series delivered in Germany, elicited discussions which have enriched the account.

My main concern is determined by the question of how in the Old Testament man is initiated into knowledge of himself. I have tried to present the characteristic texts, and not to ignore any statements that are in any way significant. My purpose was to produce a reader that would make the biblical documents accessible to everyone concerned with anthropological problems, even those without previous specialist knowledge. In addition, I hope the working over of the considerable specialist literature may further theological research into its basic as well as its detailed problems. Old Testament ideas have not infrequently been traced down to the New Testament; but this is at most a preparation for a comprehensive biblical anthropology; these indications are really only the expressions of a wish for New Testament expansion and correction. Even the investigation of the Old Testament alone, however, can expand the questions raised by a systematic anthropology and can stimulate and deepen its insights. It is part of the unique character of most of the biblical testimony that it speaks to its readers directly. I hope that my account will bring out, and not obscure, these impulses towards man's self-knowledge.

Everything that is essential in this anthropology, everything that brings new clarity or that points us a step forward, comes from the Bible itself and the one to whom it witnesses. It is my hope, therefore, that the work may awake anew for many people the joy of discovery in the book of books itself. For I know that this study exhausts only the merest fraction of the wealth of what the Bible has to tell us about man.

Heidelberg, Epiphany 1973   HANS WALTER WOLFF

TRANSLATOR'S NOTE

The biblical quotations have been taken from the Revised Standard Version; but its wording has been modified where this was necessary for a correct rendering of the author's text.

I

Introduction

1. *Questions*

Will every generation set out anew to seek for and discover man? The task can doubtless be crowded out for a long time, because the world around us seems to demand all our energies as an object of research; and man's questionings about himself may in the process be appeased by enquiries into his past and his future. Must man first of all fall sick before he discovers himself to be the object of essential investigation? Must a human society first perceive the extremity of its danger before noting that no field has been subject to so little research as contemporary man?

Why does the progress of science and technology not only penetrate into new light but also into new darkness? Why is the misuse of scientific and scholarly knowledge and methods assuming threatening form, not only in the practice of the natural sciences but even in the so-called humanities? Why is research designed for the use of man – in medicine, chemistry, pharmacology, sociology, psychology and theology – suddenly by-passing man altogether? The pressure of problems, the opportunities for gain, specialized questions, total planning, statistics, tradition – all these things distort the eye for man in our time. And all of a sudden, in the middle of the mass consumption of requisites and remedies, Utopias and psychoanalyses, an elemental hunger breaks out for the anthropology that has been so long neglected. Who is man? Where can we find him in the thicket of clever plans and misguided impulses, on the way from youthful ardour to frigid old age, between the lust for aggression and the suffering of the oppressed? What does he know about his condition, his time and his place in the world? In all the abundance of his knowledge, has man's most fundamental being become for him in the end the most alien of all?

The question of how the problem of a reliable doctrine of man can be surmounted at all in the scholarly sense is an imperative one. For here the scholar is faced with that extreme borderline case in which the impossibility of objectification presents an insoluble problem. Just as it is impossible for a man to confront himself and to see himself from all sides or for a person who is still developing to know of himself whose child he is, just so certainly does man fundamentally need the meeting with another, who investigates and explains him. But where is the other to whom the being man could put the question: who am I?

2. *Preliminaries*

During and after National Socialism's evil misinterpretation of man, certain scholars have rediscovered this other person in their dialogue with the Bible. Karl Barth[1] pointed with unprecedented thoroughness and conviction to the place where man could know himself to be truly understood and could discover his real humanity. The Old Testament writings as pioneers of the way and the New Testament as the testimony of witnesses lead to the encounter with the God who is 'completely defined in Jesus'.[2] The younger generation is beginning to draw the conclusions from Barth's perceptions, in which the alternative between theism and atheism, between metaphysics and nihilism, in which man was left to himself, has already been overcome. There God was asserted or denied as the 'Up-there where man doesn't exist',[3] but the biblical witnesses know nothing of any 'divine inhumanity'. Even in the Old Testament Yahweh already shows his godhead through his bond with man in word and deed. In this way the Other enters human history, the Other who enquires anew of every fresh generation: 'Man, where are you?'[4] and before whom every fresh generation can ask yet again 'What is man'?[5] 'Who am I?'[6]

In 1948 Karl Barth complained in his biblical reflections on anthropology:

> The time does not yet seem to have arrived when the dogmatician can accept with a good conscience and confidence the findings of his colleagues in Old and New Testament studies.[7]

Learned disquisitions on biblical anthropology had certainly been in existence for long enough.[8] Did these in Barth's view overwhelm the questions of the biblical witnesses too much with their own questions or even with their own theses? The early postwar years brought at first small, outwardly quite modest exegetical studies.[9] Their authors were thinking of the contemporaries for whom man had been turned into a riddle by an inhuman distortion. In the search for a criterion they took their stand on the claims to binding force made by the biblical statements (and especially the basic Old Testament ones), though they did not fail to recognize their historical character.[10] More extensive investigations soon followed. They pursued the unique features of Old Testament thinking about man,[11] enquired into the nature of man in the light of basic anthropological concepts,[12] or tried to discern the physical and spiritual image of the Hebrew and the course of his life.[13] In the wake of generally increasing specialization, a number of extensive monographs followed, dealing with particular anthropological problems; concepts like soul, spirit or flesh, and themes like death, the experience of desolation, or the position of man and woman were treated in detail.[14]

The prerequisites for a new, more comprehensive biblical anthropology seem to be met. Moreover there is a demand for one. For already the schemes of systematic theology for an anthropology must face the problems of current philosophical anthropology, as well as those of psychology, sociology and political science,[15] without having our present exegetical recognitions available as a connected whole.

3. *Methods*

How can this be achieved today? The Old Testament is not based on a unified doctrine of man, nor are we in a position to trace a development in the biblical image of man. The fact that every individual document presupposes a particular view of man could be a challenge to a systematic of biblical anthropology. On the other hand there is an urgent wish to put to the texts a selection of current questions or even 'all the possibilities'.[16] In both cases we should neither meet the requirements of a historical interpretation of the ancient texts nor do justice to the force of our present problems. Biblical anthropology as a scholarly task will seek its point of departure where there is a recognizable question about man within the texts themselves. The whole breadth of the context must be drawn upon in order to work out the specific answers. It will become evident that the essential contributions bear the character of dialogue and that the consensus in their testimony about man is, in spite of all mutations in its linguistic form, astonishing from the point of view of the history of thought. In his dialogue with God above all, man sees himself as called in question, searched out and thus not so much established for what he is as called to new things. Man as he is is anything but the measure of all things.

This already brings us to a basic point which has to be considered from a methodological point of view: here anthropological problems cannot be solved by screening off theology, but only in complete openness to the divine witness of the Bible. Indeed, in correction of the fashionable anthropologization of theology, the scholar will have to be alive to the possibility of a theological understanding of anthropological phenomena.[17] He discovers the chance of entering into dialogue with the other, a dialogue through which he begins to understand his being as man.

4. *Plan*

Both in general and in particular, it is only the investigation of the texts that will clarify the function of a biblical anthropology. The more we succeed in discovering the questions, insights and expectations of the authors of the Old Testament writings, the more they will be able to withstand the contemporary dangers of too narrowly formulated questions or the missing of concrete problems; and the more they will help to pin-point what belongs essentially to the nature of man.

We shall hope in three major sections to include all the important answers to the questions that arise among the biblical witnesses themselves about the nature of man, his life and his destiny in the world around him. In the first place the statements about man's creation will stimulate us to investigate the basic anthropological concepts of the Old Testament; they clarify the various aspects and dominating features of human existence. The wisdom literature and the psalms of lamentation and thanksgiving are actuated by the question about the life of man in all its important phases between birth and death. The question about man's real destiny in his world lies behind many of the legal texts and prophetic sayings.

In following this path of investigation we shall take care not to be guided by questions which are alien to the Old Testament itself. It is only in this way that our understanding of the New Testament aspects of anthropology can also be furthered and that the starting point and the execution of present-day anthropological schemes can be subjected to a critical investigation.

PART ONE

THE BEING OF MAN
An anthropological language primer

Preliminary Remarks

What we shall be investigating here are the Hebrew names for man's organs, his limbs, and his appearance as a whole. We shall be starting from the various individual concepts. In this way we shall arrive at a language primer for the anthropology of the Bible.

When the most frequent substantives are as a general rule translated by 'heart', 'soul', 'flesh', and 'spirit', misunderstandings arise which have important consequences. These translations go back to the Septuagint, the ancient Greek translation, and they lead in the false direction of a dichotomic or trichotomic anthropology, in which body, soul and spirit are in opposition to one another.[1] The question still has to be investigated of how, with the Greek language, a Greek philosophy has here supplanted Semitic biblical views, overwhelming them with foreign influence.[2] Old Testament linguistic usage must be clarified at this point.

This task demands insight into the premises of the Semitic imagination and mind. Two of these presuppositions have fundamental significance and may therefore precede the discussion of all more specialized points.

1. Concepts like heart, soul, flesh and spirit (but also ear and mouth, hand and arm) are not infrequently interchangeable in Hebrew poetry. In poetic parallelism, they can be used by turns for the whole man, almost like pronouns (Ps. 84.2):

> My soul longs, yea, faints
>   for the courts of Yahweh,
> my heart and flesh
>   sing for joy to the living God.

The variants indicate different aspects of the same subject in a way that is sometimes hardly recognizable. Thus a man's organs or members can also be replaced completely smoothly by pronouns (Prov. 2.10f.):

> Wisdom will come into your heart,
>   and knowledge will be the delight of your soul;
> discretion will watch over you;
>   understanding will guard you.

In Psalm 6.2–4 I – my bones – my soul – I stand parallel to one another. This has been well characterized as the '*stereometry* of expression'.[3]

> The teachers believe that there is no better way of presenting their subject-matter . . . , not by the use of terms which are clearly differentiated one from the other, but by the opposite means, namely by the juxtaposition of words related in meaning.[4]

This stereometric thinking pegs out the sphere of man's existence by enumerating his characteristic organs, thus circumscribing man as a whole (Prov. 18.15):

> An understanding heart acquires knowledge
> and the ear of the wise seeks knowledge.

Different parts of the body enclose with their essential functions the man who is meant.

2. Stereometric thinking thus simultaneously presupposes a synopsis of the members and organs of the human body with their capacities and functions. It is *synthetic* thinking,[5] which by naming the part of the body means its function. When the prophet cries (Isa. 52.7):

> How beautiful upon the mountains
> are the feet of him who brings good tidings,

it is not the graceful form of the feet that he means, but their swift movement: 'How beautiful it is that the messenger is hurrying over the mountains!' Feet, says the Hebrew, but he is thinking of the approach by leaps and bounds. In Judg. 7.2 Israel's dreaded self-praise is expressed in the sentence: 'My own hand has helped me.' What is meant of course is Israel's own efforts – its own strength. The member and its efficacious action are synthesized. With a relatively small vocabulary, through which he names things and particularly the parts of the human body, the Hebrew can and must express a multiplicity of fine nuances by extracting from the context of the sentence the possibilities, activities, qualities or experiences of what is named.[6]

It is in this way that our language primer of biblical anthropology will have to light up the richness of meaning of the words describing man. Synthetic and stereometric thinking must be carried over into our analytical and differentiating language. We shall see that the stereotyped translation of a Hebrew term by the same word inevitably leads the understanding astray in most cases; it misses all too often the real statement that is being made about man. The opening up of the wide semantic range of the main anthropological concepts is calculated, on the other hand, to open up a first means of access to the biblical picture of man; for with the essential organs there emerge at the same time man's typical capabilities and characteristics – and thus the typical aspects of what it means to be a human being. What is meant by that in this first section is '*hominitas* as the *sine qua non* for humanities';[7] that is to say 'the nature of man' as the essential premise for man's 'humanity'.[8]

II

nepeš – Needy Man[1]

The traditional English Bible generally translates *nepeš*, one of the basic words of Old Testament anthropology, as 'soul'. In so doing it goes back, like the French *âme* and the German *Seele*, to the Greek Bible's most frequent translation of *nepeš*, *psyche*, and to the Latin Bible's rendering, *anima*. *nepeš* occurs 755 times in the Old Testament and on 600 occasions the Septuagint translates it by *psyche*.[2] This statistical difference shows that even the ancient writers noticed that the word bore another meaning in not a few places. Today we are coming to the conclusion that it is only in a very few passages that the translation 'soul' corresponds to the meaning of *nepeš*.

Notwithstanding, an almost definitory use of the Hebrew word to signify human existence cannot be from the outset denied. The Yahwist's account of the creation uses it in this way (Gen. 2.7):

> Yahweh God formed man of dust from the ground, and breathed into his nostrils the breath of life; and man became a living *nepeš*.

What does *nepeš* (which we shall from now on be referring to as *n.*) mean here? Certainly not soul. *n.* is designed to be seen together with the whole form of man, and especially with his breath; moreover man does not *have n.*, he *is n.*, he lives as *n.* Which aspect of human existence is being viewed in this way? For the moment the text we are using for our definition can only invite us to pace out the whole human area that *n.* encompasses.

Access to the fullness of meaning lent by the synthetic way of thinking[3] may be opened up for our analytical understanding when we ask: what part of the human body can be identified with the being and behaviour designated as *n.*? Methodologically we shall have to ask, in looking at the text, whether the context really allows us to deduce from it a particular physical organ. We shall then have to go on to enquire where the argument picks out particular functions and characteristics of that part of the body, and how the word finally brings out, more or less clearly, a particular aspect of human existence in general. We must always bear in mind that this is an outline of our method of arriving at an understanding, and is certainly not the pattern of a historical semasiology. The history of meaning can only bring out particular changes for a limited linguistic phase.[4] In general stereometric-synthetic thinking sees a part of the body together with its particular activities and capacities, and these in their turn are conceived as being the distinguishing marks of the whole man. We must therefore always remember that the Hebrew uses one and the same word where we need widely differing ones. In each case the textual context of the instance decides.

1. *Throat*

We shall start from the image in Isa. 5.14:

> The underworld wrenches wide its *nepeš*,
> and opens its mouth beyond measure.

The synonymous parallel talks about the mouth. As far as the *n.* itself is concerned, we are told that it is wide open. This is a clear indication that *n.* here means the gullet, the jaws, or the throat. In the same way Hab. 2.5 can say about the rapacious man:

> He opens his *nepeš* wide as the underworld
> and is like death and has never enough.

According to this, *n.* is a term for the *organ that takes in food* and satisfies hunger. The great thanksgiving liturgy in Ps. 107 talks in its first strophe about

> the hungry and thirsty
> whose *nepeš* fainted within them (v. 5),

and who ought to thank Yahweh (v. 9),

> For he satisfies the thirsty *nepeš*
> and the hungry *nepeš* he fills with good things.

The context of *n.* mentions its hunger and thirst, its fainting and its being satisfied, its dryness and its being filled, thus showing unequivocally that what is being talked about is not the 'soul' but the 'throat'.

> All the toil of man is for his mouth,
> yet his *nepeš* is not satisfied,

says Ecclesiastes 6.7. 'Mouth' in the parallel and the statement about the being satisfied (cf. Ps. 107.9) remind us again of the 'throat', though here as of a perpetually needy organ which cannot be satisfied by human effort. The preacher therefore teaches (Eccles. 6.9):

> Better is the sight of the eyes
> than the wandering of the *nepeš*,

where what is meant is the insatiable desire of the throat. When, therefore, together with the organ, its specific characteristic is thought of, that characteristic seems to be in the first place primarily the greedy need. Ps. 143.6 compares the *n.* with the parched land. Isa. 29.8 talks about a hungry and thirsty man who dreams that he is eating and drinking, but when he awakes his *n.* is empty and dry; cf. Isa. 32.6bβ. In his *n.* man realizes that he cannot live of himself (Prov. 10.3):

> Yahweh does not let the righteous *n.* go hungry,
> but he repulses the craving of the wicked.

Again the argument shows clearly that the throat is meant, but at the same time it also shows that the word stands for the needy man *per se*. The satisfied *n.* of the righteous man can stand in antithesis to the empty belly of the wicked (Prov. 13.25). And what does *reḥab-nepeš* mean when, according to Prov. 28.25, it 'stirs up strife', whereas 'he who trusts in Yahweh will be well fed'? What is meant is doubtless the 'wide jaws' that stand for the man who wants to supply his needs with immoderate greed (cf. Hab. 2.5). 'Their bread (serves) their *n.*', that is to say, 'their gullet' (Hos. 9.4).

n. as the organ of the needy man is also demonstrated by its being called the 'parched throat' which Yahweh refreshes and satisfies 'like a watered garden' (Jer. 31.12, 25). Thirst, water and *n.* often belong together (Prov. 25.25):

> Like cold water to a thirsty throat
> is good news from a far country.

Cf. Ps. 42.1f. and the 'dry throat' in Num. 11.6.

In its very function as the organ that feels hunger and thirst, *n.* is also the seat of the sense of taste (Prov. 27.7):

> A sated *n.* stamps on honey with his feet,
> but to a hungry *n.* everything bitter is sweet.

The hungry *n.* (v. 7b) that tastes everything bitter as sweet is of course the throat, with which the root of the tongue and the palate are associated as organs of taste. But it is not the throat (v. 7a) that 'stamps'; it is the man whose behaviour is determined by the throat's satiety. The parallelism of the satisfied and the hungry *n.* (which is made possible by synthetic thinking) must be differentiated in translation because of the differing statements: 'the sated man' must be set over against the 'hungry throat' (Prov. 16.24):

> Pleasant words are like a honeycomb,
> sweetness to the *n.* and healing to the body.

n. side by side with the body and with the experience of sweetness is again designed to point clearly to the organ of taste, and yet in the simile for the 'pleasant words', the needy man as a whole is clearly envisaged, with the hint at his sensitivity and vulnerability.

The *n.* tastes what is horrible as well as what is pleasant.[5] Israel grumbles (Num. 21.5b):

> There is no food and no water,
> and our *n.* feels loathing at this worthless food.

Here *n.* is the designation for man with respect to his hunger and his sense of taste. Cf. Zech. 11.8bβ. It is significant in this context that when Yahweh's loathing is talked about, it is his *n.* that is mentioned (Prov. 6.16).[6]

But the *n.* does not only count as the organ for taking in nourishment; it is also the organ of *breathing*. This is quite clear in the case of the female camel in Jer. 2.24: 'In the lust of "her"[7] *n.* she pants for breath.' Again and again we are told that the action of the *n.* is *nph*=to blow, breathe or pant. Thus the throat of a fainting mother pants heavily (Jer. 15.9); the hope of the godless 'is to breathe out their *n.*' (Job 11.20), where the organ of breathing and the breath itself are viewed together; as they are in Job 41.21, where the crocodile's *n.* kindles coals.[8]

When we are told that the *n.* of the dying Rachel 'departed' (Gen. 35.18), it can only be the breath that the writer is thinking of. In I Kings 17.21f. the *n.* returns to the child of the widow of Zarephath, of whom v.17 had reported that there was no breath (*neˢama*) left in him. In this archaic anatomy, therefore, the throat stands without terminological distinction for both the windpipe and the oesophagus. When 'the floods rise to the *n.*', there is danger of drowning (Jonah 2.5; Ps. 69.1; cf. Ps. 124.4f. and *ṣawwāʾr* in Isa. 8.8; 30.28).

It is only *n.* as the organ of breathing that makes the verbal use of the root *npš* (niph.) – which only occurs three times – comprehensible. We are told in II Sam. 16.14 that David, being exhausted after his strenuous flight, 'breathed again' (*wayyinnāpēš*), 'took breath', 'recovered himself' at Jordan. According to Ex. 23.12, the son of the slave and the stranger are to 'take breath' and rest from their labours on every seventh day, just as, according to Ex. 31.17, Yahweh too stopped and 'took breath' after six days of creation. It is worth considering whether the root *npš* was not originally biliteral (the preceding *n* being added at a later stage, as perhaps in *nph* as well) and was thus as *pš* an onomatopoeic representation of the violently hissing breath.[9]

In Accadian too *napašu* means to blow, to snort, to take breath,[10] and *napištu* means in the first instance the throat, both of men and animals, and then life, the basis of life, and the living being;[11] in Ugaritic *npš* also repeatedly means the jaws, the throat or the gullet, and then appetite, desire, the feelings and the living being.[12] Arabic *nafsun* can mean both breath and appetite, and can then be the term for life, the feelings and the person.[13] The semasiology of the Hebrew *n.* shows over and above these indications wide parallels in the related Semitic languages.

J. H. Becker (*Nefesj*, 1942) has contested the basic meaning of throat (which was maintained by L. Dürr, '*nepes*', 1925),[14] and took breath to be the earlier basic meaning (similarly M. Seligson, 1951). This controversy is probably to no purpose, since for Semitic peoples eating, drinking and breathing all took place in the throat; so it was the seat of the elemental vital needs in general.

2. Neck

Over against the copious evidence for the inside of the neck and the vital functions which take place there, the rarer use of *n.* for the external neck could be secondary. We see how easy the transition is for Hebrew thinking alone through the parallel use of *ṣawwā'r* (neck) and *n.* in the phrases about the threateningly rising floods.[15] Ps. 105.18 is thinking solely of the outer neck:

> They forced his feet into fetters,
> his *n.* was put into iron.[16]

That this is the neck and not 'his soul'[17] is strongly suggested, both by the 'iron' and by the parallel statement about the feet. When in Isa. 51.23 the tormentors of Israel say: 'Bow down, that we may pass over,' the *n.* that is addressed means the neck, especially since the sequel demands:

> Make your back like the ground,
> like a street for wanderers.

In Ps. 44.25, then, *n.* is doubtless also the 'neck' which is 'bowed down to the dust', since in the same verse the 'body cleaves to the ground'. Accordingly in Ps. 119.25 *n.* is probably also the neck which cleaves to the dust, and is therefore the man who is utterly cast down and who cries out for revival according to Yahweh's word.

What are we intended to understand by the 'houses of the *n.*' in the list of adornments belonging to the daughter of Zion in Isa. 3.20? These are not infrequently named after the parts of the body that they adorn. So we ought to think of a kind of necklet[18] rather than amulets, which we should have to think of as hollow objects in the form of 'a little house on the neck'.[19] The parts that are in danger are the parts adorned.

Should the phrase 'strike the *n.*' (Gen. 37.21; Deut. 19.6, 11; Jer. 40. 14f.; and frequently elsewhere)/have a more concrete meaning than 'to imperil life' – namely to 'cut a person's throat'?[20] There is no doubt that *n.* in Jer. 4.10 is meant in this sense: 'The sword is at our necks.' Does the saying to Mary in Luke 2.35, 'A sword will pierce through your own soul', preserve in *psyche* a Semitism that goes back to *n.*, neck?[21]

As well as the sword, the rope also endangers the neck. The witch, or necromancer, of Endor asks Saul (I Sam. 28.9):

> Why do you want to lay a noose for my *n.*,
> to bring about my death?

Even though *n.* may also have been understood as a personal pronoun, yet the pictorial language still allows a concrete part of the body to be thought of in the background. Similarly in Ps. 124.7:

> Our *n.* escaped like a bird
> from the net of the fowlers.

Cf. Prov. 18.7b. Thus *n.* as the neck also indicates the man who, being humbled and endangered, is in need of help.

3. *Desire*

When, therefore, the throat or neck are mentioned, there is frequently an echo of the view of man as needy and in danger, who therefore yearns with his *n.* for food and the preservation of his life; and this vital *longing, desiring, striving* or *yearning* can, even when the *n.* is mentioned, dominate the concept by itself. This is clearly the case where a man's *n.* lies outside his own person. In the lament in Ps. 35.25 the petitioner quotes his enemies, who are already saying about him: 'Aha, our *n.*!' and who would like soon to be able to say, 'We have swallowed him up.' If a man has here become the *n.* of his opponent, he cannot be his throat or neck; he can only be his longing or desire, and here his positive 'enjoyment', whereby we ought also to think back to the *n.* as the organ of taste.[22] When Prov. 13.2b defines the *n.* of the treacherous as 'violence', *n.* means there too only their striving and desire. Prov. 23.2 teaches:

> You put a knife to your throat
> if you are a *ba'al n.*

In the context it is the possessor of lust that is thought of, that is to say the man whose behaviour is entirely determined by the desires of the throat, by voracious hunger or greedy appetite.

n. is associated with noticeable frequency with words which have the root *'wh*, which in piel and hithpael mean wish, desire, craving for. When the craving of the *n.* is for early figs (Micah 7.1), the eating of meat

(Deut. 12.15, 20; I Sam. 2.16), or, beyond that, the drinking of wine (Deut. 14.26), then the throat may still be meant as well as the seat of the desire. But when evil (Prov. 21.10), the kingdom (II Sam. 3.21; I Kings 11.37) or God (Isa. 26.9) becomes the object of the wishes, or when there is no object at all (Prov. 13.4, 19), then *n.* means longing *per se*, the human urge of desire as the author of longing (*'wh*). It is similar with the phrase *nś' n.*, 'to raise the *n.*' It may come from observation of a man greedily craning his neck. This idea seems to be still present in Hosea's words about the priests (4.8):

> They feed on the sin of my people;
> they raise the *n.* for their iniquity.

If what is being thought of here is sacrifice for sin and guilt, the raising of the *n.*, parallel to 'feed on', could be a visual expression of the desirous craning of the neck. But generally the phrase refers to the desire for objects which are not eatable in the narrower sense – the land (Jer. 22.27), vanity (Ps. 24.4), sons and daughters (Ezek. 24.25), so that *nś' n.* generally means: to direct one's desires towards, to long for. Thus in other respects as well, the organ with its specific impulses recedes behind the whole man and his corresponding behaviour. Gen. 34.2f. says of Shechem and Dinah: 'He saw her, he seized her and lay with her and violated her. And his *n.* clove to Dinah . . . he loved the maiden and spoke encouragingly to her.' When his *n.* clove to her, it is obviously the violent desire for a permanent bond. Fatherly love (Gen. 44.30) and love of a friend (I Sam. 18.1) are also the work of the *n.*[23]

n. is as a rule the still unslaked desire, which urges action. It is this that makes possible the remarkable maxim (Prov. 16.26):

> A worker's *n.* works for him;
> his mouth urges him on.

n., parallel to mouth, is the throat in action, the hunger that urges a man to work. Deut. 23.24: 'When you go into your neighbour's vineyard, you may eat your fill of grapes according to your *n.*' When the man has eaten his fill, *n.* as the unsated desire has reached the limits set for it.

The *n.* as such stands for unlimited desire. When a man wants to part company from a woman who is a prisoner of war, he is according to Deut. 21.14 only allowed to dismiss her 'in accordance with her *n.*' (*lᵉnapšāh*), that is to say in complete conformity with her free desire and will; in the same way slaves were set free, Jer. 34.16 tells us, 'according to their *n.*' (*lᵉnapšām*), that is to say at their own choice. How commonly *n.* is used in the sense of a free wish is shown by the phrase *im yēs napšᵉkem*, that is to say, 'if it pleases you' (Gen. 23.8; II Kings 9.15).

But still more frequently *n.* means man in his ardent desire, which is like the parched longing of the man who is dying of thirst. This is how the *n.* thirsts in Ps. 42.1f. – that is to say the longing desire for the living God felt by the author of the lament. And so, according to I Sam. 1.15, does the childless Hannah pour out her *n.* – that is, her unsatisfied desire – to Yahweh. The Deuteronomic command to love Yahweh with the whole of the *n.* (Deut. 6.5 and passim) means accordingly that man should carry the whole living force of his wishes and all his longing desire into his love for the one God of Israel. Cf. Mark 12.30. 'To fight with one *psyche* for the faith of the gospel' (Phil. 1.27) means: striving in common.

4. *Soul*

It is only a short step from the *n.* as specific organ and act of desire to the extended meaning, whereby the *n.* is the seat and action of other spiritual experiences and emotions as well. Ex. 23.9 exhorts Israel:

> You shall not oppress a stranger;
> You know the *n.* of a stranger,
> for you were strangers in the land of Egypt.

This is the place where we could translate *n.* by 'soul' for the first time. For the writer is thinking not only of the stranger's needs and desires but of the whole range of his feelings, arising from the alien land and the danger of oppression in his state of dependence. Job is also thinking of the soul as the central organ of suffering man when he asks his 'friends' (Job 19.2): 'How long will you torment my *n.*?' According to this, the *n.* is the typical organ of sympathy with the needy (Job 30.25). As the suffering soul especially, and as the tortured mind, the *n.* is the precise subject of the psalms of lamentation; it is frightened (6.3), it despairs and is disquieted (42.5f., 11; 43.5), it feels itself weak and despondent (Jonah 2.7), it is exhausted and feels defenceless (Jer. 4.31), it is afflicted (Ps. 31.7; cf. Gen. 42.21) and suffers misery (Isa. 53.11). The *n.* is often described as being bitter (*mar*), that is to say embittered through childlessness (I Sam. 1.10), troubled because of illness (II Kings 4.27), enraged because it has been injured (Judg. 18.25; II Sam. 17.8) or distressed in some other way (Prov. 31.6); the choice of the word 'bitter' certainly reminds us of *n.* as the organ of taste (Prov. 27.7, see pp. 12f. above), but the context in the cases just quoted and in many similar ones shows clearly that here it is the state of mind that is being thought of.

Other emotions too are primarily expressed by the *n.*; it feels hate (II Sam. 5.8; of Yahweh as well: Isa. 1.14) but also love (S. of S. 1.7; 3.1, 2, 3, 4; of Yahweh also: Jer. 12.7). The *n.* experiences grief and weeps (Jer.

13.17), but it also rejoices and exults over Yahweh (Ps. 35.9). We must ask here whether in such cases the seat of these states of mind and moods is still identified with the throat, as the place of vital needs, and its sobbing, censuring and rejoicing. The not uncommon phrase about the *n.*'s 'being short' (*qṣr*, Num. 21.4; Judg. 16.16; of Yahweh too: Judg. 10.16; Zech. 11.8) and then also about its 'making long' ('*rk* hiph.; Job 6.11) are certainly derived from the notion of the throat's short and long breathing, but it has become such a generally accepted expression for impatience and patience that here too our understanding demands the rendering 'soul' for the subject, *n.*

With this the *n.*'s content of meaning has been considerably extended; but it does not go beyond the sphere marked out by the stirrings of the mind and the emotions; and here it is not uncommon for there to be a reminiscence of the physical organ and its particular functions.

5. *Life*

This reminiscence becomes still clearer in a highly extensive sector of the *n.* occurrences. If *n.* designates the organ of vital needs, which have to be satisfied if man is to go on living, then it is easy for synthetic thinking to see that *n.* further means 'life' itself. In Prov. 8.35f. the argument enforces this translation: wisdom says:

> He who finds me has found life (*ḥayyīm*)
> and has obtained favour from Yahweh.
> But he who misses me violates his *n.*;
> all who hate me love death (*māwet*).

In the antithesis to the preceding sentence, *n.* appears as an exact synonym for 'life', and in the parallel to the following stichos, *n.* forms the contrasting word to 'death'. In Ps. 30.3 we read: 'O Yahweh, thou hast brought up my *n.* from the underworld.' The synonymous continuation goes on: 'thou hast called me into life (*ḥiyyītanī*)', thus confirming that in what has gone before *n.* means nothing less than the life of the worshipper himself. In Prov. 19.8, too, none of the meanings we mentioned earlier will fit:

> He who gets wisdom loves his *n.*
> he who keeps understanding 'finds'[24] good things.

As in Prov. 8.35f., wisdom is related to life itself as the good *per se*. In Prov. 7.23 too:

> as a bird rushes into a snare
> without knowing that his *n.* is at stake,

n. no longer means the neck (cf. I Sam. 28.9; Ps. 124.7; Prov. 18.7), but the life, since this simile in the great warning discourse also serves only as a guide to 'life' (7.2a) and as a guard against death (v. 27).

That the meaning 'life' can, in distinction from the last example, be separated entirely from the idea of 'neck' or 'throat' is proved surprisingly by the definition in Deut. 12.23: '<u>The blood is the *n.*</u>' With this the complete identification of blood and life has taken place, as justification for the precept that the blood – namely the life – is not to be eaten with the flesh. Lev. 17.11 puts it almost more clearly still: 'The *n.* of the flesh is in the blood.' The Priestly document also associates the *n.* as the life with the blood, as in Gen. 94f.

This secondary assignment of the *n.* as the life to the blood instead of to the throat makes some phrases comprehensible which are hard to understand if one takes the process of breathing as the starting-point – the phrase which speaks about the emptying out of the *n.* (*'rh* hiph. and piel, Ps. 141.8; Isa. 53.12: to death) as if it were a liquid (cf. Gen. 24.20) or of the pouring out of the *n.* (*špk* hithpael, Lam. 2.12: the children of Jerusalem have poured out their *n.* 'on their mothers' bosoms'; cf. Job 30.16).

The definition of blood is already evidence that *n.* means the life *per se*, both animal and human (Deut. 12.23; Gen. 9.4f.). It is clearly in this context that Lev. 24.17f. declares:

> He who kills the *n.* of a man
> shall be put to death.
> He who kills the *n.* of a beast
> shall make it good.

Both follow from the basic rule 'a *n.* for a *n.*' (v. 18b.). Here that can only mean, one life substitutes for another, one's own when a man has been killed, a living animal for a dead one. The older administration of justice is already familiar with this meaning of life for *n.* in the *lex talionis*,[25] as the Book of the Covenant demonstrates (Ex. 21.23f.): 'If an accident occurs, you shall give life for life, eye for eye, tooth for tooth, hand for hand, foot for foot.' In military life too the man on guard is responsible with his life for the man whom he has to watch: 'your *n.* shall be for his *n.*', I Kings 20.39 (cf. v. 42). Deut. 24.6 commands: 'No man shall take a mill or an upper millstone in pledge; for he would be taking the *n.* in pledge.' Anyone who takes away from a man the tools that are essential to support everyday life is taking away the life itself.

This use of *n.* in the legal precepts about the safeguarding of life corresponds to a usage that is very widespread linguistically. When anyone asks for his own or another man's life, he asks for the *n.* II Kings 1.13; Esth. 7.3; I Kings 3.11; if he asks for death, he says, take my *n.* from me (Jonah 4.3; cf. I Kings 19.4). In this way set phrases grow up: 'to seek someone's *n.*' (*biqqeš n.*) means 'to seek someone's life' (Ex. 4.19; I Sam. 20.1; 22.23; 25.29; II Sam. 4.8; 16.11; I Kings 19.10, 14; Jer. 4.30; 11.21; 38.16; Ps. 40.14); *millēṭ n.* means 'to save someone's life' (II Sam. 19.6; I Kings 1.12; cf. Gen. 19.17; 32.31). Anyone who has narrowly escaped death has carried off 'his life as a prize' (Jer. 21.9; 39.18; 45.5). Satan knows (Job 2.4): 'All that a man has he will give for his *n.*', that is to say, for his life. This means the uninjured, healthy life. When Yahweh nevertheless gives Job's bone and flesh into Satan's hand, he also sets him a limit: 'spare his *n.*', that is to say, his bare life. The not uncommon phrase 'to take his *n.* in his own hand' (*śīm napšō beḳappō*: Judg. 12.3; I Sam. 19.5; 28.21; Job 13.14; cf. Ps. 119.109) means the readiness to put one's life in danger of one's own accord.

Rich and abundant though this use of *n.* for life is, we must not fail to observe that the *n.* is never given the meaning of an indestructible core of being, in contradistinction to the physical life, and even capable of living when cut off from that life. When there is a mention of the 'departing' (Gen. 35.18) of the *n.* from a man, or of its 'return' (Lam. 1.11), the basic idea, as we saw on p. 13 above, is the concrete notion of the ceasing and restoration of the breathing. When Yahweh leads up the *n.* from the underworld (Ps. 30.3; 86.13), the idea is the return to healthy life of the whole man who has, through his illness, already been exposed to the power of death.[26] Though much is said about *n.* as the life, any cult of life or death is lacking, and with it also every speculation about the fate of the 'soul' beyond the borders of death.[27]

On the other hand it is acknowledged in prayer that the *n.* as the life of man remains at the disposition of Yahweh and is subject to his power of deliverance:

For thou dost not give my life up to the underworld (Ps. 16.10).
Yea, God will ransom my life from the power of the underworld,
yea he wrests me away (Ps. 49.15).

With vivid clarity Abigail prays for David (I Sam. 25.29):

Let the life (*n.*) of my lord be bound in the bundle of life (*ṣerōr haḥayyīm*) in the care of Yahweh your God; but the lives (*n.*) of your enemies he shall sling out as from the hollow of a sling.

Precious things like silver are kept in the 'bundle' (Gen. 42.35; Prov. 7.20). The 'bundle of life' is a protection against the loss of the *n.*

6. *Person*

We come across yet another new sense of *n.* when it is presupposed that man *is n.* and not, as up to now, that he *possesses n.*[28] We see the differences most clearly in those texts which have something to say about the relation between *n.* and life (*ḥayyīm*). We have just met sayings where *ḥayyīm* and *n.* are treated as synonyms (e.g., Prov. 8.35f. and see pp. 18f. above); but in Prov. 3.22 we have:

[Discretion and wisdom] will be life (*ḥayyīm*) for your *n.* and adornment for your neck.

The translation 'life' for *n.* is impossible here, since life is only promised to it. *n.* therefore does not say what a man has, but who the person is who receives life (*ḥayyīm*): 'person', 'individual', 'being'.[29] Legal texts from the Law of Holiness make this interpretation clear. Lev. 17.10: 'Every man . . . who eats any blood (of him it is true that) I will set my face against the *n.* that eats blood.' Here *n.* has to be translated as person,[30] even though we should note that the person here is called *n.* in his function as a person who eats (cf. 17.15). But this association is quite frequently missing. Lev. 20.6 talks about the *n.* as the person who turns to the spirits of the dead, and 22.4 about an unclean person. In Lev. 23.30 we read: 'Every *n.* who does any work on this same day, that *n.* I will destroy from among his people.' In this general sense *n.* means the single person, the individual as distinct from the ethnic unit; cf. also Lev. 19.8; 22.3; Num. 5.6; 9.13; and frequently elsewhere. It is not by chance that the Israelite would have seen *n.* – as the throat which by eating and breathing satisfies the vital needs of every individual – as being simply the appropriate term for the individual person as well.

This, however, also makes a plural formation *nepāšōt* possible, when a number of individuals is meant. We find it consequently in the middle of the legal texts just quoted, in Lev. 18.29:

For whoever shall do any of these abominations, the *nepāšōt* that do them shall be destroyed from among their people.

When Jer. 43.6 lists the people who are taken to Egypt, the text first of all speaks particularly about 'the men, the women, the children, the princesses', and goes on: 'and the whole *n.* whom Nebuzaradan . . . had left with Gedaliah . . . also Jeremiah . . . and Baruch'. Here *n.* is a collective expression for a whole group of individuals, just as it is in Gen. 12.5, where the Priestly document enumerates what Abram took with him from Haran to Canaan: Sarai, Lot, all their possessions and the *n.*, under which here the 'personnel' is grouped together. This collective use of *n.* is shown very clearly where numbers are mentioned: the offspring of Leah number 33 *n.* (Gen. 46.15), of Zilpah 16 *n.* (v. 18), of Rachel 14 *n.* (v. 22) and of Bilhah 7 *n.* (v. 25); all the offspring of Jacob who came to Egypt were 66 (v. 26) or 70 *n.* (v. 27).

This collective use of *n.*, as well as the plural usage, is exemplified particularly in the later literature. Of 44 instances, 20 come from the Priestly document (KBL 626). When Gen. 9.5 formulates: 'Your blood, namely your *nᵉpāšōt*, I will require of every living being,' this is an express defence of the human individual (cf. v. 6). According to Num. 19.18 the purifying water is to be sprinkled on the tabernacle, 'upon all the furnishings, and upon all *nᵉpāšōt* who were there', that is to say expressly on every individual. Ezek. 13.19 distinguishes *nᵉpāšōt* who ought not to die from those who ought not to live.

This statement suggests a detachment of the concept *n.* from the concept of life; stress lies on the individual being as such. This makes the extreme possibility of speaking of a *n. mēt* (Num. 6.6) comprehensible. Here the writer is not thinking of a 'dead soul', or of a 'slain life', but simply of a person who has died – a dead individual, a corpse; a Nazirite must not go near one during the whole period of his consecration. Even more striking is that in certain cases *n.* can mean the corpse of a human individual even without the addition of *mēt* (dead), as we can see from Num. 5.2; 6.11; cf. Num. 19.11, 13.

It is this possibility of using *n.* that first shows us that the phrase *nepeš ḥayyā* contains no superfluous epithet. This is what the Priestly document calls aquatic creatures (Gen. 1.20f.; also Lev. 11.10, 46; Ezek. 47.9), land animals (1.24), animals in general (Gen. 9.10, 12, 15)[31] and men and animals together (Gen. 9.16), as living creatures. (According to Gen. 1.30 the *n. ḥayyā* is 'in' the animals, so that here we ought to think of the 'breath of life'.)

In the Yahwist's account of the creation (Gen. 2.7) we saw man expressly defined as *n. ḥayyā*; he is so not simply on the basis of his creation out of the dust of the earth; he only becomes so because the God Yahweh breathes the breath of life into his nostrils. It is only the breath produced by the Creator that makes him a living *n.*, which is to say, therefore, a living being, a living person, a living individual. It is under this aspect, then, that man is here more closely defined. According to the tendency of the statements in Gen. 2.7, *n. ḥayyā* introduces no *differentia specifica* for animal life; then the subsequent definition in 2.19 of animal life as being *n. ḥayyā* as well would hardly be possible. But at the same time man is, through God's endowment with the breath of life, distinguished as living individual from the *n. mēt*, as a lifeless structure or corpse.

7. *Pronouns*

If in the contexts mentioned *n.* without any additional epithet simply means the individual person, it can easily come about that *n.* now merely takes the place of the personal or reflexive pronoun. The transitions are fluid. The modern reader will be inclined to see the pronominal character as being already present even in places where for the ancients the nominal content was still clearly to be heard. Consequently, even according to today's interpretation, instances of the pronominal meaning vary between 123 and 223.[32] Here too it seems to me less important to draw an exact borderline than to observe the particular character of the synthetic-stereometric way of thinking, which permits different nuances of meaning to go hand in hand to a great extent.

In Gen. 12.13 the Yahwist makes Abram say to Sarai: 'Say you are my sister, that it may go well with me (*lī*) because of you, and that my *n.* may survive on your account.' The parallelism of the last two sentences suggests that 'my *n.*' should be understood as a variant to the personal pronoun 'I' ('so that I may survive on your account'). Although we translate it in this way as a general rule, the factual difference in the Hebrew should remain clear: the 'I' is brought out in relief through *n.* with its centre in the person, with whose life the Yahwist has been concerned since the definition of Gen. 2.7.[33] Typical of the difficulty of *this* pronoun's meaning is the alternation with a simple pronominal suffix or preformatively or afformatively formed verbal subject, which we find in the words of Lot in the Yahwist's account (Gen. 19.19f.):

> Thou hast shown me ('*immādī*) great favour
> in upholding me (my *n.*) in life;
> but I cannot flee to the hills . . . ,
> behold, yonder city is near . . . ,
> let me escape there . . .
> that I (my *n.*) may be maintained in life!

Where the word 'life' occurs, *n.* is used as pronoun. Even a far-off echo of the throat, thirsty for life, cannot be entirely ignored. It is not by chance that the plea 'let me live'! is in Hebrew 'Let my *n.* live!' (I Kings 20.32). Correspondingly, in dying it is the *n.* that is at stake. Thus Samson cries as he pulls down the pillars of the Philistines' house (Judg. 16.30): 'May I die with the Philistines!' where the pronoun 'I' again means 'my *n.*' Balaam ends his discourse (Num. 23.10): 'May I (my *n.*) die the death of the righteous!' *n.* stands for the person whose life is in danger. From this starting point, in poetry *n.* can stand parallel to the usual pronoun with almost the same meaning:

> Behold God helps me
> the Lord alone upholds me (my *n*.) (Ps. 54.4);
> A fool's mouth is his ruin
> and his lips are his snare (the snare of his *n*.) (Prov. 18.7).

In spite of all this, it is important for the whole feeling of the language for us to keep in mind the total range of meaning, from neck (in the noose, see above p. 15) down to life and person.

How can we explain the fact that in the story of Jacob's stealing of the blessing, the author of Isaac's blessing is always his *n*. (Gen. 27.4)? '. . . bring it (the venison) to me that I may eat it so that my *n*. may bless you before I die.' Verse 19: 'that your *n*. may bless me'; and again in vv. 25 and 31. Nothing in the whole range of *n*.'s meaning for which we have found evidence justifies us in thinking here of a particular power and endowment of soul, in connection with which magical ideas are supposed to have been preserved.[34] We ought much rather to think here of the simple pronominal use; the context gives it sufficient content; in all four passages there has been talk immediately beforehand about the eating of the desired venison – and on the first occasion Isaac's death is mentioned immediately afterwards. Isaac's 'I' that blesses is as *n*. the desirous and satisfied person, who is still alive but who is already facing death.

Job says (16.4):

> I also could speak as you do,
> if you stood here for me.

The pronouns in the last stichos read: 'your *n*. for my *n*.', bringing with them a suggestion of the vital need. Thus in the pronominal usage we should enquire in each case into the accompanying undertones and overtones – whether 'my transgression' in Micah 6.7 means 'the transgression of my (greedy) *n*.' ('my transgressing life' parallel to 'my revolt'= *piš'i*); or whether Jonathan loves David 'as himself', i.e., as his own life (I Sam. 18.1); or whether in Isa. 3.9 'woe to them!' is, in the form: woe to their *n*., still an echo of 'woe to their greedy life!'

The meaning of *n*. is most strongly generalized into a personal pronoun where the word appears in a synonymous parallel to 'flesh', 'spirit' and 'heart'. But even in these cases we can see that specific statements of emotional desire (Prov. 2.10) or the longings of the needy (Ps. 84.2) are being made about people as *n*.[35]

If we survey the wide context in which the *n*. of man and man as *n*. can be observed, we see above all man marked out as the individual living being who has neither acquired, nor can preserve, life by himself, but who is eager for life, spurred on by vital desire, as the throat (the organ for receiving nourishment and for breathing) and the neck (as the part of the body which is especially at risk) make clear. Although in this way *n.* shows man primarily in his need and desire, that includes his emotional excitability and vulnerability. The semantic element 'vitality', which also applies to the animal, has largely contributed to the fact that *n.* can be a term for the person and the enumerable individual, from which, in extreme cases, the meaning 'corpse' follows. *n.* is never the author of specific spiritual activities.

The fact that *n.* points pre-eminently to needy man, who aspires to life and is therefore living (which also makes him comparable with the animal) is indirectly confirmed by the observation that considerable strata of the Old Testament (such as the older strata of the Pentateuch, up to and including Deuteronomy) avoid speaking of Yahweh's *n.*[36] Where later language, mainly prophetic and poetic, mentions Yahweh's *n.*, it stresses his being aroused (Judg. 10.16; Zech. 11.8) to anger and scorn (Isa. 1.14; Ps. 11.5; Prov. 6.16; Lev. 26.11, 30; Jer. 6.8; 9.8; 14.19; Ezek. 23.18) as well as love (Jer. 12.7), his unfettered desire (Job 23.13; Jer. 15.1; 32.41; I Sam. 2.35) or his living self (Amos 6.8; Jer. 51.14; see pp. 17f. above).

Finally, it must be pointed out that it is before Yahweh that man's dialogue with his *n.*, that is to say with his self, takes place. In Ps. 103.1 he calls upon himself to give praise:

> Bless Yahweh, O my *n.*,
> and all that is within me
> bless his holy name!

Thinking of the organ of praise and the contrast to the inner life, we might translate: 'Bless Yahweh, O my throat.' If we see the totality of the inner life as being stressed, and think of the reason for praise as lying in Yahweh's kindnesses touching the whole of man, we can translate: 'Bless Yahweh, O my life!' In any case the knowledge of Yahweh's saving acts makes the man of understanding free to turn his vital, emotional, needy and desirous self to joyful praise.

The dialogue originating before Yahweh between the man who has become quick to hear and his vegetative self can also, in the song of lament, take the form of self-exhortation (Pss. 42.5, 11; 43.5):

> Why are you cast down, O my *n.*,
> and why are you disquieted within me?
> Hope in God; for I shall again praise him.

Here *n.* is the self of the needy life, thirsting with desire (cf. 42.1f.).

Thus, before Yahweh, man in the Old Testament does not only recognize himself as *nepeš* in his neediness; he also leads his self on to hope and to praise.

bāśār – Man in his Infirmity[1]

Whereas *nepeš* is applied to God in at least a bare three per cent of its occurrences in the Old Testament, there is not a single instance in the case of *bāśār*. On the other hand the *bāśār* of animals in incomparably more often mentioned than their *nepeš*. *bāśār* occurs 273 times[2] altogether, and 104 of these instances –that is to say more than a third – relate to animals.[3] This alone shows that *bāśār* (henceforth simply *b*.) is the term for something that is broadly characteristic of both man and beast. Methodologically, therefore, this would seem to be a good starting point.

1. *Flesh*

Isa. 22.13 describes Jerusalem's carelessness:

> Behold, joy and gladness,
>> slaying oxen and killing sheep,
>> eating *b*. and drinking wine.
> 'Let us eat and drink,
>> for tomorrow we die.'

It is clear that *b*. means the flesh of slaughtered cattle and sheep. Isa. 44.16 talks about *b*. as the meat that is eaten roasted. In the first instance *b*. means the flesh of living beasts. Thus Job 41.23 describes the *b*. of the crocodile:

> The dewlaps of his flesh stick close together,
>> sealed closely to him, immovably.

The flesh that is mentioned most frequently is the flesh of sacrificial animals, in ritual regulations (Lev. 4.11; 7.15–21; Num. 19.5 and frequently elsewhere). It is significant of this that *b*. is not mentioned in any other book nearly so frequently as in Leviticus.[4]

It is possible to talk about human *b*. as food, just as it is about animal flesh. One of the curses on a disobedient Israel is (Lev. 26.29):

> You shall eat the flesh of your sons,
>> and you shall be compelled to eat the flesh of your daughters.

We are told about those who violated Israel (Isa. 49.26a):

> I will give your oppressors to eat of their own flesh,
> and they shall drink their own blood like wine.

The Yahwist's account of the creation of the woman from one of the man's ribs (Gen. 2.21bβ) talks about *b.* as a piece of flesh belonging to the human body, in contrast to the bones: 'He closed up its place with flesh.' In descriptions of the whole human body, *b.* forms a part. It is mentioned side by side with the bones ('*eṣem*) (Job 2.5): 'Touch his bone and his flesh', where *b.* primarily means what is externally visible, as distinct from the bones, as the inner structure. The skin ('*ōr*) is especially mentioned as a third feature in Lam. 3.4:

> He has made my flesh and my skin waste away,
> and broken my bones.

Job 10.11 adds, as a fourth, the sinews (*gīdīm*):

> Thou didst clothe me with skin and flesh,
> and knit me together with bones and sinews.

In order to depict the living being, the breath as the spirit of life (*rūaḥ*) must finally be added as fifth element (Ezek. 37.5f.):

> Thus says Yahweh to these bones . . .
> I will lay sinews upon you,
> and will cause flesh to come upon you
> and cover you with skin,
> and put breath in you.

Thus *b.* as flesh, differentiated in different degrees, can mean a part of man's bodily substance. In a special sense we find the *b.* of the foreskin mentioned (Gen. 17.11, 14). If we enquire whether *b.* as 'a piece of flesh' can also mean a particular organ or limb, without its actually being more closely defined, it is noteworthy that here only the male sexual organ, the penis, is definitely in question. In Lev. 15.2f., 7,[5] *b.* is probably already the male organ, and then in v. 19, correspondingly, the female one. 'When any man has a discharge on his *b.*, his discharge is unclean' (Lev. 15.2). The meaning in Ezek. 16.26 (where Jerusalem, the faithless wife, is addressed) is indisputable:

> You play the harlot with the Egyptians,
> your neighbour with the swelling member (*b.*).

And it is still more unequivocal in Ezek. 23.20, where we read of Jerusalem as the faithless paramour – here too in her relationship to the Egyptians (v. 19):

> She was full of desire towards her libertines
>   whose penis (*b*.) is like the ass's penis (*b*.) and whose
>   issue is like the stallion's issue.

zĭrmā for the ejaculation (cf. *zerem*, cloudburst, rainstorm) makes it certain that *b*. means the male member here. A stronger image for lust as an indication of the 'power of political conspiracy' can hardly be imagined.[6] It should be noted for the further development of the word's meaning that this pregnant euphemistic use of *b*. is not employed in any positive sense, to depict the power of generation, but only to bring out faithlessness and impurity.

2. Body

Since *b*. stands primarily for the visible part of the body, it can then also mean the human body as a whole.[7] According to Num. 8.7, in the course of the Levite consecration, one should 'let a razor go over all their *b*.', that is to say, over the whole of their body. Eliphaz says, meaning the same thing, 'The hair on my *b*. stood on end' (Job 4.15). In the instructions for dealing with a leper, Lev. 13.2ff. distinguishes more precisely between 'the skin of his body' (*'ōr b°śārō*) and the hair on it (v. 4). But in Lev. 19.28 *b*. once more means the body together with its skin: 'You shall not make any scratches in your flesh (*b*.) . . . or tattoo any marks upon you' (here *b*. is already fading into a synonym for the personal pronoun). When Ps. 102.5 describes how the poet is wasting away, 'My bones cleave to my *b*.,' then the petitioner is giving factual expression to his condition: he is just 'skin and bone'. When Ahab, after rending his clothes, puts the garment of repentance 'round his *b*.' (I Kings 21.27), it is his naked body that is meant.

The whole body, not only its externally visible parts, is under discussion in Ps. 38.3a:

> There is no soundness in my *b*.
>   because of thy indignation.

(Here *b*. is synonymous with 'bones' in v. 3b.) Accordingly medicine is for the whole body (Prov. 4.22):

> [The words of wisdom] are life 'to him who'[8] finds them,
>   and medicine to his whole *b*.

Again the parallelism is moving *b*. in the direction of the personal pronoun; cf. also Ps. 119.120:

> My *b*. trembles for fear of thee
>   and I am afraid of thy judgments.

Like *nepeš*, therefore, *bāśār* points towards man *per se*, but now in his bodily aspect.

Gen. 2.24 can say of man that he will 'cleave to his wife and they will become one *b*.', that is to say, a common body, a 'fellowship for life'.[9]

3. *Relationship*

Here *b*. is used for flesh in the sense of what binds people together and what can then be an almost legal term for 'relationship'. Thus Judah points out to his brothers that Joseph 'is our brother, our own *b*.' (Gen. 37.27); that is to say, he is our (nearest) relation (cf. Neh. 5.5: 'our *b*. is as the *b*. of our brethren'). A more frequent 'formula expressing relationship'[10] is 'my bone and my flesh': Gen. 29.14; cf. Gen. 2.23; Judg. 9.2; II Sam. 5.1; 19.12f.[11]

Lev. 18.6 sums up the prohibition of all sexual intercourse with blood relations: 'None of you shall approach the flesh (*šĕ'ēr*) of his *b*. to uncover his privy parts.' Here *šĕ'ēr*, as the physiological term for flesh with the blood circulating through it, is clearly thrown into relief against *b*. as the legal term for a member of the family.[12] The circle of blood relations (*b*.) is defined in Lev. 25.49 as the tribe (*mišpāḥā*, family group). Isa. 58.7 talks about not only the hungry, the homeless and the naked, but also 'your own *b*.', from whom anyone who wants to 'fast' in the true sense will not withdraw himself; the context suggests that by *b*. we should not only think of relations in the legal sense, but of our fellow-men, who are in general related to us in kind. In Deutero-Isaiah (40.5, 6; 49.26b) and in Ps. 145.21, at least, *kol-bāśār* means 'the whole of mankind'.

This is also pre-eminently the case in the story of the Flood in the Priestly document, as Gen. 6.12 (beside 6.5 J) shows.[13] Admittedly the Priestly document unites the world of men and the world of animals under the term *kol-b*. in Gen. 6.17 and 9.16f., as those who are affected by the judgment of the Flood and as God's partners in the covenant; cf. also Num. 18.15.

The document defines *b*. more closely as the living being 'in whom is breath' (Gen. 6.17) or as 'living creatures' (9.16, *nepeš ḥayyā*).[14] *b*. is not the term for a corpse, which is generally called *nĕbēlā* and not infrequently 'bones' or 'skeleton' (*'aṣāmîm*, *'aṣāmōt*, Amos 6.10; Ezek. 6.5; Gen. 50.25; Ex. 13.19).

The way in which *b*. stresses the relationship in kind of all living things makes understandable the remarkably positive meaning which *b*. takes on in the promise in Ezek. 11.19b (36.26b): 'I will take the stony heart out of their flesh (*b*.) and give them a heart of *b*.' (i.e., a fleshy heart). The heart of flesh is here clearly the living heart, in contrast to the stony one.[15] This use of *b*. in the sense of a positive valuation of human behaviour is absolutely unique.

4. *Weakness*

Otherwise *b.* characterizes human life in general as being in itself weak and frail. Ps. 56.4 confesses:

> In God I hope without a fear,
> What can *b.* do to me?

In v. 11 in the same phrase *b.* is replaced by 'a man'. Afterwards *b.* describes the human being in contrast to the being of God as weak and unreliable.

Job asks God (Job 10.4):

> Hast thou eyes of flesh (*b.*)?
> Dost thou see as man sees?

Thus God's *b.* is never spoken of; on the contrary, *b.* very often stands for something typically human, in contrast to the God of Israel. Jer. 17.5, 7 sets in antithesis:

> Cursed is the man who trusts in man
> and makes *b.* his arm . . .
> Blessed the man who trusts in Yahweh.

II Chron. 32.8 writes even about the mighty king of Assyria, Sennacherib:

> With him is but an arm of flesh;
> but with us is Yahweh our God, to help us.

In these cases *b.* always describes restricted, insufficient human power in contrast to the surpassing power of God, which is alone worthy of trust.

'Flesh' is dependent on God's power to give life, on his breath; if he withdrew it from created being

> all flesh (*b.*) would perish together
> and man would return to dust (Job 34.14f.).

b. is really man as a being who is in himself weak and incapable (cf. also Gen. 6.3). But for that very reason God sets limits to his anger: 'He remembered that they were but flesh (*b.*)' (Ps. 78.38f.). Before God in his holiness, however, man as *b.* is not only one who is frail, but also one who is liable to sin and for whom, therefore, the voice of the living God is unendurable (Deut. 5.26):

> For who is there of all flesh, that has heard the voice of the living God speaking out of the midst of the fire, as we have, and has still lived?

Under the scorching wind of God's judgment all *b.* withers like grass (Isa. 40.6). In the Priestly document the Flood descends in judgment on *kol-b.* because 'all flesh' as such 'had corrupted their way upon the earth'

(Gen. 6.12). That is why it is 'all flesh' that also brings the weight of sin before God (Ps. 65.2f.).

Thus even in the Old Testament *b.* does not only mean the powerlessness of the mortal creature but also the feebleness of his faithfulness and obedience to the will of God.[16]

Ethical frailty is added to the frailty of the creature. It is not the Qumran texts, when they talk about 'guilty flesh' (*beśār 'aśmā* 1 QM 12.12) and 'the flesh of unrighteousness' (*beśār 'āwel* 1 QS 11.9), that are moving for the first time towards the Pauline recognition that 'nothing good dwells in my flesh' (Rom. 7.5, 18). In complete contrast to this 'flesh' is the 'spirit' (Isa. 31.3); but the spirit is also the flesh's hope (Joel 2.28).

rūaḥ – Man as he is Empowered[1]

A mere glance at the statistics shows that *rūaḥ* can be distinguished from *nepeš* and *bāśār* in two ways. In the first place, *rūaḥ* is to a large extent the term for a natural power, the wind, this meaning being applicable in no less than 113 out of 389 instances (378 Hebrew and 11 Aramaic).[2] In the second place *rūaḥ* more often refers to God (136 times[3]) than to men, animals and false gods (129 times), that is to say in about 35% of all instances, whereas *nepeš* is only applied to God in 3% of the cases in which it is used,[4] and *bāśār* never applies to God at all. I may note that it is typical that *rūaḥ* never appears at all in the book of Leviticus, whereas we come across *bāśār* in Leviticus more often than in any other book of the Bible.[5] Consequently *rūaḥ* (henceforth *r.*) must from the very beginning properly be called a theo-anthropological term.[6]

1. Wind

But first it is not unimportant even for the anthropology to make the meteorological meaning of *r.* clear. It does not mean the air as such; it means the moving air. Thus the *r.* in Gen. 1.2 moves over the waters, like the hovering eagle (Deut. 32.11), the trees in Isa. 7.2 'shake' before the *r.*, and in Gen. 3.8 the '*r.* of the day' is the cool, refreshing breeze in which it is pleasant to stroll about in Palestine, after the midday heat. The Yahwist knows the *r.* above all as the power which brings about alteration; in Ex. 10.13 the east wind brings locusts; in v. 19 it blows a strong sea wind into the Reed Sea; in Ex. 14.21 a powerful east wind dries out the Reed Sea; in Num. 11.31 the wind brings quails with it. Here the *r.* is always Yahweh's instrument. In the Priestly document too (Gen. 8.1) God makes a wind blow over the earth, so that the flood waters subside.

Only in exceptional cases does *r.* appear parallel to the (mortal) *bāśār* in the sense of the weak puff of wind 'that passes and comes not again' (Ps. 78.39; cf. also Isa. 41.29); as a rule in these cases Israel talks about *hebel* as the breath that is evanescent – a mere nothingness (Ps. 62.9; 144.4; Eccles. 1.2; and frequently elsewhere). On the other hand it is characteristic that *r.* as the divinely strong stands in contrast to *bāśār*, as human weakness (Isa.31.3a; Gen.6.3). Thus the stormy *r.* breaks forth with a deluge of rain and hail as the instrument of Yahweh's wrath (Ezek.13.13). The *r.* snatches up the prophet, lifts him and sets him down in another place (Ezek.3.12, 14; 11.1; cf. I Kings18.12; II Kings 2.16).

What we have to remember is that *r.*, particularly as wind, as distinct from *hebel* and *bāśār*, generally means a mighty phenomenon standing at Yahweh's disposal.

2. Breath

The 'wind' (*r.*) of man is in the first place his breath. Consequently *r.* is not infrequently parallel to *neśāmā* (e.g. Isa.42.5):

> Thus says Yahweh ... who spread forth the earth ... who gives breath (*neśāmā*) to the people upon it and *r.* to those who walk in it

(cf. also Isa.57.16; Job34.14; and also Gen.7.22). This wind, as man's vital power, is also 'given' by Yahweh; he 'forms' (*yṣr*) the *r.* within man (Zech.12.1). There is no *r.* in the idols of wood or stone – that is to say, they have no breath and therefore no vital power, which would first of all make it possible for them to 'awake and arise' (Hab.2.19; cf. Jer.10.14= 51.17). Only when Yahweh infuses the *r.* as breath into the bones covered with sinews, flesh and skin, will the bodies live (Ezek.37.6, 8–10, 14). 'When his *r.* departs he (man) returns to his earth' (Ps.146.4). According to Eccles.12.7, the *r.*, for its part, returns to the God that gave it. We are told in Judg.15.19 that Samson was in danger of dying of thirst until God made a spring break out; Samson drank from it, 'his *r.* returned, and he revived'; cf. I Sam.30.12. It is therefore possible to talk about the going out and the return of the *r.* very much as in the case of the *nepeš*[7] (cf. the synonymous use of *nepeš* and *r.* in Job12.10). We can see here the stereometry of synthetic thinking, which approaches a phenomenon from different sides. In *nepeš* the organ of breathing and the process of breathing itself are seen together. In *r.*, however, it is the 'wind' which proceeds from Yahweh and returns to him that also constitutes the breath of man's life. Job34.14f.:

> If he should take back his[8] *r.* to himself,
>   and gather to himself his breath (*neśāmā*),
> all flesh would perish together,
>   and man would return to dust.

Similarly Ps.104.29, with the continuation in v.30:

> Thou sendest forth thy Spirit,
>   they are created.

The image of the female camel in Jer. 2.24 shows how *r.* as the breath and *nepeš* as the organ of breathing are to be seen together and yet distinguished from one another: 'In the lust of her[9] *n.* she pants for breath' (i.e., for air to breathe – *r.*).

Life and death depend on the *r.* That is why, in the Priestly Document's story of the Flood, living things are called 'flesh in which is the breath of life (*r. ḥayyīm*)'.[10] In a concrete sense the smell of a person's breath can be meant; Job, for example, complains when he is dangerously ill (19.17):

> My breath (*r.*) is repulsive to my wife,
> I smell loathsome to my own sons.

We are compelled to think of the quickness of the breathing when the Yahwist, in a few psychologically skilful strokes, describes Jacob's violent reversal of feeling after his sons have returned from Egypt, telling that Joseph is alive (Gen. 45.26f.):

> But his heart remained cold,[11] for he did not believe them. But when they told him all . . . and when he saw the wagons which Joseph had sent to carry him, the *r.* of their father Jacob revived.

In other words, his breathing became strong once more – he 'breathed again'.[12]

3. *Vital powers*

We saw how *r.* as the breath of man is frequently inseparable from the *r.* of Yahweh (Job 34.14f.; Ps. 104.29f.).[13] But it must now be remembered that the *r.* of Yahweh as a whole means more than the enlivening 'wind' which becomes the breath of man. Here too the transitions are fluid, as we can see in Ps. 33.6:

> By the word of Yahweh the heavens were made,
> and all their host by the *r.* of his mouth.

Here *r.* acts as a synonym for word in so far as both proceed from the mouth. But at the same time *r.* is more than moving air. Yahweh's breath is the creative *power of life*. As life-giving power, Yahweh's *r.* also determines man's life-span (Gen. 6.3), In addition it has power over natural forces. It is this that Ex. 15.8 is celebrating:

> At the blast (*r.*) of thy nostrils the waters piled up,
> the floods stood up in a heap.

When Yahweh's *r.* descends on the great judges, it makes Othniel (Judg. 3.10) go out to battle and save Israel; it enables Samson to tear a lion to pieces (14.6; cf. 13.25); *ṣlḥ* (to become efficacious) is here applied to the *r*. of Yaweh in its character as highly activating power – as when it seizes upon Saul, so that he is 'turned into another man' (I Sam. 10.6). Besides these acts of power, Yahweh's *r*. produces other abilities, above all the charisma of prophecy, for example in Balaam in Num. 24.2f.; this applies, however, only to certain layers of narrative; in contrast, it is not true for classical pre-exilic prophecy, where according to Hos. 9.7 the prophet as a man of *r*. sees himself mocked.

When Pharaoh in Gen. 41.38 looks for 'a man . . . in whom is the *r*. of God', he means a discreet and wise man, in the sense of economic policy (vv. 33, 39). With the *r*. of God, therefore, an extraordinary endowment falls to man's lot. When the *r*. of Yahweh comes upon Ezekiel (11.5) it brings with it Yahweh's address to him and the commission to proclaim Yahweh's word; authorization takes place when Yahweh's *r*. falls on the prophets – the other way of describing it is 'the hand of Yahweh was upon him' (1.3).[14] It is in this light that Yahweh's address to the Servant in Isa. 42.1 can be understood:

> I give him my authority (*rūḥi*)
> that he may bring my justice to the nations.

With Yahweh's *r*. we must be constantly aware of the aspect of power; so when this *r*. rests on the shoot of Jesse in Isa. 11.2 we should think of his authorization. It is only through this awareness that the multifarious fine distinctions become understandable in which not only the *r*. of wisdom, understanding, counsel and knowledge can be talked of, but also the *r*. of might and fear of Yahweh; so that one does better to translate *r*. in all cases by 'power' or 'authority' rather than by spirit. Even where the 'good *r*. of Yahweh' primarily assists the insight, it is as *r*. still pre-eminently a 'gift', an overwhelming of weakness and incapacity, like that which is also accomplished through manna and water (Neh. 9.20). We are frequently told that Yahweh 'gives' (*ntn*)[15] his *r*. to men, or that he fills a man with the divine *r*. (*ml'* piel); this can also evoke artistic gifts (Ex. 31.3; 35.31; cf. 28.3). Joel (2.28) prophesies the pouring out of the spirit of Yahweh on all flesh, that is to say on everyone in Israel.[16] This is a proclamation of an unreserved authorization and the clothing with prophetic gifts, a proclamation made to people of both sexes, all ages, and indeed all social classes. The supreme privilege of knowledge of God, just because it is something that no one (as flesh) has of himself, is to be granted to all classes of people equally (cf. Gal. 3.28). Thus the term, in being a theological one, becomes an anthropological one at the same time. The authorized person is incomprehensible without the energy of the divine *r*.

4. Spirit(s)

Now it is also possible, however, to talk about the *r.* as an invisible *independent being*, which is not absolutely conceived of as being Yahweh's *r.* but which is none the less completely at his disposal. Thus Yahweh says, according to II Kings 19.7, 'I will put a *r.* in him (the king of Assyria), so that he shall hear a rumour and return to his own land.' The lying *r.* which deludes Ahab's prophets (I Kings 22.21–23) is then also a being sent by Yahweh which operates in men, primarily through speech. *r.* is like an assembly of powers which can be distributed to a great many people. It is in this sense that Yahweh also talks (in Num. 11.17) about the *r.* resting on Moses, some of which he takes away in order to give it to the seventy elders. As a result not only the elders (v. 25) but even people who were not with them, like Eldad and Medad, unexpectedly fall into a prophetic ecstasy (v. 26). Moses rejects Joshua's protest and exclaims (v. 29): 'Would that Yahweh would make all the people prophets, that Yahweh would put his spirit upon them all!' Here, therefore, ecstasy appears as a gift of participation in the *r.* resting on Moses, although Moses himself is not an ecstatic. The idea of the lending of a spirit no doubt belongs to the sphere in which Elisha too can ask to inherit a double share of Elijah's spirit (II Kings 2.9f., 15).[17] In the Priestly document the appointment of Joshua as Moses' successor takes place under appeal to him who is 'the God of the vital spirits (*rūḥōt*) of all flesh' (Num. 27.16; cf. 16.22). Both the *r.*, as the vital power of every man, and unusual gifts and authority are at God's disposal. Particularly the texts that talk about the *rūḥōt* as independent beings make this clear.

5. Feelings

When we turn to the question of the meaning of the human *r.*, it is impossible to exaggerate the distance that separates 'breath'[18] from 'spirit' as the organ of knowledge, understanding and judgment. The rise and fall of the breath is namely in the first place to be seen together with the movement of the feelings. When the Queen of Sheba saw the wisdom of Solomon, his palace, the food, the officials, their clothing, and the burnt offerings in the temple (I Kings 10.5), 'there was no more *r.* in her'. That is to say, her breath stopped, she lost her self-possession, she was beside herself. 'The lack of *rūaḥ* characterizes the state of unconsciousness, of disconcerted astonishment.'[19] Attitude of mind is documented in the *r.* 'You turn your *r.* against God,' Eliphaz accuses Job (15.13), meaning his excitement and ill-humour (LXX: *thumos*). When, under persuasion, the *r.* 'relaxes' (Judg. 8.3) then the angry excitement diminishes. Jezebel notices, according to I Kings 21.4, that Ahab's *r.* had turned away. She meant that he was ill-humoured. When Yahweh 'hardens' Sihon's *r*. (Deut. 2.30), he made him behave inflexibly. Just as *nepeš* and *r*. come together in the breathing process,[20] so similar states of excitement can be paraphrased by both words. Just as it is possible to talk about the *nepeš* being short and long, it is also possible to speak of the *r*. being short and long (Prov. 14.29):

> He who is longsuffering has great understanding,
> but he who is impatient exalts folly.

Here *qᵉṣar-rūaḥ* (the person who is short of breath through excitement) is in opposition to the *'erek 'appayim*, he who has 'long breath'. Cf. Prov. 14.17; Job 21.4 (of Yahweh, Micah 2.7). We are told that when Israel was oppressed in Egypt it was *qōṣar rūaḥ*, and this 'shortness of *r*.' is a reference to the diminishing vitality, that is to say despondency and down-heartedness. But *r*. is also used to describe other attitudes of mind. Eccles. 7.8 says: 'The patient in spirit is better than the proud in spirit.' The man with a 'patient' or 'long' *r*. is preferred to the one with a 'proud *r*.' The 'greatness of the *r*.' is far removed from 'spiritual greatness'; it is indeed the arrogant attitude that according to Prov. 16.18 goes before a fall. Job speaks (7.11) out of the 'straits' of his *r*. – that is to say out of his distress of mind; and immediately afterwards about the bitterness, that is to say the grief (*mar*), of his *nepeš*. Gen. 26.35 can also report the *mōrat r*. – the bitter suffering – of Isaac and Rebecca. In Isa. 26.9 the yearning desire of the *nepeš* corresponds to the searching longing of the *r*. Thus *r*. can frequently designate a person's spiritual disposition (Prov. 18.14):

> A man's courageous will (*r*.) can endure sickness;
> but a dejected spirit (*r*.) who can bear?

When according to Isa. 19.14 Yahweh brought about a 'spirit of confusion' among the princes of Egypt, the passage means the state of mind that goes with drunkenness.

But what does it mean when Joshua is named briefly in the Priestly document as 'a man in whom is the *r*.' (Num. 27.18)? A man of reliable bearing? A man of gifts and authority? A man of spirit? The Priestly document interprets itself in Deut. 34.9 by calling him 'full of the *r*. of wisdom, for Moses had laid his hands upon him'. The man 'in whom is the *r*.' therefore points here to the man who is endowed with the vital power of wisdom.

6. *Will*

This has led us beyond the sense of *r*. as an attitude of mind, in which the word is largely related in meaning to *nepeš*. The special character of the human *r*. emerges when we find that *r*. generally means the powerful blast of the wind and the enlivening and authorizing efficacy of Yahweh. In this way *r*. is not only suited for depicting movements of feeling; it is still more adapted to be the bearer of energetic actions of the will.

When Ezra 1.5 speaks of the exiled 'whose *r*. God had stirred to go up to rebuild the house of Yahweh which is in Jerusalem,' it is the will that *r*. stands for. But Jer. 51.11 shows that the will to destroy can be meant, just as much as the will to build up: 'Yahweh has stirred up the r. of the kings of the Medes, because his purpose is towards Babylon's ruin, to destroy it.' The *r*. as driving force within man is in the first instance ethically neutral. Num. 5.14, 30 talks about the *r*. of jealousy which can overcome a man. Hosea accuses Israel on account of the *r*. of harlotry, as the seducing impulse which leads to a turning away from God (4.2), or as the binding force that does not permit the return to him (5.4). The Yahwist singles out Caleb from the refractory wilderness generation, because in him there was 'a different *r*.', so that he followed Yahweh completely (Num. 14.24). The talk about 'another will' is significant for the ethical-religious neutrality of the anthropological concept *r*. When Ps. 32.2b calls the man happy 'in whose *r*. there is no indolence', the presupposition is that the will can be both lazy and strong. Ps. 51 prays first for a firm and steadfast will (v. 10b.) and then for a free and ready will (v. 12b); between these sentences stands the plea that God will not take away the *r*. of his holiness – that is to say his incomparable vital power – [21] from the petitioner (v. 11b). The strength and the freedom of the human will are, according to this, dependent on the effect of Yahweh's efficacious power. In the promise to Ezekiel, the 'new *r*.' (36.26; cf. 11.19) is the *r*. of Yahweh himself (36.27). Just as in Ps. 51.10 the prayer for the clean heart precedes the prayer for the firm will, so in Ezek. 11.19; 36.26 the gift of the new heart and the new will are linked together; cf. also 18.31. If in the case of the new heart the point is the pure guidings of the conscience,[22] in the case of the *r*. it is the steadfast power of the will to act accordingly. The usual translation, which speaks of the new, steadfast 'spirit', does not bring this out sufficiently.

It is only seldom that *r*. corresponds to what we call 'spirit'.[23] In Isa. 29.24 the context could point to it:

> Those who erred in spirit (*r*.) come to understanding,
> and those who murmured accept instruction.

The goal of understanding on the path of knowledge suggests 'spirit' for *r*. Similarly in Isa. 19.3:

> The spirit (*r*.) of the Egyptians within them will be disturbed,
> its plans will be confounded.

The parallel to 'plans' suggests the knowing and judging 'spirit' for *r*. But even in these two instances the aspect of will is by no means excluded, just as in Isa. 29.24 'those who err in spirit' are 'those who murmur' and in Isa. 19.3 the spirit that is 'disturbed' forms plans.

In addition, both texts show once more how much man as *r*. can only be rightly understood out of God's communication with him. It should be remembered that *r*. stands twice as often for wind and for the divine vital power as for man's breath, feeling and will. Most of the texts that deal with the *r*. of God or man show God and man in a dynamic relationship. That a man as *r*. is living, desires the good and acts as authorized being – none of this proceeds from man himself.

V

lēb(āb) – Reasonable Man[1]

The most important word in the vocabulary of Old Testament anthropology is generally translated 'heart'. In its commonest form, *lēb*, it occurs 598 times in the Hebrew Old Testament; and in the form *lēbāb* 252 times. In addition the Aramaic *lēb* occurs once, in the book of Daniel, and *lᵉbab* seven times.[2] Altogether, therefore, it can be found 858 times, which makes it the commonest of all anthropological terms. Moreover, in contrast to the other main concepts, it is almost exclusively applied to man. Where *bāsār* refers to animal flesh in more than a third of all its instances, *lēb(āb)* is only applied to animals five times, and four of these are in a comparison with the human heart (II Sam. 17.10; Hos. 7.11; Dan. 4.13; 5.21); only once does it refer exclusively to animals (Job 41.24). And whereas *rūaḥ* is more often applied to God than to man, and means the wind in almost a third of its instances, there are only 26 mentions of the heart of God, 11 of the 'heart of the sea', one mention of the 'heart of heaven' and one of the 'heart' of the tree.[3] So there remain 814 passages which deal exclusively with the human 'heart' – that is to say, more than there are for *nepeš* as a whole (755 instances).

But it is to be feared that the usual translation 'heart' for *lēb(āb)* (henceforth *l.*) leads our present-day understanding astray. The extreme relevance of the word for anthropology demands a semantic re-examination on the basis of the argument of the respective passages, that is to say here, on the basis of the connections between the statements that are made.

1. *Heart*

For our analytical understanding of the synthetic way of thinking, it is again advisable to start from the question, what ideas about the *l.* as a physical organ are to be found in the Old Testament?

The account of Nabal's death in I Sam. 25.37f. seems to me the most interesting:

> His heart (*l.*) died within him,
> and he turned to stone.

And about ten days later Yahweh smote Nabal;
and he died.

The modern reader finds this confusing. In the first sentence he thinks
that when the heart stopped beating the man died, and *rigor mortis* set in.
But then he learns that Nabal went on living for another ten days. The *l.*,
therefore, dies ten days before the man himself. The man Nabal survives
the death of his organ, the *l.*, for ten days. This shows that the writer is
not thinking of the heart stopping beating in our contemporary medical
sense; for that would mean the man's immediate death. Neither here nor
elsewhere [4] does the Old Testament suggest that it is aware of a connection
between the beating of the pulse and the *l.* In our text the body's turning
to stone is associated with the death of the *l.*; here, in view of the fact
that Nabal lived for another ten days in this state, we can only think of
paralysis. To a doctor that would suggest a stroke. After a stroke a man can
easily live for another ten days. The ancient narrator therefore thought of
the heart here as a central organ which made it possible for the limbs to
move. The 'beating' of the heart is not observed here – nor are the brain,
the nerves or the lungs known to ancient Israelite anatomy. In its function,
l. corresponds accordingly in our passage to certain parts of the brain. It
is important to remember this for our later question about the essential
functions which the Hebrews most frequently assign to the 'heart'.

Moreover it is clear that I Sam. 25.37 already looks for *l.* not in the head
but in the 'internal parts' of the body (*beqirbō*). Hosea is more precise
when he proclaims, as his God's threat to Israel:

I will fall upon them like a bear robbed of her cubs,
I will tear open the lock of their heart (Hos. 13.8).

Here 'lock' probably means the basket-like structure of the ribs which
encloses the heart. II Kings 9.24 clearly determines the anatomical place of
the heart when Jehu 'shot Joram between his arms, so that the arrow
protruded from his heart again'. 'Between his arms' here means much the
same as 'between his shoulder-blades'. In II Sam. 18.14 Joab thrust three
spears 'into Absalom's heart', after which he continued to hang living on
the oak tree until ten armour-bearers killed him; here the region of the
heart is thought of as being in the chest. Elsewhere too the 'heart' stands
for the 'breast', as when Aaron bears the breastplate of judgment on his *l.*
(Ex. 28.29f.).

A further contribution to the anatomy of the heart is offered solely by
Jeremiah, when he speaks on one occasion about 'the walls of the heart'
(4.19). The context tells that the prophet becomes aware of an approaching
cry of war. Its purpose is to announce a coming catastrophe. He is then

struck down by a heart attack. For there is no other way of interpreting the words which he groans:

> My innards, my innards! I writhe in pain!
> Oh, the walls of my heart!
> My heart is beating wildly;
> I cannot keep still.

Apparently violent pain or constriction in the region of the heart is here producing a suffocating sense of fear. This is the way that the paroxysm is described which is one of the symptoms of angina pectoris. Perhaps, therefore, 'the walls' of the wildly beating heart are a reference, not so much to the chest as to the pericardium 'inside' the body, which feels as if it is going to burst when the heart is beating wildly with fear. In view of the more than 800 mentions of the human heart in the Old Testament, it is surprising that no more than the passages mentioned contribute anything to its anatomy.

We learn little about the physiology of the heart either, beyond what we have already noticed; and what we do learn is only in connection with some disorder. Jeremiah groans once more under the onslaught of Yahweh's word (23.9):

> My heart is broken within my breast,
>   all my bones shake.

The true prophet, unlike the false one, must even risk his health (cf. 8.18). In Ps. 38.10 a man who is seriously ill complains:

> My heart throbs, my strength fails me;
>   and the light of my eyes – it also has gone from me.

The 'throbbing' of the heart is described by the onomatopaeic word $s^e harhar$, which means, *not* the regular heart beat, but a racing or fluctuating movement (shr gal means roving about). Everything goes black in front of a man's eyes when he is in deadly fear because of the violent and irregular beating of his heart. Thus it was primarily in sickness that Israel learnt to recognize the heart as the central and crucially vital organ (cf. also Isa. 1.5; 57.15; Ps. 37.15).

But this was true in over-exertion as well. To give an exhausted traveller a bite of bread and to strengthen him by so doing is therefore called in Hebrew 'strengthening his heart' (Gen. 18.5; Judg. 19.5, 8).[5] Jezebel shouts at Ahab as he lies listlessly on his bed: 'Arise, and eat bread, so that your heart may recover!' (I Kings 21.7; cf. Acts 14.17; James 5.5; Luke 21.34).

The heart is always recognized as being an inaccessible, hidden organ inside the body. This makes the relatively frequent biblical talk about the 'heart of the sea' comprehensible. In Prov. 30.18f. we read:

> Three things are for me incomprehensible;
> four I do not understand:
> the way of an eagle in the sky,
> the way of a serpent on a rock,
> the way of a ship in the heart of the sea
> and the way of a man with a maiden.

Here the writer describes four paths that have not been previously pioneered and are therefore not discernible in advance. 'The heart of the sea' means here the high seas, the unexplored, open seas (see also Prov. 23.34; Ezek. 27.4, 25–27; 28.2; cf. Ex. 15.8). For coastal shipping, routes are familiar because the shores are visible, but a voyage into the open seas leads into the unknown. When we read, in Jonah 2.3, 'Thou didst cast me . . . into the heart of the seas,' the writer is thinking of the fathomless 'depths' of the 'high seas' too (see also Ezek. 28.8; Ps. 46.2). Correspondingly, the 'heart of the heaven' means its heights, which are unattainable by man; thus Moses reminds the people in Deut. 4.11 of the experience at Horeb: 'You . . . stood at the foot of the mountain, while the mountain burned with fire to the heart of heaven.' According to II Sam. 18.14 Absalom hangs 'in the heart' of the oak, that is to say in the dark, innermost branches of the foliage. Accadian *libbu* can mean the palm tree's 'cone of vegetation'.[6] In all these cases, therefore, the heart stands for the inaccessibly unexplorable – for anything that is quite simply impenetrably hidden.

Numerous sayings about man presuppose this view, which takes its starting point from the anatomical position of the heart. For example, we read in the story about David's anointing in I Sam. 16.7 that Yahweh warns Samuel, in connection with Jesse's eldest son Eliab, who is the first to appear: 'Do not look on his appearance or on his great stature . . . man looks on the outward appearance, but Yahweh looks on the heart.' The heart is therefore contrasted with the outward appearance. Although it is concealed from men, it is here that the vital decisions are made. For Prov. 24.12, *l.* is the place of unknowable impulses, in contrast to the externally articulate word:

> If you say, 'Behold, we did not know this',
> he who weighs the heart perceives it.

It is only before God that what is hidden from the eye of man cannot be concealed:

The underworld and the realm of the dead lie open before Yahweh,
how much more the hearts of men (Prov. 15.11).

He knows the secrets of the heart (Ps. 44.21).

Cf. Ps. 139.23; Jer. 17.9f.

Even if all these texts presuppose a certain notion of the physical organ
l., yet they all – with the sole exception of the Nabal story – envisage far
more than the anatomical position and the physiological functions of the
heart. The essential activities of the human heart are in the Bible mental
and spiritual in kind.

Which acts, then, are ascribed to the heart?

2. *Feelings*

In the first place they affect the sensibility and the emotions, and therefore
correspond to what we would ascribe to feeling and mood – the irrational
levels of man. This may be understandable if we start from the excited
condition of the sick heart. In Ps. 25.17 a sufferer prays:

Relieve the constriction of my heart,
and bring me out of my distresses.

The first sentence (*ṣārōt lᵉbābī harḥēb*[7]) means literally: 'Expand the
narrow places of my heart.' Here the pains of angina and its anxiety
coincide. But in Ps. 119.32 talk about the 'enlarging' of the heart, that is to
say the relieving of its cramp, has already left the idea of physical recovery
far behind:

I will run in the way of thy promises,
for thou enlargest my heart.

tarḥib libbī means here in the widest sense: 'Thou freest me.'[8] The tranquil
heart contributes to the health of a man's whole life (Prov. 14.30):

A tranquil heart is the life of the flesh,
but passion makes the bones rot.

l. is here attitude of mind, a man's mood, or his temperament. This is
what Prov. 23.17 means when it admonishes:

Let not your heart be stirred up over sinners,
but continue in the fear of Yahweh all the day.

The heart that is stirred up is a man who reacts emotionally, or gets
excited. The cultivation of obedience is contrasted with unbalanced
feelings.

In addition, the heart is the seat of certain states of feeling, such as joy
and grief. In this sense the heart is described as being good (*yṭb*) or bad

(r"), when a man is feeling well disposed (Judg. 18.20; 19.6, 9; Deut. 28.47; Prov. 15.15) or ill-tempered (Deut. 15.10). Hannah's heart is sad at first because of her childlessness (I Sam. 1.8), but after Samuel's birth she rejoices: 'My heart exults in Yahweh' (I Sam. 1.2; cf. Ps. 13.5). The heart is the place of the cheerfulness that comes from wine (Ps. 104.15): 'Wine gladdens the heart of man.' Cf. Zech. 10.7. A wedding day is 'the day of the gladness of the heart' (S. of S. 3.11). The state of the heart dominates every manifestation of life (Prov. 15.13):

> A glad heart makes a cheerful countenance,
> but by sorrow of heart the spirit (*rūaḥ*) is broken.

Prov. 17.22 even teaches:

> A cheerful heart promotes health,
> but a downcast spirit (*rūaḥ*) wastes away the body.

Courage and fear are also realized in particular movements of the heart. If courage fails 'the heart quivers like leaves in the wind' (*nw*ʿ, Isa. 7.2), it is faint (*rkk*, Isa. 7.4; Deut. 20.8), it melts (*mss*, Deut. 20.8) like wax (Ps. 22.14), it turns to water (Josh. 7.5). Cf. Josh. 2.11; 5.1; Isa. 13.7; 19.1. If a man is overcome by fear, the Hebrews say, his heart 'goes out' (Gen. 42.28), it leaves him (Ps. 40.12) and drops down (I Sam. 17.32). These phrases show how little the writers continue to think of the physical organ and how *l.* has actually taken on the meaning of 'courage' (cf. II Sam. 17.10). He that hopes in Yahweh 'strengthens his heart', that is to say, he acquires courage (Ps. 27.14). In the Joseph story, the Yahwist tells that after the brothers have told what has happened to Joseph, Jacob's heart became limp, or powerless (*pwg* describes the lack of energy of someone who is depressed, Ps. 38.8; Ps. 77.2 the weakness of a raised hand; cf. Hab. 1.4) that is to say, Jacob's courage was exhausted.[9]

3. Wish

It is possible to talk about the *l.*'s *desire and longing*, just as it is in the case of *nepeš*. Ps. 21.2 expresses thanks on behalf of the king:

> Thou hast given him his heart's desire
> and hast not withheld the request of his lips.

Since here (instead of *nepeš*: see pp. 15f. above) the heart is mentioned next to the lips, the writer will have been thinking of the inner, secret wishes. In the same way Prov. 6.25 is thinking of the secret longing for a neighbour's wife: 'Do not desire her beauty in your heart.' The strength of a longing heart must not be overstrained (Prov. 13.12):

> Hope deferred makes the heart sick,
> but a desire fulfilled is a tree of life.

In a remarkable phrase, Job in his oath of purity (31.7) disputes that 'his heart has gone after his eyes', that is to say that his secret lust was ever roused by what came before his eyes. Just as in this sentence the eyes stand for what is seen, so the heart stands for the hidden desire. Cf. also Job. 31.9. Num. 15.39 talks about the tassels on the corners of the Israelites' garments, which are to have the following meaning for them:

> When you look upon them, you shall remember all the commandments of Yahweh, to act according to them, not to run after your own hearts and your own eyes, when you follow them in your unfaithfulness.

Here the lusts of the secret imaginings (the heart) are set beside the visible enticements (of the eyes). Just as the heart can 'fall' into despondency (I Sam. 17.32), so it can also 'rear up' in arrogance (*rwm* Deut. 8.14; Hos. 13.6; cf. Dan. 5.20–22). Arrogance is 'swelling' of the heart (*gōdel lēbāb*, Isa. 9.9); pride of heart is presumption (*zᵉdōn lēb*, Jer. 49.16).[10] This linguistic usage is worth noticing as the background to the single New Testament passage which speaks about the heart of Jesus (Matt. 11.29): 'I am gentle and lowly in heart.' The counter-images of *hubris* in the Old Testament are an urgent injunction to the imitation of Jesus.

The groups of texts dealt with in this section have not mentioned *l.*'s essential characteristics. As the organ of emotional impulses, we found it in direct proximity to *nepeš* and *rūaḥ*. Like those words, it can sometimes be generalized into a personal pronoun; and many emotional processes, such as trembling, dwindling away or being restless can certainly be described even without *l.*[11] But the stereometry of expression must still be noted, particularly in the parallelism of *l.*, *nepeš* and *rūaḥ*. We saw with the 'heart's desire' (to take an example) that secret wishes and ideas were more clearly touched on than with the 'soul' (Ps. 21.2; Num. 15.39). The oppressed *rūaḥ* that wastes away the body (Prov. 17.22; cf. 15.13) reminds us more of the diminishing vital powers when it is set against the cheerful heart.[12] But what is the specific thing about 'heart' – the characteristic note that still echoes at the back of those statements about joy and grief, courage and fear, desire and arrogance, and in the usages which are now almost solely pronominal?

4. Reason

In by far the greatest number of cases it is intellectual, rational functions that are ascribed to the heart – i.e., precisely what we ascribe to the head and, more exactly, to the brain; cf. I Sam. 25.37.[13] Here the word is clearly distinguished from *nepeš* and *rūaḥ*. We shall see that just as *rūaḥ* means 'vital power' (in contrast to the infirmity of the 'flesh') rather than spirit, *l.* is frequently better rendered by 'spirit' than by 'heart'. We must guard against the false impression that biblical man is determined more by feeling than by reason. This mistaken anthropological direction is all too easily derived from an undifferentiated rendering of *l.* The Bible sets before men clear alternatives, which have to be recognized. It is highly significant that *l.* occurs by far the most frequently in the wisdom literature – 99 times in Proverbs alone, 42 times in Ecclesiastes, and in the strongly didactic Deuteronomy 51 times.[14]

It is positively by definition that Deut. 29.3 presupposes that the heart is destined for *understanding* (*lāda'at*), in the same way that the eyes are destined for seeing and the ears for hearing; cf. 8.5. It is failing to fulfil its primary function if its insight (*bîn*) fails through callousness (Isa. 6.10). Prov. 15.14 describes the essential business of the heart in the biblical sense: 'The wise heart seeks knowledge.' Cf. Prov. 8.5; 18.15. Prov. 16.23 says: 'The heart of the wise makes his speech judicious.' Ps. 90.12 defines as the aim of life:

> To number our days – so teach us –
> that we may bring home a heart of wisdom.

In Job 8.10 Bildad comes to speak of the wisdom of the patriarchs with the words:

> They teach you, and speak to you,
> and utter sayings out of their heart.

The reference is to their capacity for perception and the treasure of their knowledge, not, as one might think, to their moods and feelings.

Such fullness of perception comes from receptive hearing. That is why Solomon's great wisdom consists in the fact that he does not ask for long life, riches, or the lives of his enemies, but for 'a hearing heart' (I Kings 3.9–12). It is the wise and discerning heart because of its capacity for hearing.[15] This makes him capable of the heavy task of ruling justly over a great and difficult people[16] and of 'discerning between good and evil'. In this way his 'heart' also then acquires the 'breadth' (*rōḥab lēb*) to grasp the fullness of all world phenomena (I Kings 4.29–34).[17] In our language *mind* is exactly the right word at this point.[18] For its characteristics are an international culture, comprehensive scholarship (botany, zoology, law, politics, educational theory), an accurate power of judgment and the high art of poetic language.

For the perceptive reason (Prov. 18.15) the heart and the ear stand parallel to one another:

A heart of insight acquires knowledge,
and the wise ear seeks knowledge.

Ear and heart are often mentioned together: Deut.29.4; Isa.6.10; 32.3f.;
Jer.11.8; Ezek.3.10; 40.4; 44.5; Prov.2.2; 22.17; 23.12.

Insight originates in the heart. Deutero-Isaiah reminds his hearers of
God's angry but fruitless judgment over Jacob (42.25):

It flamed up round about, but he did not understand;
It scorched him, but he did not take it to heart.

Literally, the last sentence runs: 'he did not lay it upon his heart', i.e., he
did not derive insight from it.[19] In a similar sense the Yahwist can talk in
Gen.31.20 about the theft of the heart: 'Jacob stole the heart of Laban the
Aramaean, in that he concealed from him that he intended to flee.' 'To
steal the heart' (*gnb* qal) therefore means to deprive someone of insight, to
deceive him.[20]

In the same sense, the Old Testament speaks quite often of 'lack of
heart' (*ḥᵃsar l.*). The expression does not mean coldness of feeling but lack
of thought. This is the sense in which Prov.10.13 is to be understood:

On the lips of him who has understanding wisdom is found,
but a rod is the due of him who lacks heart.

Insight would be the exact translation for *l.* here. The same phrase is to be
found in Prov.24.30:

I passed by the field of a sluggard,
by the vineyard of a man without heart.

It may not be only the person without sense that is meant here; it could
be the positively stupid person, in apposition to the sluggard, or lazy man;
cf. also Prov.6.32. *timhōn lēbāb* (Deut.28.28) is confusion of mind.

Insight will lead to permanent *consciousness*. When Deut.6.6 charges
that 'These words which I command you this day shall be upon your
heart,' it means that the hearer should 'remain conscious' of them. When
talking about the words of wisdom Prov.7.3 demands in graphic terms:

Bind them on your fingers,
Write them on the tablet of your heart.

They are to remain constantly present to the mind. When Jer.17.1 says
of the sin of Judah that it is 'written with a pen of iron, with a point of
diamond it is engraved on the tablet of their heart,' then the heart has in
this way become a permanent reminder – its consciousness cannot be
erased. The turn of phrase 'to rise up into the heart' (*ʿālāh ʿal-l.*) means
something like 'to enter the consciousness'. Thus Isa.65.17 stresses the
overwhelming impression of the new heaven and the earth by saying that,

in contrast, what was before will no longer be remembered and will no more 'rise to the heart', that is to say, come to mind.[21] Jer. 3.16 says the same thing about the ark of the covenant. Paul writes similarly about his Corinthians (II Cor. 3.2f.):

> You yourselves are our letter, written in our heart, to be known and read by all men . . . a letter from Christ . . . written . . . on the fleshly tablets of the heart.

Thus the heart also becomes the treasury of knowledge and of memory. When Daniel (7.28) keeps the words firmly 'in his heart' it means in his *memory*; cf. Ps. 27.8. In the story of Samson, the woman Delilah struggles to obtain the secret of the Israelite's enormous power. She makes the solution of this riddle the touchstone of his love. According to Judg. 16.15, she says to him:

> How can you say that you love me when your heart is not with me? You have mocked me these three times, and you have not told me wherein your great strength lies.

Samson is accordingly giving evidence of his love for Delilah although 'his heart is not with her'. 'Your heart is not with me' therefore does not mean here 'you do not love me,' but 'you do not share your secrets with me', 'you do not allow me to share the treasure of your knowledge'. When Delilah pursues Samson day after day with these reproaches, 'his soul was vexed to death' and (vv. 17f.):

> he opened his whole heart to her, and said, 'A razor has never passed over my head . . .' (Then) Delilah recognized that he had opened his whole heart to her.

Clearly 'to open his heart to her' means to part with his *knowledge*.

Thinking also takes place in the heart – reasoning, reflecting and considering. *śîm 'et-lēb le* means: to direct his attention to something or someone (I Sam. 9.20; 25.25; Hag. 1.5). When in Ex. 14.5 Pharaoh's 'heart' is turned towards the people, it is his attention or his interest that is meant. Hosea accuses Israel in the name of his God (7.2):

> They do not say to their hearts
> that I know of all their weakness.

That is to say, they do not reflect. In I Sam. 27.1 'David said to his heart'; under this introductory heading he has all kinds of reflections, makes plans, and considers various factors:

> I shall still perish one day by the hand of Saul; there is nothing better left for me than to escape to the land of the Philistines; then Saul will cease to seek me all over Israel.

A whole strategy can therefore be thought through when a man 'says to his heart'. Cf. Gen. 24.45; 27.41, and in I Kings 12.26f. the considerations that lead Jeroboam to his decision in v. 28. In Gen. 17.17 we are told that, after his son was promised to him, Abraham 'fell on his face and laughed; for he said in his heart, "Shall a child be born to a man who is a hundred years old?"' Instead of 'he said in his heart', we should say 'after reasonable consideration he said to himself'. In the same way the fool thinks that he is drawing quite sensible conclusions when he 'says in his heart "There is no God"' (Ps. 14.1). In Prov. 28.26 the heart as the organ of its own reflections is confronted with the accumulated wisdom of experience:

> He who trusts in his own heart is a fool;
> but he who walks in wisdom is delivered.

Hos. 7.11 takes the intellectual functions of the heart one step further. The prophet sees that:

> Ephraim is like a dove,
> which lets itself be led astray, without heart.

What does 'without heart' (*'ēn lēb*) mean? The sequel explains: 'Calling to Egypt, going to Assyria.' The state of Israel is becoming the victim of an ill-considered seesaw policy. Accordingly 'without heart' means without a clear *sense of direction*. In Hos. 4.11 the prophet complains:

> Wine is taking the heart from my people.
> They enquire of a thing of wood,
> and their staff gives them oracles.

People who rely on the use of mindless oracles have lost their heart, that is to say they have been robbed of their understanding or, to be more precise, they have lost their power of judgment and direction. Moreover the robber is wine. As everyone knows, it does not detract from a cheerful mood, but it does rob a man of his understanding. That is why the author of Proverbs warns (23.31f.):

> Do not look at wine when it is red . . .
> At the last it bites like a serpent . . .
> Your eyes will see strange things
> and your heart utter absurdities.

In contexts such as these, heart can in general be translated by '*understanding*'. Cf. Eccles. 10.2f.; Prov. 19.8. Job defends himself against his all too clever friends (12.3):

> I have understanding (*l.*) as well as you;
> I am not inferior to you.

'Men of understanding' are consequently called *'anšē lēb* (Job 34.10), which means wise men, not stout-hearted, brave men, or men of feeling. In Job 34.34 the wise man is therefore also a synonymous parallel to 'the man of heart'.[22]

I hope that this selection of texts may have been able to suggest the wide range and the fine shades of meaning with which the 'heart' in Hebrew describes the seat and function of the reason. It includes everything that we ascribe to the head and the brain – power of perception, reason, understanding, insight, consciousness, memory, knowledge, reflection, judgment, sense of direction, discernment. These things circumscribe the real core of meaning of the word *l.*

5. *Decisions of the will*

Some of the last-mentioned texts, which talked about *l.* in its capacity for judgment and a sense of direction, suggested that there is an easy transition in the use of the word from the functions of the understanding to the activity of the *will*. The Israelite finds it difficult to distinguish linguistically between 'perceiving' and 'choosing', between 'hearing' and 'obeying'. The linguistic difficulty that ensues for our more differentiating mode of thought comes from the factual impossibility of dividing theory from practice. Thus the heart is at once the organ of understanding and of will.

By *planning* (*ḥšb* piel) the Hebrew has in mind the transition from deliberation to action. Prov. 16.9 shows both the execution of the plan and its limitations:

> A man's heart plans his way
> but Yahweh directs his steps.

In Ps. 20.4 *l.* is the synonymous parallel to 'plan' (*'ēṣā*):

> May he grant you your heart's desire,
> and fulfil all your plans!

In Gen. 6.5 the Yahwist talks about the forming of the plans of the heart which are only evil.

Since the criteria of plans and actions have to be considered in the heart, *l.* comes to take on the meaning 'conscience', for example in I Sam. 24.6: 'Afterward David's heart smote him, because he had cut off the corner of Saul's garment.' In the same way, in II Sam. 24.10 it is the heart as conscience that beats, or smites David. The reason given for the 'beating' of the heart in the respective contexts shows that the writer does not mean the beating of the heart, either in the physiological sense, or in the sense of excited emotions; what is being described is the reaction of the ethical judgment formed by the conscience. The prophetess Huldah says to King Josiah in II Chron. 34.27: 'Because your heart has been softened and you humbled yourself before God when you heard his words and wept, I have heard you.' The passage talks about the softening of the *l.* because, instead of remaining hard, it was moved; this is interpreted as penitence, through the listening to God's word. The conscience is called *lēb* in the Bible because it is a perceptive organ. In Ps. 51.10 the guilty man joins his plea for a pure heart with the request for the new creation of a pure conscience, meaning that his life should take its bearings from the conscience. The prayer that follows for a 'steadfast spirit' adds the wish for the enduring power to implement to a corresponding degree what the conscience has perceived.[23]

The heart is the place of *decision*. In II Sam. 7.27 David says he has 'found his heart' to pray to God. How is this literal translation to be understood? 'Find his *l.*' certainly does not mean that he has found courage; in view of the succeeding, final sentence it means that he has arrived at his decision, and has arrived at it on the basis of his knowledge. Prov. 6.18 shows the heart as being the organ which brings already conceived plans to fruition through decision: Yahweh hates, among other things,

> a heart that devises wicked plans,
> feet that make haste to run to evil.

Because it is in the heart that the decision is made between corruption and wise advice (Prov. 4.20–27), the heart should be protected with the greatest vigilance (v. 23):

> Above all guard your heart,
> for from it flow the springs of life.

Hardness of heart develops at the same place as decisions of the will; the heart is hardened and becomes insensitive and inflexible (Ex. 4.21; 7.3,15; 9.7; Deut. 2.30; Isa. 6.10; and frequently elsewhere).

The common phrase *dibber 'al-l.*, 'to speak to the heart', 'to appeal to the heart', belongs to this same context. It is in the first place part of the language of love; but it does not mean fine words without any particular aim, but an appeal which is an attempt at a change of will (Hos. 2.16f.; Gen. 34.3). It can then also mean 'to appeal to the conscience' (Judg. 19.3; Gen. 50.21).[24] In any case it is the invitation to a decision; cf. Isa. 40.2; II Chron. 30.22; 32.6. 'To speak to the heart' in the Old Testament consequently means: to move someone to decision.

From this point it is not far to *intention* as something that happens in the heart. Nathan says to David, when he is considering the building of the temple (II Sam. 7.3): 'Go, do all that is in your heart.' That is to say, do what you intend to do. Jonathan's armour-bearer says to him, after he has unfolded his military plans (I Sam. 14.6f.): 'Do all that is in your heart; behold I am with you; "As is your heart so is mine."'[25] With this he declares: do what you mean to do; I will act according to your intentions. Isa. 10.7 pronounces judgment on Assyria: 'It is in his heart to destroy.' The link with the final infinitive shows that the destroying is 'within his intention'. Ps. 24.4 answers the question as to who may ascend Yahweh's hill with: 'He who has clean hands and a pure heart.' That could mean anyone who has neither done evil nor intended to do so; cf. Pss. 17.3; 139.23; Prov. 21.2.

The Priestly document talks about the heart as the *impulse of the will* in Ex. 35.21; 36.2: the men working on the tent of meeting are called people 'whose hearts had stirred them up to come to do the work'. This is the way in which willingness is described. According to the Yahwist's description in Num. 16.28, Moses introduces his threat of punishment to the refractory Dathan and Abiram with the words: 'Hereby you shall know that Yahweh has sent me to do all these works, and that it does not come from my own heart.' *lōʾ millibbî* means here 'not of my own (arbitrary) impulse'. The Deuteronomic preachers are stressing that love of God should come of its own accord when they charge their hearers in Deut. 6.5: 'You shall love Yahweh your God with all your *l.* and with all your *nepeš* and with all your might.' Just as *nepeš* means true longing and desire, so *l.* means here the *conscious devotion of the will* (cf. Deut. 4.29; 10.12; 11.18; and passim). The aspects of consciousness and of will must definitely be seen together at this point. For the devotion can be the object of testing. Deut. 8.2 reminds its hearers of the path by which Yahweh led Israel through the wilderness for 40 years, 'testing you, to know what was in your heart, whether you would keep his commandments, or not'. Here *obedience* on the basis of knowledge of the commandments is tested 'in the heart'. When Absalom steals 'the hearts of the men of Israel' (II Sam. 15.6 *gnb* piel), he is robbing them of their conscious liking, obedience and allegiance which ought to be paid to his father David; cf. I Kings 12.27. The admonition in Prov. 23.26 is also thinking of decision of the will:

> My son, give me your heart,
> and let my instructions be pleasing in your eyes.

David's sons are judged according to whether 'their hearts are wholly with Yahweh' (*lēbāb šālēm ʿim yhwh*) as David's is (I Kings 8.61; 11.4; 15.3, 14; II Kings 20.3). The Deuteronomist is thinking here of complete and unconditional obedience.[26]

This view of the heart is put in pictorial terms in the prophetic demand for circumcision for Yahweh's sake and for the removal 'of the foreskin of your hearts' (Jer. 4.4). This illustrates the new return – indeed the surrender – to Yahweh. Deut. 10.16 explains the expected event still further by indicating that the people's previous 'stubbornness' will now be ended: 'Circumcise therefore the foreskin of your heart, and be no longer stubborn.' Jer. 3.10 contrasts a deceptive, hypocritical or merely outward conversion (*beseqer*) with one which takes place 'with the whole heart' (*bekol-l.*), with a sincere devotion that could also stand up to an examination of the hidden intentions. Thus Joel (2.12) calls for 'a return with all your heart', that is to say for a change brought about by a clear decision of will (cf. Jer. 29.13). The Deuteronomist is continually charging the people to fear God and serve him sincerely 'with the whole heart' – exhorting them, that is, to a conscious surrender of the will (cf. I Sam. 12.24).

The prophet Ezekiel recognizes that man cannot renew his heart by himself. He promises in the name of his God (11.19; cf. 36.26):

> And I will give them another (new) *l.*
> and put a new *rūaḥ* within them;
> I will take the stony heart out of their body
> and give them a heart of flesh.

The rest of the passage shows that here *l.* also probably means perception and a sense of spiritual direction – indeed conscience; but it means more than that. For 11.20 (cf. 36.27) goes on:

> that they may walk according to my statutes
> and keep my ordinances and obey them.

The heart of stone is the dead heart (cf. I Sam. 25.37), which is unreceptive and makes all the limbs incapable of action. The heart of flesh is the living heart, full of insight, which is at the same time ready for new action. The new *rūaḥ* brings to the perception and will of the heart the new vital power to hold on steadfastly in willing obedience.[27] When Ezekiel demands (18.31): 'Get yourselves a new heart and a new spirit!' his call is based on God's previous offer of life (vv. 23, 31f.):

> I have no pleasure in the death of the wicked.
> Why will you die?

The call is interpreted antithetically (v. 31a): 'Cast away from you all the obstinacy with which you have rebelled against me!' In contrast to this the invitation to get a new heart is an exhortation to accept the offer of a purposeful willingness for new obedience.

Finally, 'heart', like the other main anthropological concepts,[28] can also stand for man's self, for the person as such. When Jer. 23.16 warns against false prophets:

> Do not listen to the words of the prophets,
> they do but delude you;
> they speak visions of their own *l*.
> not from the mouth of Yahweh,

visions of their own hearts means simply 'their own views', the vision which comes from themselves;[29] but at the same time one hears the under-tone – visions which accord with their human knowledge or even their self-conceit. Ps. 22.26 is a call to the thank-offering meal:

> The afflicted shall eat and be satisfied;
> those who seek him shall praise Yahweh,
> may 'their'[30] hearts live for ever.

This means little more than 'long may they live'.

Even where *l.* fades almost into a personal pronoun, we should remain conscious of the particular aspect of man under which man as heart is being contemplated. We saw that *l.* least of all means the emotions; on the contrary, it much more frequently means (and indeed this is its specific characteristic) the organ of knowledge, with which is associated the will, its plans, decisions and intentions, the consciousness, and a cònscious and sincerely devoted obedience.

We can see that the spectrum of meaning of this most frequent anthropological term is a particularly broad one. But though it undoubtedly embraces the whole range of the physical, the emotional and the intellectual, as well as the functions of the will, yet we must clearly hold on to the fact that the Bible primarily views the heart as the centre of the consciously living man. The essential characteristic that, broadly speaking, dominates the concept is that the heart is called to reason, and especially to hear the word of God.

6. The 'heart' of God

The statements about the 'heart' of God are worth thinking about because they always concern God's relationship to man. The heart of God is most often mentioned as the organ of God's distinct will, against which man is judged. A man of God proclaims the word of Yahweh to the priest Eli (I Sam. 2.35):

> I will raise up for myself a faithful priest,
> who shall do according to what is in my heart and in my mind.

ka'ᵃšer bilᵉbābī ūbᵉnapšī means: according to my will and my desire. Very similarly, Yahweh says to Jehu in II Kings 10.30:

> Because you have zealously carried out what is right in my eyes, and

entirely as it is in my heart, your sons into the fourth generation shall sit on the throne of Israel.

Acts which are exactly what is 'in Yahweh's heart' also correspond exactly to his will, just as whatever is right in his (incorruptible) eyes does. Samuel says to Saul (I Sam. 13.14):

> Your kingdom shall not continue;
> Yahweh has sought out a man after his own heart;
> and Yahweh has appointed him to be leader over his people.

'*iš kilᵉbābō* is the man who is in accordance with God's will; cf. Jer. 3.15. On the other hand, the serving of false cultic sites is not in accordance with Yahweh's command, since 'it never entered his *l*.', that is to say, it was not one of the decisions made by his will (Jer. 7.31; 19.5; 32.35).

Just as God's distinct will (against which he judges men) is seen in conjunction with his heart, so is the *plan* of his future actions: 'A day of vengeance is in my heart' (Isa. 63.4). This is an expression of decision; cf. Jer. 23.20; 30.24. The same is true of the promise (Jer. 32.41):

> I will rejoice in doing them good,
> and I will plant them in this land in faithfulness,
> with all my heart and all my soul.

We know this turn of phrase from the preachers of Deuteronomy, who expect of the hearts of men complete devotion, together with complete engagement of the will.[31] Correspondingly God's *l*. and God's *nepeš* are spoken of here to attest his steadfast will and his longing desire – in this case with regard to his plan for the future, to which his whole will is completely committed. Cf. II Sam. 7.21.

Ps. 33.11 praises the absolute reliability of Yahweh's plans for the future:

> The counsel of Yahweh stands for ever,
> the plans of his heart to all generations.

Others texts which speak of the heart of God express the fervour of his kindness towards man. Thus Lam. 3.33 says almost accusingly of God in view of the miseries of the Exile: 'He does not afflict or grieve the sons of men from his heart.' The phrase *lō' millibbō* ('not from his heart') corresponds exactly to Moses' self-defence in Num. 16.28,[32] and means 'not of his own accord', 'not according to his own original will'. If Yahweh has to take action against Israel, then 'strange is the deed! . . . alien is the work!' (Isa. 28.21), which is demanded of him by Israel's apostasy.

The idea that God himself suffers under the wickedness of men is already expressed by the Yahwist in Gen. 6.6. Because human plans are evil, God is sorry that he created man, 'and it grieved him to his heart'.

His will to create is deeply injured; he is hurt to the innermost core of his being (cf. also Jer. 48.36a, b).

At the end of the story of the Flood, Yahweh's resolve never again to curse the earth is introduced by the Yahwist with the sentence (Gen. 8.21) 'Yahweh said to his heart'. This is the way we found statements of reflection, of consideration and of decision introduced when it was men who were involved.[33] Here Yahweh forms the good resolution that corresponds to his original will to create, against which man has offended, according to 6.6.

The more rational function of the *l.* is more evident still in Jer. 44.21, where we are told that Yahweh was aware of all kinds of cultic abominations: 'Yahweh took note of it and it entered his heart.' *'ālāh 'al-l.* does not correspond to our phrase 'to take something to heart'; it means 'to come home to a person', 'to notice', and is here parallel to *zkr*, 'to think of'.[34]

Job is amazed at the attention God focuses on man (7.17):

> What is man, that thou dost make so much of him,
> and that thou dost even set thy heart upon him?

On *šīt lēb 'el* see p. 49 above. Job 34.14 questions that God 'directs his heart towards himself', that is to say, that he thinks about himself. With his heart God devotes his observation, his perception, his attention and his care to his creation. (Only Job 10.13 talks about the heart of the hidden God.)

We may mention in this connection a remarkable late Deuteronomic interpretation of the presence of God in the temple at Jerusalem. In I Kings 9.3 (=II Chron. 7.16) a saying of Yahweh's to Solomon after the consecration of the temple runs:

> I have consecrated this temple which you have built,
> by leaving my name there for ever;
> my eyes and my heart also shall be there for all time.

The well known Deuteronomic saying about the name of God dwelling in the sanctuary is explained and supplemented by an otherwise unknown expansion. The presence of the eyes proclaims that God notices everyone who comes to the holy place; in so far the saying represents the granting of Solomon's plea in I Kings 8.29: 'that thy eyes may be open day and night over this house'. But what is the intention of the quite unusual additional promise of the presence of the heart of God? It no doubt promises – beyond what has been said hitherto – God's 'sympathy' and 'favour',[35] that is to say his innermost and entire good will. Cf. also Ps. 78.72.

Hosea speaks in an incomparable way of God's heart as the place of revolutionary, vital decisions. Neither the demonstrations of Yahweh's love nor his punishments have been able to persuade his people to turn towards him for long (Hos.11.1–7). So the final judgment seems inevitable. But at this very point begins one of the greatest sayings in the Old Testament, proclaimed by Hosea as the word of his God (11.8f.):

> How can I give you up, O Ephraim! . . .
> My heart turns over within me,
> my compassion is mightily kindled.
> I will not execute my fierce anger . . .
> For I am God and not man . . .

Here God first reprimands himself: ' . . . how could I?' And the passage ends in an official renunciation of punishment. This is justified by the statement that instead of the well-merited, annihilating cataclysm, a cataclysm or upheaval takes place in God's heart. The word *hpk* for cataclysm is a reminder of the Sodom story (Gen.19.25; cf. Amos 4.11; Deut.29.23) and is used here for God's reversal of feeling: 'My heart is overthrown within me.' This means the overthrow of God's deliberate decision. God's unqualified mercy turns against his decision for judgment. God's heart, i.e., his free resolve of love, turns against his decision of anger. So Hosea promised that decision in the heart of God which has been sealed for all nations in Jesus Christ. Thus without knowledge of the heart of God man's real situation is incomprehensible.

What we have to remember is that in the Old Testament it is only Job 10.13 that speaks of God's heart as hidden; that there is hardly any talk of its feelings; more about its noticing, thinking and planning; and very clear and repeated statements about its normative will, its determined inclination towards man and the power of its decision for mercy.[36]

VI

The Life of the Body[1]

For Old Testament man, life is essentially manifested in the breath (*nešāmā* 24 times, in addition Aramaic *nišmā* once) and, incomparably more often, in the blood (*dām* 360 times). Both terms are distinguished from others[2] by the fact that they have almost always retained their physical or concrete basis meaning as terms of vegetative physiology.

1. *Breath*

Job (27.3) establishes that the *nešāmā* is the mark of the living person as distinct from the dead one:

> My breath (*nišmātī*) is still in me,
>   and the breath (*rūaḥ*) of God is in my nostrils.

When we are told in I Kings 17.17 that the sickness of the widow of Zarephath's son worsened so much that there was finally no breath (*nešāmā*) left in him, this means that he died (vv. 18ff.). So it is not surprising that the word becomes the term for life *per se*. Josh. 11.11 records the capture of Hazor by Joshua: '"He"[3] smote with the edge of the sword all persons (*kol-hannepeš*) who were in it, utterly destroying them; no life (*nešāmā*) remained.' With its reminder of the breath, *nešāmā* is apparently a more precise way of referring to life than *nepeš*. At the same time, the transition to the meaning 'living thing' is a fluid one. It has taken place when *nešāmā* becomes the object of destruction (Josh. 10.40; cf. 11.14; Deut. 20.16), or when it appears in the plural as the object of Yahweh's creation (*nešāmōt* Isa. 57.16). Living creatures are in this way exactly defined in Hebrew as creatures that breathe. Ought this basic meaning to be forgotten in a single passage, Prov. 20.27?[4]

> The *nešāmā* of man is a lamp of Yahweh,
>   searching all the secret chambers of the body.

Here one is inclined to interpret the *nešāmā* as 'spirit', since it makes the searching possible; but that would be an unusual meaning even for *rūaḥ*.

We should therefore rather accept the conjecture which reads *nōṣēr* for the first word instead of *nēr*, lamp.[5]

> Yahweh watches over the breath of man,
> he searches all the innermost parts of the body.

This establishes the synonymous parallelism, which is also decisively favoured by the basic meaning of *neshāmā*. Yahweh thereby counts as the protector as well as the Creator of the breath.

Breath as the characteristic of life shows that man is indissolubly connected with Yahweh.[6] Everything to do with man is earthly and material, even though it is formed by Yahweh himself; but man's existence as living being is thanks to Yahweh's infusion of the breath of life. Yet the Yahwist does not speak of the breath of Yahweh (cf. also Isa.42.5). But it should be noted that no fewer than eight other passages do so, though admittedly they are late ones: 'The breath of the Highest has brought me to life', Job 33.4; cf. 34.14; 32.8 (makes wise); 37.10 (forms ice). But Yahweh's breath is not only creative power; his breathing also brings judgment (Job 4.9; II Sam. 22.16; Ps. 18.15; Isa. 30.33). Isa. 57.16 makes Yahweh's anger find its limits in the remembrance of the 'creatures of breath' whom he has created (cf. Gen. 2.7 and Isa. 42.5ff.). The breath of animals is never expressly mentioned; it is only in Gen. 7.22 that it is included according to the context. The business of all human breath is to praise God (Ps. 150.6):

> Let everything that breathes praise Yahweh.

Thus breath as the basic function of human life is to keep man bound together with his Creator and preserver, with the God of wrath and the God of mercy.

2. *Blood*

Like the breath, the blood plays no part in the intellectual or even in the emotional life in the Old Testament.[7] In view of the fact that *dām* occurs 360 times, this is to our ideas as remarkable as the circumstance that it is thought of together with man's *nepeš*,[8] rather than with his 'heart'. It counts mainly as being the seat of the vital physical life *per se*. Talking about criminals, Prov. 1.18 says:

> These men lie in wait for their own blood (*dāmām*),
> they set an ambush for their own lives (*napšōtām*).

Thus blood stands for the bare life of man. Ps. 72.13f. prays for the righteous king:

> May he save the lives (*napšōt*) of the needy . . .
> let their blood (*dāmām*) be precious in his sight.

Thus blood which has been shed and has not been covered up cries from the ground (Gen. 4.10). It is a substitute for the cry of need of the mouth that has been silenced (Job 16.18, cf. Gen. 37.26). The animistic power of the blood (in which life has gone out of the murdered man and which cries out for revenge) goes on working in the Old Testament, since it finds a hearer in Yahweh. An account rendered for the blood is an account rendered for the life which has been demanded (Gen. 42.22). It is true of a man as well as of an animal that 'the life of every creature is its blood' (Lev. 17.14; Deut. 12.23; Gen. 9.4–6).[9]

Consequently sacral law includes in its thinking all crimes against the blood, not only in the cultic and ritual sphere but also in the social one. Both are assigned to the sphere of Yahweh, as the guardian of life. That the thinking of the sacral law plays a prominent part as regards the blood can be seen merely from the fact that *dām* is found most frequently in Leviticus (88 times) and Ezekiel (55 times).[10]

The tasting of blood in the eating of meat is forbidden without exception (Gen. 9.4; Lev. 3.17; 7.26; 19.26; Deut. 12.16, 23; 15.23). After Saul's battle with the Philistines, when the people fall upon the booty of sheep, oxen and calves, even enjoying the blood, it is this – that the people ate the meat together with the blood – that is reported as being a sin against Yahweh (I Sam. 14.32f.; cf. Ezek. 33.25). According to Lev. 17.3ff. it is not enough (as was the usual practice in the case of game like hart or gazelle) simply to let the blood of sacrificial animals 'pour out upon the earth like water' (Deut. 12.15f., 22, 24); the priest is to sprinkle it on the altar of Yahweh (Lev. 17.6). This expresses with cultic-theological stringency that man is entitled only to the meat that comes from the earth and returns to the earth, while the life belongs to Yahweh alone.[11] In Yahweh's eyes, the neglect of the ritual commandment is no less serious than the murder of a person; it is blood guilt, the crime of the shedding of blood, which is punishable by the death penalty (Lev. 17.4; cf. Num. 35.33).

Gen. 9.4–6 also views the tasting of animal blood and murder as going together. The shedding of human blood is especially stressed as a crime against the 'image of God'.[12] So *dām* (Lev. 17.4), but especially the plural form *dāmīm*, comes to be the ethical-legal term for blood guiltiness, for the 'violently shed blood of another'.[13] Thus Isaiah complains (1.15): 'Your hands are full of blood (guiltiness, *dāmīm*).' Hosea threatens Jeroboam II with Yahweh's judgment (1.4): 'I will punish the house of Jehu for the blood (guiltiness) of Jezreel,' and he sees the crime against God's rights as culminating in 'murder upon murder' (4.2). Nahum (3.1) and Ezekiel (22.2; 24.6, 9) call Jerusalem 'the city of blood-guiltiness', because of its political brutality.[14] Cf. Deut. 19.10; Prov. 28.17:

A man who is burdened with the blood of another (*dam-nepeš*) is a fugitive until death; let no one help him.

The fundamental interweaving of the shedding of blood, blood-guilt and the consequences of that guilt found its tersest expression in the legal formula: *damāw bō* – his 'blood (guilt) is upon him' (Lev. 20.9, cf. 11–13, 16, 27); or: 'Your blood guilt (*dāmeka*) is upon your head' (II Sam. 1.16; I Kings 2.37). This establishes the guilt of the condemned person and the innocence of the man who carries out the death penalty, as it is commanded by Yahweh (cf. II Sam. 16.8; I Kings 2.32ff.).[15]

That the blood sprinkled on the altar becomes a means of expiation for the guilty, is explained in the ordinances in Lev. 4.5–34; 16.14–19; 17.11. It only has this power through Yahweh's decree, just as in Ex. 24.6, 8 it becomes the 'blood of the covenant' which Yahweh makes with Israel.

Everything that is said about breath and blood[16] in the anthropology of the Old Testament is instruction in an ultimate reverence for life. But this reverence is not derived from the manifestations of life itself; it is based on the fact that the breath and the blood belong to Yahweh, and therefore life without a steady bond with him and an ultimate tending towards him is not really life at all.

VII

The Inner Parts of the Body[1]

1. *Bowels*

The cavity for the inner organs of the body is usually called *qereb*. We already found the most important of these organs, the heart, localized here (I Sam. 25.37).[2] The body's 'inner parts' can even be identical with the heart, as in Prov. 14.33:

> Wisdom abides in the heart of a man of understanding,
> but it is 'ineffective'[3] in the inner parts of fools.

Cf. Jer. 31.33. But *qereb* basically includes all the inner parts belonging to the trunk, as opposed to the head and the limbs (Ex. 12.9, in connection with the Passover lamb). *mēʿîm* (which according to Jer. 4.19 also includes the heart[4]) means primarily the abdomen and the intestines, as well as the internal sexual organs (Gen. 15.4). The abdomen as womb is frequently called *beṭen* (Judg. 16.17 and frequently elsewhere; more precisely *reḥem*); but *beṭen* can also mean the male abdomen (Judg. 3.21f.). To it belong the reproductive organs and the stomach, which have no name of their own.[5] Cf. besides Gen. 25.24 ('there were twins in Rebecca's *beṭen*') and Job 19.17 ('the sons by my *beṭen*') Prov. 13.25:

> The righteous has enough to satisfy his appetite,
> but the belly (*beṭen*) of the wicked suffers want.

The digestive processes take place in the *beṭen* (Prov. 18.8):

> The words of the slanderer are like delicious morsels;
> they penetrate into the inner chambers of the body.

ḥadrē-beṭen is here the innermost parts of the body, which are hidden from the normal person. *ḥeder* otherwise means the bedchamber (Ex. 7.28 and frequently elsewhere) and also the dark, inner rooms of the temple (I Chron. 28.11); so here the inner rooms of the trunk are called 'dark chambers'. It is these that Yahweh searches, according to Prov. 20.27.[6] This indicates once more that the inside of the body too is of less interest anatomically and physiologically than psychologically, in the broadest

sense of the word.[7] As an example we might cite Jer. 4.14: 'How long shall
your evil thoughts lodge in your inner parts (*qereb*)?' Apart from the heart,
only a few inner organs are mentioned. The Old Testament has no special
words for lungs, stomach and intestines, though it has for liver, bile and
kidneys.

2. Liver

The liver is well known as being the largest gland in the human and animal
body; its weight (about $1\frac{1}{2}$ kg. or $3\frac{1}{2}$ lbs.) gave it its name: *kābēd*, liver,
belongs to the root *kbd*, 'to be heavy' (cf. Acc. *kabattu*, 'liver', *kabātu*, 'to
be heavy', and Ugaritic *kbd*[8]). In the area of the Accadian language the
liver is the most important organ after the heart and it is mentioned with
extreme frequency.[9] It is therefore all the more noticeable that in the Old
Testament[10] the liver is only mentioned 14 times, 13 of them in connection
with animals: the lobes of the liver, as sacrificial parts, 11 times (Ex. 29.13,
22 and 9 times in Leviticus),[11] the liver of the hart which has been
pierced by the hunter's arrow, once (Prov. 7.23) and, finally, the examination of the liver, once (Ezek. 21.26); this is mentioned as being one of the
oracular practices of the king of Babylon. Now, the examination of the
liver took on enormous importance in the Accadian region as is proved by
textbooks on the examination of the liver and by as many as 32 models of
the liver from the palace at Mari, among other things.[12] Is the reserve of
the Old Testament to be explained as opposition to the heathen practice
of soothsaying?

In Prov. 7.23 the man who is seduced by a strange woman is compared
with the stag who is caught fast in a trap 'till an arrow pierces him through
the liver'. This means that he must die, says the context (vv. 22–27).
According to this the liver is known to be a highly sensitive and vital
organ. Only once does the transmitted text speak of men's liver (Lam. 2.11):

> My eyes are spent with weeping
>   my innermost parts (*mēʿîm*) are in turmoil.
> My liver is poured out on the ground
>   because of the destruction of the daughter of my people.

This is a way of describing measureless grief; in his sorrow the poet is no
longer in control of his innermost feelings; his very life is poured out with
his liver. (In Pss. 16.9; 30.12; 57.8; 108.1 the reading should perhaps be
kābōd instead of the Masoretic text's *kābēd*.[13] Then the liver would here be
the subject of rejoicing, as it often is in Accadian.[14])

3. Bile

The liver produces bile. Only the learned poet of the book of Job mentions the gall bladder once (*m^erērā*, 16.13) and the bile twice (*m^erōrā*, 20.14, 25), both words being appropriately formed from the root *mrr*, 'to be bitter'. Job 20.14 says about the process of digestion and the liver's secretion in man:

> His food is transformed in his bowels (*mē^eīm*);
> it turns to the gall of asps in his inner parts (*qereb*).

If a man's gall bladder is pierced by an arrow his life is in great danger (Job 16.13; cf. 20.25).

4. *Kidneys*

Next to the heart, the kidneys are the most important internal organ in the Old Testament. They are mentioned 31 times; on 18 of these they are part of the body of sacrificial animals (16 times in Exodus and Leviticus, in addition Deut. 32.14 and Isa. 34.6); on 13 occasions they are part of men. Appropriately enough, the kidneys are only referred to in the plural (*k^elāyōt*), even where only one is in question; in Lev. 3.4, 10, 15 and frequently elsewhere 'the two kidneys' are expressly mentioned.

The kidneys are the one organ referred to particularly in Ps. 139 as being created by God (v. 13):[15]

> It is thou who didst form my kidneys,
> thou didst knit me together in my mother's womb.

When Yahweh chastises a man he shoots his arrow into his kidneys (Job 16.13; Lam. 3.13). The image is reminiscent of the piercing pain of renal colic. Is Job 19.27 talking about the shrinking or the 'longing' of the kidneys? The meaning of *klh* is not clear from the context. At all events this passage is the last in which the physical aspect is considered.

More frequently the kidneys are the seat of the conscience. Ps. 16.7 thanks Yahweh for counselling him, and because his kidneys chastise him in the night, that is to say his conscience reproves him. Jer. 12.2 describes to God the characteristics of the godless:

> Thou art only near their mouth,
> but far from their kidneys.

They talk about God, but he is not allowed to have any influence on their private decisions. Yahweh is called the one that proves the heart and kidneys no fewer than five times (Pss. 7.9; 26.2; Jer. 11.20; 17.10; 20.12).

The deeply troubled poet of Ps. 73 also mentions his kidneys as well as his heart as the most sensitive of organs (v. 21):

> Then my heart was embittered,
> I was sharply pricked in the kidneys.

But as the organ of right judgment they can also become an organ of praise (Prov. 23.16):

> My kidneys will rejoice
> when your lips speak what is right.

Thus the inner parts of the body and its organs are at the same time the bearer of man's spiritual and ethical impulses.

VIII

The Form of the Body[1]

1. *Limbs*

The same thing is true of man's extremities as of his internal organs – that the individual part of the body is frequently seen together with its activities and capacities. The limbs are even said to have spiritual impulses. According to Ps. 51.8, the bones that were broken 'rejoice' when Yahweh, with his forgiveness, allows joy and gladness to be felt. Only *'ₐṣāmīm* seems to act as a collective term for the limbs (Judg. 19.29; Pss. 31.10; 32.3; Job 33.19).[2]

(*a*) *regel* stands for the leg and the foot. The bodily extremity as such is meant, for example, when Abraham invites his guests to 'wash your feet' (Gen. 18.4). But when Deutero-Isaiah calls the feet of the messenger of peace lovely, he is not referring to their beautiful appearance; he means the welcome approach of the good news (Isa. 52.7).[3] And when in Gen. 30.30 Jacob says to Laban that the Aramaean's possessions have increased enormously during Jacob's service, Yahweh 'has blessed him *lᵉraglī*, that does not mean 'according to my foot' but 'according to the steps, or measures, I took – the progress I brought about'.

(*b*) *zᵉrōaʿ* means the arm as a limb of the body, when there is talk about the armlet as an ornament (II Sam. 1.10). But what is a 'man of arm' (*'īš zᵉrōaʿ*, Job 22.8)? He is a man who is 'all arm' or 'only arm' – that is to say a man of violence. Thus it is possible to talk about the 'arm' of a whole people and nation. When Moab's 'arm' is broken (Jer. 48.25) it is his fighting power that is meant (cf. v. 14), since the arm wields the sword. When Assyria lends its 'arm' to the sons of Lot, it is lending effective (military) aid.

(*c*) By far the most frequently mentioned extremity is the hand (*yād*).[4] The part of the body that grasps and can be grasped is what is meant in the *lex talionis* (e.g., Ex. 21.24; cf. Deut. 25.11f.) and in numerous other passages. When one man offers another his hand, as Jehonadab does to Jehu in II Kings 10.15, the gesture becomes the token of sincerity and mutual readiness to help the other. When Yahweh says to Satan about

Job (2.6): 'Behold he is in your hand,' he is putting him at Satan's 'disposal'. In the case of *yād*, the notion of a bodily limb recedes entirely into the background, generally speaking, giving way to the meaning 'strength', which belongs to the hand as the primary means of power; for example the Hebrew 'hand of the tongue' (*yad lāšōn*) in Prov. 18.21 must be translated: 'Death and life are in the power of the tongue.' The statement of self-praise in Judg. 7.2 can indeed be still understood in a literal translation: 'My own hand has helped me,' ('I have saved myself by my own power'; cf. I Sam. 25.26aβ). But a literal translation is impossible when we read about the inhabitants of Ai, when they are faced with their burning city (Josh. 8.20): 'There was no *yādayim* among them to flee this way or that;' for the Hebrew 'hands' means here the 'power' or the 'possibility' of flight. 'To raise the hand' can become the term for a revolutionary uprising (I Kings 11.26f.). When we read in Isa. 1.12:

> Who requires of your hand (*miyyedkem*)
> this trampling of my courts?

'hand' clearly stands for the person in respect of his exertion.[5]

The right (*yāmīn*) and the left hand (*śᵉmō'l*) are distinguished, for example, in the description of the embracing of the beloved (S. of S. 2.6):

> His left hand is under my head,
> and his right hand embraces me.

But they also represent the contrast between strength and weakness (Gen. 48.14), wisdom and foolishness, or happiness and unhappiness (Eccles. 10.2).

(*d*) *'eṣba'* means both the finger of the hand and the toes of the foot. The giant in Gath (II Sam. 21.20) had 'six fingers on each hand, and six toes on each foot, twenty-four in number'. The finger is more useful than the whole hand for making secret signs; Prov. 6.13 puts the sign with the finger beside the wink with the eyes and scraping with the feet. When idols are not only called the work of men's hands but expressly the work of their fingers as well (Isa. 2.8; 17.8), they are no doubt thereby being exposed not only as being the works of man's own powers and capacities, but also as being the products of his art, formed by the fingers. Thus when the heavens are praised as being the work of God's fingers (Ps. 8.3) this is perhaps an allusion to the artistic filigree-work in the delicate web of the constellations.

(*e*) The head (*rō'š*) makes it possible to count the individual in an assembly of people (Judg. 5.30; cf. Ex. 16.16; Num. 1.2 from skull, *gulgōlet*). The head represents a danger point for the life of the individual (Judg. 9.53); that is why the bodyguard is called 'defender of the head'

(I Sam. 28.2, *šōmēr lᵉro'šī*). To bow the head is an act of humiliation (Lam. 2.10). Conversely, raising the head means the end of the humiliation – a raising up, a recognition, or a restoration to office (Gen. 40.20; Ps. 3.3; and frequently elsewhere), when it is not an attitude of arrogance and a feeling of superiority (Ps. 140.9f.). The head becomes the image of everything high (Gen. 8.5; 11.4; Isa. 2.2) and dominating (Judg. 11.8; Isa. 9.14; Micah 2.13).

2. *Stature*

If the figure of a man is to be described in his whole stature, he is surveyed 'from the sole of the foot even to the head' (*mikkap regel wᵉᶜad-rō'š*, Isa. 1.6) or more precisely 'to the crown of the head' (*qodqōd*, Deut. 28.35; II Sam. 14.25; Job 2.7). At first glance a man's great height brings him respect – Eliab, David's eldest brother, for instance (I Sam. 16.7), or Saul, who 'from his shoulders upwards was taller than any of the people' (I Sam. 9.2; 10.23).

The Israelite seems in general not to have been especially tall. Bones found in a mass grave in Gezer suggest that the average height of the men was 1.67 m. (about 5 ft. 6 in.) and that of the women 1.60 m. (about 5 ft. 3 in.).[6] Thus not only did David face a giant in the Philistine champion who (according to I Sam. 17.4) was six cubits and a span tall (about 2.70 m., nearly 9 ft.), but the Israelites thought that they were smaller than other peoples in general. According to Amos 2.9 the previous inhabitants of Canaan were in height 'as tall as the cedars and . . . strong as the oaks', and in Deut. 1.28 Israel calls them a people 'greater and taller than we'. The difference in size between Israelites and Canaanites becomes one of the main themes of the spies in Num. 13.32f., when they report 'all the people that we saw . . . are men of great stature. And there we saw the giants (the sons of Anak belong to the giants); and we seemed to ourselves like grasshoppers, and so we must have seemed to them.'

But Yahweh does not look upon the size of the human form and does not want a man to be ruled by it in his judgment of others either (I Sam. 16.7; Prov. 25.6). He is capable of levelling down the tall and making the small great (I Sam. 2.7f.; Ezek. 21.31; Ps. 75.7). Thus man's greatness is only to a lesser degree a question of his stature. Anyone who does not realize that does not know the real man.

3. *Beauty*

When is a person beautiful? The question begins to be asked in Solomon's time. The adjective *yāpeh*, which the Old Testament uses 28 times in all for human beauty, occurs no less than 12 times in the great literary works of this period, the Yahwist's story of the rise of David and the subsequent court history, and a further 11 times in the Song of Solomon;[7] we must also take into account the not infrequent use of *ṭōb* to mean beautiful (e.g., Gen. 6.2; Ex. 2.2; I Kings 1.6; cf. Gen. 24.16). But these very writers who pay so much attention to the human side of life, know that attention to beauty is as old as time. The fathers of the giants of primeval times already choose themselves wives according to their beauty (Gen. 6.2). The most beloved of the mothers of Israel too are for the Yahwist always beautiful: Sarah (Gen. 12.11, 14), Rebecca (24.16) and Rachel (29.17). The ancient narrator does not conceal the fact that feminine beauty is also part of the history of human error (Gen. 6.1–4), indeed that it can be highly dangerous (12.11–14). Here beauty is in the first place a question of appearance (*mar'eh* 12.11; 24.16) and form (*tō'ar* 39.6) – that is to say of colour, and the lines of the body.

The same is basically true of male beauty, with which Joseph (Gen. 39.6) and above all David are credited (I Sam. 16.12, 18; 17.42). The attributes of beauty among contemporaries are more closely scrutinized. Even the fame of Absalom's incomparable beauty is based on the fact that 'from the sole of his foot to the crown of his head there was no blemish in him' (II Sam. 14.25); only his abundant hair is given special mention:

> When he cut the hair of his head (for at the end of every year he used to cut it, because it was so heavy that he had to cut it), he weighed the hair of his head, two hundred shekels by the king's weight.

That was about 2.3 kg., over 5 lbs. David is accounted beautiful particularly because of his eyes and his ruddy, light brown colouring[8] (I Sam. 16.12; 17.42). I Sam. 16.18 gives him as an illustration of the ideal of perfection. At the same time what the writer praises before his beautiful form (*'īš tō'ar*) is that he can play the lyre and is a man of parts, skilful in war and ready of speech; after the mention of his fine presence we are only told that Yahweh was 'with him'; without this last point, which is in no way at a man's own disposal, man's being is apparently imperfect. If we compare the tenth-century ideal of perfection with that held towards the end of the Old Testament period, in the second century, as we find it in Dan. 1.4, here too lack of blemish and a handsome appearance are important; but the writer goes on to stress:

> suitable for instruction in every kind of wisdom, intelligent and of a quick understanding, and suitable for service in the king's palace – and they are to be instructed in the writing and language of the Chaldaeans.[9]

The descriptive poems in the Song of Solomon give us the most exact information about the external characteristics of beauty. When the girl describes her lover in the Song of Solomon 5.10–16, her glance wanders from his head down to his thighs:

My beloved is all radiant and ruddy,
    distinguished among ten thousand.
His head is the finest gold,
    His locks are as the leaves of the date palm,
                                    black as a raven.
His eyes are like doves beside the waterbrooks,
    bathing in milk, sitting beside pools of water,
His cheeks are like beds of spices
    where fragrant herbs grow.
His lips are lilies,
    dropping liquid myrrh.
His arms are barrels of gold,
    set with chrysolites.
His body is ivory work,
    encrusted with lapis lazuli.
His legs are marble columns,
    set on bases of gold.
His stature is like Lebanon,
    choice as the cedars.
His palate (kiss?) is full of sweetness,
    his whole being is bliss.
This is my beloved and this is my friend,
    O daughters of Jerusalem.

The picture of the beloved is framed by a general impression of colour, size, strength and sweetness. If we examine it in detail, we find that the form and colour of certain features is stressed: the deep black hair, the milky whiteness of the eyes, the golden colouring of the face, arms and thighs, the ivory fairness of the body; then the lines of the curls, the lips, formed like the cup of a lily, the barrel-like arms and the pillars of the thighs. The scent of the cheeks and the movement of the eyes, bathed in milk, breathe life. The beauty is measured, not only against animals and plants, like doves, scented herbs and cedars, and against features of the landscape, like brooks, pools and Lebanon, but also against the creations of the architect and the jeweller, like pillars and their bases, marble and ivory, jewellery and goldsmith's work.[10]

Love songs addressed to the woman are commoner. In the Song of Solomon 7.1–5 we read how the lover's glance moves lingeringly upwards, from the feet to the hair of the head:

> How beautiful are your feet in your sandals,
>   O daughter of princes!
> The curves of your thighs are like jewels for the
>   throat,
>   the work of a master hand.
> Your navel is a rounded bowl
>   – may the mixed wine never be lacking –
> Your belly is like a heap of wheat
>   encircled with lilies.
> Your two breasts are like two fawns,
>   twins of a gazelle.
> Your neck is like an ivory tower.
>   Your eyes are as pools in Heshbon . . .
> Your nose is like the tower of Lebanon
>   overlooking Damascus.
> Your head crowns you like Carmel,
>   and the hair of your head is like royal purple,
>   bound to the weaver's loom.[11]

Apart from the vivid comparisons with nature (a heap of wheat encircled with lilies, twins of a gazelle), the masterpieces of visual art dominate the description. When the neck, and then the nose as well, is described as a tower, it is not so much the appearance that is in the writer's mind as the attitude of proud inaccessibility, which is perhaps designed to stress the beloved's virginity.[12]

How lively the picture of the beloved can be is especially evident in the Song of Solomon 6.5b–7:

> Your hair is like a flock of goats,
>   springing down from Gilead.
> Your teeth are like a flock of ewes
>   that come up from the watering place,
>   all of them have twins.
> Your temples gleam like a piece of pomegranate
>   behind your veil.[13]

Thus joy over the beauty of the beloved also produces beautiful language.

Yet beauty is at most only the penultimate thing. It can not only be dangerous (Gen. 12.11ff.), it can also be deceptive. Prov. 11.22 teaches us to see more deeply:

> Like a gold ring in a swine's snout
>   is a woman who is beautiful but shameless.

Prov. 31.30 points to what is more enduring:

> Charm is deceitful and beauty is fleeting,
> but a wise woman – she is to be praised.

And Isa. 53.2f. says even of the Servant of God who 'has borne our griefs and carried our sorrows' that

> He had no imposing stature and no majesty
> that we might have regarded him,
> no beauty in which we could rejoice.
> He was despised and rejected by men.

The beauty of Jerusalem, which is coupled with harlotry, is open to accusation (Ezek. 16.14f.). At the judgment the daughters of Zion have to exchange beauty for shame (Isa. 3.24).[14] Thus even the form of the body and God's dialogue with man cannot be divided from one another.

IX

The Nature of Man[1]

A man's 'face' is far more important than his 'head' in the Old Testament.[2] It is always called *pānīm*, in the plural, thus reminding us of the manifold different ways in which a man can give his attention (*pnh*) to his counterpart; events are reflected in the features of the face (e.g. Gen. 4.5); the partner can be already addressed through the play of expression (e.g. Gen. 31.2, 5). In the 'face' as the *pānīm*, man's 'turnings towards' another, his organs of communication, are gathered together; and among these the eyes, the mouth and the ears are the most important. Among all the organs and limbs, is it not here that we ought to come close to finding out what man's being consists of, and what distinguishes him from all other created beings?

1. *Seeing and hearing*

Let us try to find out from some illustrative texts what kind of communication emerges as being the really human one. Among the songs of lament, Ps. 38 is the cry of need of a man who sees his end approaching. To all the other symptoms of his illness is added the failure of his eyesight (v. 10). But at the height of his lamentation the psalm runs (vv. 13f.):

> But I am like a deaf man, I do not hear,
>> like a dumb man who does not open his mouth.
> Yea, I am like a man who no longer hears,
>> and in whose mouth there are no more answers.

The man who is threatened with becoming deaf and dumb must fear for his very humanity. It is the hearing, the hearing above all (vv. 13a, 14a), that makes man – that, and the corresponding opening of the mouth, the being able to answer (13b, 14b).

From a quite different aspect, the wisdom writings recognize the hearing as being the root of true humanity. Prov. 15.32 teaches:

> He who ignores warnings casts away his life (*nepeš*),
>> but he who heeds admonition gains wisdom (*lēb*).

The same is true according to Prov. 18.21a: 'Death and life are in the power of the tongue.' Since human life is reasonable life, the hearing ear and the properly directed tongue are the essential organs for man.

In so far the central Deuteronomic 'Hear, O Israel' (Deut. 6.4) is picking up the oldest call to the patriarchs and the voices of the prophets, as the word which is the essential ground of human life and its renewal. For the ear and the mouth provide not only the specifically human exchange between men, but also that between Yahweh and Israel, between mankind and its God.

Thus the Servant of Yahweh in Isa. 50.4f. can stand as prototype for humanity *per se*:

> The Lord Yahweh has given me the tongue of a scholar;
> So that I might know how to 'answer'[3] him that is weary,
>   he raised up a word.
> Morning by morning he wakens my ear
>   to hear as those who are taught.
> The Lord Yahweh has opened my ear,
>   and I was not rebellious, I did not shrink back.

The eye is certainly not infrequently mentioned in conjunction with the ear (Prov. 20.12):

> The ear to hear with and the eye to see,
> Yahweh has made them both.

Cf. Ps. 94.9. Seeing as well as hearing is necessary in order to perceive the acts of Yahweh (Ex. 14.13f.; Deut. 29.2–4; Isa. 43.8). But the opening of the eye comes through the word (Ex. 14.13f., 30f; Isa. 43.8–13 [note esp. v.12]; 30.20f.). Thus the supreme importance of the ear and of speech for true human understanding is unmistakable.

2. Ear

The Hebrew liked to adorn the ear with jewellery (Gen. 35.4; Ex. 32.2f.; Ezek. 16.12). But a legal act fixing lifelong possession could be ratified in the ear: when a slave so loved his master and his master's family that he wanted to stay in his house instead of being freed after six years, 'then his master shall bring him to the door or the doorpost; and his master shall bore his ear through with an awl; and he shall be his slave for ever' (Ex. 21.5f.; cf. Deut. 15.17). In the book of Job, Eliphaz lets us experience how, starting from the ear, the whole person is activated (4.12–15):[4]

> Now a word stole to me secretly,
>   my ear received the whisper of it,

> in the broodings of night visions,
>   when deep sleep falls on men.
> Dread came upon me and trembling,
>   making all my bones shake;
> A spirit glided over my face,
>   the hair of my body stood up.

Just as here the auditory reception of the word by the wise man through the ear changes the whole state of the body, so the hearing determines a man's behaviour and state of health generally (cf. for example Gen. 3. 8–10). For that reason it is the fundamental sign of Solomon's wisdom when he finds the plea for the hearing heart[5] more important than long life, riches, victory, or honour. 'Constitutive for man's humanity is the faculty of hearing.'[6] Speech must not be allowed to thrust itself into precedence (Prov. 18.13):

> If one gives answer before he hears,
>   it is his folly and shame.

It is not in a mirror that a man recognizes himself truly; it is in the call that comes to him and in the promise that he receives. Moses indeed asks: 'Who am I that I should go to Pharaoh and bring the sons of Israel out of Egypt?' – but he only understands himself for the first time in his acceptance of the task and in the exhortation of his God (Ex. 3.11ff.). Jeremiah's self-recognition 'I am inexperienced' is corrected and superseded by his commission (Jer. 1.6f.). Self-knowledge does not come about through self-reflection but through the call which opens up a new vista.[7]

The man who, having closed his ears, takes himself as starting point and never moves away from himself not only loses his humanity among men; he also sets himself up as God in opposition to God;[8] thus he becomes godless even in his piety (Prov. 28.9):

> If one turns away his ear from hearing the law
>   even his prayer is an abomination.

He misunderstands what the petitioner in Ps. 40.6 understood:

> Sacrifice and offering thou dost not desire;
>   but thou has given me ears.

In their own way, the Deuteronomic preachers trace life back to the hearing of Yahweh's word by interpreting the manna tradition anew (Deut. 8.3):[9] 'Man does not live by bread alone but . . . by everything that proceeds out of the mouth of Yahweh.' Failure to hear would be a denial of life (Deut. 32.47; cf. Amos 8.11; Isa. 55.10f.). The opening of the ears of the deaf is part of the redemption of the End-time (Isa. 35.5).

3. Mouth

But the word, once it has been heard, expects an answer. Israel proves itself to be the people of God by declaring its readiness in response to the divine address[10] (Ex. 19.7f.; 24.3, 7; and frequently elsewhere). Judgment follows when the call receives no answer (Isa. 65.12). The Yahwist recognizes man's privilege as lying simply in the fact that he is allowed to speak (Gen. 2.18–23): this takes place on the basis of God's word in its providing care ('It is not good that man should be alone'), after which the gifts of the Creator are brought to him. His speaking begins when he names the created things, thus responding to the gifts. His words only become worth quoting at the moment when he joyfully recognizes the help which is really his (2.23). With the word, which is a response to the perfected gift, man is for the first time a whole man. Later the person whose life is successful is described as being the man who rejoices in the Torah of Yahweh and repeats it meditatively to himself (Ps. 1.2). Ps. 71.24 sees the fulfilment of life in that 'my tongue tells of thy righteousness all the day long'.

Thus the mouth, which expresses what ear and eye had perceived, becomes the organ which distinguishes man above all other creatures. The animal also has an ear as such, as well as an eye. It is in man's speech that his ear evinces itself as being a truly human ear and his eye as being a human eye.[11]

Whereas the ear and the eye only have one word each in the Old Testament, a whole collection of parts of the body represent the instrument of speech. A comprehensive word for it is *peh*, mouth, with which man also eats and tastes (Ezek. 3.3), but above all speaks; thus *peh* can be simply 'the speaker' (Ex. 4.16: Aaron is Moses' speaker; Isa. 1.20; 40.5; Jer. 9.11; Hos. 6.5: the prophets are Yahweh's speakers). *śepātayim* often has the same meaning (Prov. 4.24):

> Put away from you the falseness of the mouth,
> and put the folly of the lips far from you.

śāpā, being the term for the touchable lips (Isa. 6.7), also stands for language as such (Isa. 19.18: the language of Canaan). The same is true of *lāšōn* (Zech. 8.23: the language of the nations), the tongue, which, as part of the body, can cleave to the roof of the mouth with thirst (Lam. 4.4) but which above all means true (II Sam. 23.2; Isa. 35.6) or false speech (Pss. 5.9; 12.3; 109.2; Isa. 59.3; Prov. 6.17). The palate too (*ḥek*) is not only the seat of the sense of taste (Ps. 119.103) but also the instrument of speech (Job 6.30; 31.30; Prov. 5.3; 8.7; cf. Job 33.2). Finally the throat (*gārōn*), with which man also drinks (Jer. 2.25), belongs to the organ of speech too

(Isa.58.1; Pss.69.3; 149.6). No human activity, therefore, is given the name of so many organs as speech.

On the other hand there is no other part of the human body of which so many different activities are predicated as the human mouth, with its lips, tongue, palate and throat, in so far as these are organs of speech: speaking (*dbr* piel), saying (*'mr*), calling (*qr'*), commanding (*ṣwh* piel), teaching (*lmd* piel), instructing (*yrh* hiphil), admonishing (*ykḥ* hiphil), accusing (*rīb*), swearing (*sb'* niph.), blessing (*brk* piel), cursing (*'rr*), calling someone accursed (*qll* piel), singing (*šīr*), praising (*hll* piel), rejoicing (*rnn*), considering (*ydh* hiphil), praying (*pll* hithp.), crying, complaining (*zᵉq*, *ṣᵉq*, *spd*), murmuring (*hgh*); and others in addition. Most of these verbs are not applied to other created things. This will no doubt be enough to show that with the human organ of speech we are coming particularly near to man's specific being. The capacity for language provides the essential condition for the humanity of man.

4. *Speech*

The question as to the right use of language is whether this essential condition is actually realized (James 3.2): 'If any one makes no mistakes in what he says, he is a perfect man, able to bridle the whole body also.'

What counts as being the right word for the proverbial wisdom of the Old Testament?

It is first of all the word that comes from hearing; see p. 76 above on Prov. 18.13, and also 19.20:

> Listen to advice and accept warning
> that your end may be the end of a wise man.

Cf. 15.32; 13.18.

Then there is the word at the right time (Prov. 25.11):

> A word in season
> is like apples of gold on silver platters.

Cf. 25.12f., 20; 15.23.

In the third place there is the quietly thought out, restrained word (Prov. 29.20):

> Do you see a man who is hasty in his words?
> There is more hope for a fool than for him.

Cf. 10.19; 13.3.

Fourthly, there is the temperate, kindly word (Prov. 25.15):

> With patience a ruler may be turned from his purpose,
> and a gentle tongue will break bones.

Cf. 16.24.

Lastly, like all wise actions, right speech requires the fear of God (Prov. 1.7; 9.10; 15.33). A scorching fire burns on the lips of the worthless man (16.27). But God is at work even between the word which the wisdom of man conceives in secret and that which then proceeds from his tongue (Prov. 16.1):

> The plans of the heart belong to man,
> but the answer of the tongue is from Yahweh.

Thus if man does not want to fall short of his real being, either in *hubris* or in laziness, he remains dependent on the God who in Israel began to speak with him in a human way.

PART TWO

THE TIME OF MAN
Biographical Anthropology

X

The Old Testament Concept of Time[1]

The Old Testament witnesses make us aware to a powerful degree that man lives his life in time – and in changing times. With the help of some striking examples, we shall first try to clarify how the understanding of time is related to the anthropology.

1. *The Yahwist*

Let us start with the Yahwist. The problem of time in the theoretical sense does not yet concern him; but what he has to say practically about the life of man in time is all the more remarkable. Before he tells of the creation of man at the beginning of his work (2.7), he fixes the time when it took place (2.4b): 'In the day that Yahweh God made the earth and the heavens'. The 'day' is not introduced as a point of time in the calendar – that is to say, not as a temporal concept in the sense of a physical division – but solely as the point of time of an event – the event of a divine act. He adds a negative definition of the time (v. 5): 'No herb of the field had yet sprung up – for Yahweh God had not caused it to rain upon the earth and there was no man to till the ground.' Afterwards the course of time is experienced as the scope for action, in which the events brought about by God and man give rise to changes. When man is formed and infused with life (2.7) the times begin in which circumstances alter. With a minimum of definition but with supreme vividness, the Yahwist goes on to show how time is primarily experienced by man.

In the story of the Garden of Eden, man's lifetime is filled at first with the cultivation, care and enjoyment of the garden, which has been given over to him in all its abundance (2.15f.). This period is to be limited by the death penalty, however, if through mistrust he transgresses the limits of the paradisal gift (2.17). This is what in fact happens; man arrogantly usurps the place of God (3.1ff.). But there is no more talk about the or- dained death penalty. Man only has to experience the misery of the person who takes his life into his own hands, godlessly and therefore without any restrictions (3.15-19). But the period of his life (3.19)[2] which was determined at his creation from the stuff of the earth (and which he is never to succeed in extending permanently; vv. 22, 24) is not shortened. He is merely expelled from the garden (3.22–24); but he is clothed by God himself in a garment made of skins, and is therefore far better protected than he was with his self-made apron of fig leaves (3.21; cf. v. 7). Thus against the background of the richly deserved death penalty, his lifetime appears as time undeservedly conferred on him – and protected time.

The same is true of Cain. It is true that the blood of his brother cries out for revenge; he is forced to go in fear of being slain by anyone who finds him (4.10, 14). But Yahweh himself secures the life that the murderer has forfeited with a mark of protection, threatening his slayer with sevenfold revenge (v. 15). Even the fratricide, therefore, experiences the gifts of a lifetime, and a protected lifetime.

After the Flood the condition of man's thought and will[3] is 'evil from his youth'; the reason for the divine will towards destruction is therefore unchanged (cf. Gen. 8.21 with 6.5). Now Yahweh alters his decision again in man's favour; he no longer wants to destroy all life, but declares (8.22): 'In the future while earth remains, seedtime and harvest, cold and heat, summer and winter, day and night shall not cease.' The cultivation of the land depends on the recurrence of the daily and yearly times and seasons. Mankind is granted the blessing of the variation offered by time's divisions. Here the Yahwist does for once express himself in fundamental terms about 'all the days of earth'. As the lifetime of man, these days are an unalterably ordained gift of the one who redeems from judgment. Unalterably they call forth the alterations which man needs for work and for rest, for strenuous seedtime and happy harvest (Ps. 126.6: sowing in tears and reaping with shouts of joy), for the return home and for the setting forth to the fields of labour.

Beyond this unalterable, cyclical fluctuation, however, the Yahwist observes with burning interest whatever is new – the things that have never been in existence before. In the framework of his account of history as a whole, the permanence of the conditions of life described in Gen. 8.22 as being the raising of a curse (8.21), belongs to these new beginnings. But it is striking in general how often the Yahwist notes the 'beginning' (*ḥll* hiphil) of something that has been hitherto unknown: Gen. 4.26, 'At that time men *began* to call upon the name of Yahweh'; 6.1, 'When men *began* to multiply on the face of the earth . . .'; 9.20, 'Noah *began*, as tiller of the soil, to plant a vineyard'; 10.8, Nimrod 'was the first who *began* to be a ruler on earth'; 11.6, the building of a city and a tower for protection and self-glory, as being the united work of mankind, is only 'the *beginning* of what they will do'; cf. 13.3; 43.18, 20; Num. 25.1, at the occupation of the promised land the people of Israel *began* 'to play the harlot with the daughters of Moab' and to have dealings with the idol Baal of Peor. The keen observation of any alterations which take place in the course of time is shown by the keyword 'new' (*ḥādāš*) at the beginning of Israel's history, when there arose a *new* king over Egypt who did not know Joseph (Ex. 1.8). Highly significant of the Yahwist's interest in events which coincide in time is his liking for the word *ṭerem* (not yet, before) – otherwise rare in the Pentateuch – which we already meet in Gen. 2.5.[4] Even *before* Abraham's servant had finished praying (when he went to seek a wife for Isaac), Rebecca came out (Gen. 24.15; cf. 19.4; 27.4, 33; 37.18; 45.28; Num. 11.33). In the stories of the plagues, above all, as preparation for Israel's exodus from Egypt, there is a striking use of *ṭerem* (not yet, before) when the writer is comparing events in their temporal sequence. In Ex. 9.30 Moses says to Pharaoh during the plague of hail: 'I know that you do *not yet* fear the God Yahweh.' At the plague of locusts, Pharaoh's servants ask (Ex. 10.7): 'Do you *not yet* understand that Egypt is ruined?' Finally, in the haste of their departure the people very characteristically (and with momentous consequences) take their dough *before* it is leavened (Ex. 12.34).

But even without using any distinguishing word at all, the Yahwist is still able to depict the mighty course of the history of mankind and of Israel in their mutual interaction and their decisive revolutionary changes. He does so by following up the stories of God's judgment on mankind and his patience with the promise of blessing on all the families of earth, which comes at the beginning of the story of Abraham (Gen. 12.3b). This promise is then realized in a series of provisional fulfilments; but it is as a whole still proclaimed as a kerygma of hope and stimulus for Israel and the world surrounding her.[5]

Thus for the Yahwist history is the story of an alterable and altering train of events directed towards a certain goal which, as time, above all offers man the gift of the possibility of life. Yet the Yahwist seldom uses the word 'time' (*ʿēt*) – perhaps in the compound 'evening time' (Gen. 8.11; 24.11) or 'tomorrow at this time' (Ex. 9.18), for the chronological fixing of an event[6] or – and this is more in line with his fundamental understanding of time – as 'the time to gather the flocks together' (Gen. 29.7), or as 'the time to bear children' (Gen. 38.27), where 'time' has the meaning of the favourable moment.[7]

2. *The Priestly document*

In the Priestly document we find a differentiated understanding of time based on reflection. In the first place it shows an interest in chronological and calendar data as the framework of history. For the Priestly document it is important that the people of Israel lived 430 years in Egypt (Ex. 12.40f.) and that they arrived in the Sinai desert in the third month after the Exodus (Ex. 19.1); that Abraham was 99 years old when Yahweh appeared to him and he was circumcised (Gen. 17.1, 24); that Ishmael was 13 years old at his circumcision (v. 25), whereas Isaac was only 8 days (Gen. 21.4); that Sarah died when she was 127 (23.1) and Abraham when he was 175 (25.7). For the total pattern of the Priestly document the genealogies are actually the structural principles: the *tōlᵉdōt* of Adam (Gen. 5.1), of Noah (6.9), of Noah's sons (10.1), of Shem (11.10), Terah (11.27), Ishmael (25.12), Isaac (25.19), Esau (36.1), Jacob (37.2), Aaron and Moses (Num. 3.1).[8] Taking precedence over them all, and prefixed with the same keyword, is the *tōledōt*, which is the story of the creation of heaven and earth (Gen. 2.4a).

Within this first section the work brings us a further significant statement about time. On the fourth day of creation the stars are made. Their primary function is to distinguish between day and night (1.14a), but their second purpose is to order the seasons, to determine the days and the years (v. 14b). That is to say they divide up time and make it possible to determine certain fixed dates; they fulfil functions with regard to the calendar. Consequently ordered time is one of the gifts of God's creation (cf. Pss. 74.16f.; 104.19).[9]

This theological understanding of divided time makes it possible to invest different times with a different status. Thus the Priestly document did not only place the individual works of creation within a sequence of six different days; it above all emphatically distinguished the seventh day as a day of rest after God's days of labour.[10] At the revelation of Sinai Moses first spent six days on the mountain hidden in the clouds, and it was only on the seventh day that the call of Yahweh reached him out of the midst of those clouds. Afterwards Moses remained forty days and forty nights on the mountain in order to receive Yahweh's detailed instructions (Ex. 24.16–18).

Thus the various times, as the divine gift of creation, help the priestly witness to find bearings in history and to perceive its status.

3. *Deuteronomy*

The preachers of Deuteronomy give fundamental consideration to the relation to past and future. Yet they are passionately interested in 'today'. In the sections framing the Deuteronomic Code alone (4.44–30.20) *hayyōm* (today) is to be found 35 times and *hayyōm hazze* (this present day) 6 times; in addition, in the body of the Code itself (chs. 12–26) *hayyōm* occurs 9 times and *hayyōm hazze* once. All in all *hayyōm* is found 58 times in the book of Deuteronomy and *hayyōm hazze* 12 times; that is to say, 'today' is found 70 times in all. Thus the word in its numerous variations rams home the validity of Moses' message (5.1–3):

> Hear O Israel, the statutes and ordinances which I speak in your hearing *this day* and you shall learn them and be careful to do them. Yahweh our God made a covenant with us in Horeb. Not with our fathers did Yahweh make this covenant, but with us, who are all of us here alive *this day*.

The novelty of 'today' is stressed by distinguishing it from the era of the patriarchs. But it is through the presence of the God who makes the covenant that 'today' acquires its decisive significance. To follow the word that is very near today means life and happiness for the hearer (30.11–20).

Yet if he is to perceive the utter actuality of the present hour, the hearer must not forget history either (9.7ff.): 'Remember and do not forget how you provoked Yahweh your God to wrath in the wilderness, from the day you came out of the land of Egypt . . .' The present generation is to be vividly aware of the history of Israel's recalcitrance, Moses' intercession and God's new bestowal of his purposes. Such history is not to be evaluated as 'something that is past'; it is as something fore-given, something open to reflection, without which new hearing of the word in the present will miss its mark. The man who forgets to contemplate the history that has been lived in the past is missing the future that lies in 'today' (8.19): 'If you forget Yahweh your God . . . I solemnly warn you *this day* that you shall surely perish.' Because of Yahweh's faithfulness, the God of history is, as the God of today, also the God who rules the future. In proclaiming his will towards covenant, he forms the future through his dialogue with man today (7.9–11):

> Know therefore that Yahweh your God is the true God, the faithful God who keeps covenant and steadfast love with those who love him and keep his commandments, to a thousand generations, but requites to his face 'him who hates him'[11]. . . . You shall therefore be careful to do the commandments . . . which I command you *this day*.

The individual as member of God's people participates in the goodly future; the disobedient man breaks away from it. The word that is proclaimed today expressly unites the present generation with the generations of the future, for whom the word is also valid (29.14f.):

> Nor is it with you only that I make this covenant and sworn agreement, but with him who is not here with us *this day* as well as with him who stands here with us *this day* before Yahweh our God.

Thus, for the Deuteronomic preachers, the man who lives vigilantly today is, as a member of the people of God, firmly incorporated in the events that preceded his generation, and also in what is to come. But it is in his hearing of the word that is proclaimed today and in his contemplation of the history of the fathers, that man's decision is made about his future life. Deut. 29.29 develops and consolidates this idea about present, 'past' and future in the dictum: 'The hidden things abide by Yahweh our God; but the things that are revealed belong to us and to our children for ever.' The 'hidden things' means the future; but 'the things that are revealed' is the word of promise and guidance that is promulgated in history as it is open to us.[12]

Here we see a relationship to time that is different from the one familiar to us. It emerges even more clearly in a common Old Testament turn of speech. The Israelite sees former times as the reality *before* him, whereas we think that we have them *behind* us, as the past. Ps. 143.5:

> I remember the days before me (*miqqedem*),
> I meditate on all thy works.

The future, on the other hand, does not for the Israelite lie *before* him, but 'at his back' (*'aḥar*). According to Jer. 29.11 Yahweh says:

> I know the plans I have for you,
> plans of peace and not of evil,
> that I may give you *'aḥªrīt* and a hope.

'aḥªrīt means the future as that which is behind and which follows me.[13] One detail of German usage is based on a similar attitude of mind, when it speaks of Vorfahren (those that go before), for forefathers, and Nachfahren (those that go after), for descendants. According to this viewpoint man proceeds through time like a rower who moves into the future backwards: he reaches his goal by taking his bearings from what is visibly in front of him; it is in this revealed history that for him the Lord of the future is attested.

4. *Deutero-Isaiah*

Deutero-Isaiah goes a step further in clarifying the understanding of time. He relates past and future to one another in a new way (Isa. 46.10):

> Declaring the end (*'aḥªrīt*) from the beginning,
>   and from things before us (*miqqedem*) those things that are not
>   yet done.

The end, previously hidden from men, now emerges into the light of the prophetic promises of times past. Now, for the first time, the concept of the 'future' can also consequently be formed in Hebrew: *habbā'ōt*, what is to

come (only found in Isa. 41.22; but cf. also 44.7b).[14] Future events themselves therefore move first in the direction of men; man is not of himself
facing in their direction. It is only the person who has heard the promise
who turns expectantly towards the things that have up to then lain invisibly
behind him. Now the future is also defined as 'what is new' (*ḥªdāšōt*; 42.9;
43.19); it is the hidden thing, till then unknown (48.6) which – now that it
is proclaimed – allows whatever has been before (43.18f.) to be forgotten.
Thus the prophetic promise leads our understanding of time further by
showing the way to turn towards the future, and the new things that belong to it.

In this context the ancient concept *ʿōlām* takes on increased theological
importance in Deutero-Isaiah and later in the writings of Trito-Isaiah as
well. The word does not mean eternity as timeless – that is to say unalterable – time; nor does it mean time that is still hidden at the present
day; *ʿōlām* means primarily the time that is furthest away from us, both in
the past and in the future.[15] Thus we read in Ps. 93.2:

> Thy throne is established from of old (*mēʾāz*),
> Thou art from remotest time (*meʿōlām*).

In Gen. 3.22 Yahweh says that man is not to live into the uttermost future
(*leʿōlām*); cf. Gen. 13.15; Ex. 14.13; 19.9. *leʿōlām* can then indicate the remotest point of human life – that is to say, death; and in this way it turns
into the legal term 'final' (Ex. 21.6).[16] In this sense Deutero-Isaiah can
then term 'the word of our God' final (*leʿōlām*; 40.8) and can apply the
same word to his salvation (51.6), his deliverance (v. 8), his abiding faithfulness (54.8) and his covenant (55.3). With this the threshhold term,
denoting the utmost conceivable starting point or goal, comes close to the
meaning of 'time without end'. Although time in its fleetingness may
bring painful experiences, yet the endless faithfulness and mercy of Yahweh
accords us 'unending joy' (cf. Ps. 118.1 and frequently; Isa. 51.11; 55.12f.;
61.7f.).[17]

5. *Ecclesiastes*

The later wisdom writings concern themselves intensively with the problem
of time. Deutero-Isaiah (40.6–8) had already contrasted the evanescent
nature of all flesh with the steadfastness of God's word. Job complains
(14.1f.):

> Man that is born of woman
> is of few days, and full of trouble.
> He blossoms like a flower and withers away;
> he flees like a shadow, with no continuance.

But it is in Ecclesiastes that the question of time comes to be an independent theme. The writer stresses that a time and an hour is set for all and everything. By every 'time' (*'et*) and every 'appointed hour' (*z^emān*)[18] it is not empty categories that are meant but the appropriate occasion for an event, indeed even an aspect of the event itself.[19] Eccles. 3.1–8 makes this clear:

> For everything there is an hour,
>   and a time for every matter under heaven:
> a time to give birth, and a time to die;
> a time to plant, and a time to pluck up what is planted;
> a time to kill, and a time to heal;
> a time to break down, and a time to build up;
> a time to weep, and a time to laugh;
> a time to mourn, and a time to dance;
> a time to cast away stones, and a time to gather stones
>   together;
> a time to embrace, and a time to refrain from embracing;
> a time to seek, and a time to lose;
> a time to keep, and a time to cast away;
> a time to rend, and a time to sew;
> a time to keep silence, and a time to speak;
> a time to love, and a time to hate;
> a time for war, and a time for peace.

This perception of the different times for actions that are opposed to one another comes from the experience of one of man's limitations.[20] He is not equally successful in everything at all times in the same way, because different times are appointed for success and lack of success, in the form of varyingly favourable opportunities; moreover man cannot behave at every moment in the same way, because he himself meets with things adverse to him. It is not man who fixes the different times; they fall to his lot and he cannot intervene.[21] This causes him great difficulty (3.9f.; cf. 8.6f.). God has laid this vexation upon him (3.10), for he has both appointed the times and given men their consciousness of time's changes. This makes man's dealings with time extremely complicated (3.11):

He (God) has made everything excellently for its time; also he has put remotest time (*hā'ōlām*) into man's mind (*b^elibbām*),[22] yet so that he cannot find out what God has done from the beginning to the end.

The confusing thing is this: God has given every hour its particular business, so it is excellent. But he has given man the capacity for 'enquiring beyond the present hour into past and future'.[23] This capacity – indeed this propensity – for thinking further than the present hour proves to be a severe affliction, however. For man is still not able to grasp the whole of the divine work and the meaning of the changing times. That is the reason for his difficulty in dealing with time: he ponders in the present over what has gone before and what will come afterwards, without being able to grasp the total coherence; and in the process even his own present hour eludes him. With his eyes screwed up to see into the distance, he is blind to the danger of the present moment, even if he is wise; and he becomes entangled in it, as a fish or a bird is entangled in a net (9.11f.). (Jeremiah said that the stork, the swallow and other migratory birds were wiser than the people in Israel; Jer. 8.7.) But even if man recognizes the hour when it comes, he cannot avert the destiny it brings with it; that has long been determined by one stronger than man (Eccles. 6.10).

What inferences does Ecclesiastes deduce from this? His conclusions are determined neither by nihilistic hedonism nor by sceptical resignation. Man has to face both good and evil days in the knowledge of their irreplaceable opportunities (7.14). The primary meaning of the creation of the times, as well as of human consciousness, is that man should 'fear' God (3.14), that is to say that he should fall into line with God's dispensations (7.14): 'In the day of prosperity be joyful, and in the day of adversity consider that God has made the one as well as the other.' Here the second point already finds expression: man should be completely ready and receptive for the good hours that time brings with it, both in his taking and in his giving. Eccles. 9.7–10 is the finest expression of this:

> Go, eat your bread with joy
>> and drink your wine with a merry heart;
>>> for it has ever pleased God when you do so.
> Let your garments be always white;
>> let not oil be lacking on your head!
> Enjoy life with the wife whom you love,
>> all the days of your vain life
>>> which he has given you under the sun. . . .
> Because that is your portion in life
>> and in your toil at which you toil under the sun.
> Whatever your hand finds to do,
>> do it as long as you may.

In submission to God's decrees and in receptivity towards good opportunities Ecclesiastes points to the only way in which the far-seeing sceptic can deal with his time. In what he says he absorbs essential material from the older wisdom literature (Prov. 15.15):

> All the days of the afflicted are evil,
> but a cheerful heart has a continual feast.

In the midst of the riddle that God himself sets the wise with time and its processes, it is ultimately God alone who makes it possible for man to achieve the essential and, in spite of all his difficulties, to discover the good and to enjoy it happily.

In the midst of his lamentation the man of prayer can take courage (Ps. 31.15a): 'My times are in thy hand.'

XI

Creation and Birth[1]

The time of man begins with his creation and birth. In addition to the stories of the creation in Genesis, which explain the coming into being of man as a species, we have the confessions of individuals, who bring their own birth into conjunction with God's act of creation. These relate to one another in the way that the first article of the Christian creed (I believe in God, the Father Almighty, Creator of heaven and earth) relates to Luther's declaration: 'I believe that God has created me. . . .'

1. *The creation of man according to the Yahwist*
The Yahwist's account of the creation displays no relationship at all to the process of birth. Even when Gen. 2.24 says of man and woman that 'they become one flesh', there is no further amplification of the conception and birth of a child; probably the writer is not even thinking of this; for *bāśār 'eḥād* ('a single flesh') does not mean the child in whom two people re-discover themselves as in a unity;[2] it means the physical union of man and woman, whose utter solidarity is expressed in this way.[3] The Yahwist's interest is completely directed towards those relationships in which man is compelled to recognize his humanity from the very beginning.

The relationship to God must be mentioned first here. For whatever the other relationships may be in which man is going to be living, he lives as God's creation. 'Yahweh God formed man . . . and breathed into his nostrils the breath of life; and man became a living person' (2.7).[4] The powerful anthropomorphisms stress that man receives his form and his life from God. The material of his body is completely and utterly earthly; cf. Pss. 90.3; 103.14. It is not the blood of a slaughtered god that courses through his veins, as in the Babylonian creation myths,[5] nor has man developed from the tears of the sun god, as was frequently said in Egypt from the early years of the Middle Kingdom.[6] It is solely the craftsman-ship motifs which are taken over from the creation myths that are wide-spread in the ancient East; and this stresses the distance between God and man, but also God's concrete intervention on man's behalf. The bond is shown essentially in Yahweh's word of address to man (2.16f.).

The word of God also stands at the head of man's second relationship – his relationship to animals: 'It is not good that man should be alone. I will make him a helper fit for him' (2.18). How near the beasts stand to man is emphasized in the statement that Yahweh God formed them 'out of the ground' (v. 19) – exactly what was said of man in v. 7; but the beasts do not receive the divine breath of life. They are offered to man as a help and are in this way, in intention, to some extent comparable with his fellow-man. But they do not really correspond to him. That is shown in the naming through which man orders the animal world. Giving the beasts their names is a manifestation of 'man's very first autonomy' within creation;[7] it is established through Yahweh's creative gift.

Yahweh's decision to improve man's condition only reaches its goal with the creation of the third relationship, which takes precedence over the second in importance; this decision was to give man a companion, through the creation of woman. The unique closeness of her relationship to the man is underlined above all through the fact that she is created, not from earth but out of the rib of man himself – a rib which Yahweh further forms into the woman (vv. 21f.). Man, cast into a deep sleep, does not look on at this creation. He exultantly admires the completed work as being truly related to him:[8]

> This at last
> is bone of my bones
> and flesh of my flesh.
> She shall be called Woman,
> because she was taken out of Man.

That she is called *'iššā* after the *'iš*, reflects the deep inner bond between them. It is for her that man leaves the home of his parents.[9]

The fourth relationship is the one between man and the earth. It is documented linguistically in the original text through the consonance of *'ādām* (man) and *'ᵃdāmā* (earth), in which the common etymological root *'dm*, 'to be red', appears for man's reddish brown skin and for the reddish brown of the earth.[10] This relation too is determined by Yahweh. It is a threefold one. Man is created out of the earth (2.7; cf. 3.19, 23); he has to work the soil (3.23); and he returns to the earth at his death (3.19). Moreover both the tilling of the soil and the final return to the earth are related to his creation from the earth (cf. 3.19, 23 with 2.7).

Just like the tilling of the soil and his own mortality, man's life with the woman and with the animals he has named is conditioned by his own basic relationship to his Creator, who is also the Creator of all things, but who enters into dialogue with man and with his wife as with none other of his creatures.

2. *The creation of mankind in the Priestly document*

In the account of the creation in the Priestly document the relation of man to God is also the dominating and all-embracing theme (Gen. 1.26–30). It is in this that the difference between man and all other created beings is shown. It is true that he is placed close to the beasts; he is created on the same day as the terrestrial animals (vv. 24–31), and fish and birds are also, through a blessing, given the right to multiply – a right otherwise reserved for man (cf. v. 22 with v. 28); and finally man and the land animals are assigned the same food (vv. 29f.). Yet man's special position is no less clearly brought out. The terrestrial animals, who are created immediately before man on the sixth day, proceed from the earth on the basis of a divine command to it; and God 'makes them' (*'śh*) (vv. 24f.).[11] But the man and the woman in Gen. 1 do not emerge from the depths of the earth;[12] they are completely independently created, without the materials being provided beforehand and without the co-operation of the earth (this is characterized by the threefold *br'* in v. 27),[13] by God's own personal decision (v. 26) – a decision unique in the Priestly document's whole creation account. The blessing given to man in v. 28 differs fundamentally from that conferred on the fish and the birds in v. 22, in that after they are empowered to multiply, men are entrusted with lordship over the earth and especially over all animals (v. 28b). This defines the decisive difference between man and beast, and it again derives from God's relationship to man.[14] This peculiar relationship already shows itself formally in that no other created being is deemed worthy of the divine address to such an extent as man; it is significant that when nourishment is assigned to man and beast, men are addressed (v. 29), whereas the animals are only spoken of in the third person (v. 30). Finally, it should be noted that mankind is immediately created as two sexes and is as such entrusted with the free lordship over the rest of creation (vv. 27f.).

The accounts of the creation in Gen. 1 and 2 differ widely in their philosophical premises and narrative form, centuries apart as they are in date; so their factual agreement in three essential points is all the more surprising: (*a*) Man belongs in immediate proximity to the animals. (*b*) Through the special attention God devotes towards him, man is at the same time unmistakably differentiated from the animals. (*c*) It is only man and woman together who make up a whole and useful person.

Unlike the Yahwist's account, the Priestly document sees mankind's task of multiplying until it fills and conquers the earth as being given to it simultaneously with its creation (v. 28a). Thus conception and birth belong expressly to the creation.

3. *Man's birth according to Psalm 139*

Whereas Gen. 1.28a absorbs the propagation of man into the concept of creation, Psalm 139, on the other hand, draws age-old concepts about the creation into its view of the birth of an individual. Here an archaic biology makes it graphically clear that the Creator of mankind is also the Creator of every individual person (Isa. 17.7). In what context does the psalmist arrive at this idea? Apparently he is involved in an investigation into the worship of idols, and he maintains his innocence (vv. 19–24).[15] He shows how completely and utterly he sees himself as being searched out by God; he is certain that God knows his nature completely. To make clear his certainty that man cannot flee before God into any obscurity (v. 11), since God can even penetrate the night (v. 12), he draws on his personal history of creation as proof (*kī* v. 13):

> 13   It is thou who hast formed my kidneys,
>   who hast woven me together in my mother's womb . . .
> 15   My bones were not hidden from thee
>   when I was being made in secret,
>   wrought motley-wise in the depths of the earth.
> 16   Thy eyes beheld me in my primal form.

In the context of an examination of conscience it is understandable that the psalmist should first name his kidneys – the highly sensitive organ of self-knowledge[16] – as being created by Yahweh (v. 13a). For the rest, everything that grew in his mother's womb is the work of the great weaver (*skk*); skin and muscles are seen as 'fabric'. What developed in the 'hidden places' (v. 15) does not derive from the designs and capacities of man; only the God who created it in secret also knows it, through and through, from the very beginning. His eyes already saw the embryo,[17] the worshipper's germinal form. It is noticeable in this context that, besides the womb as man's chamber of development, the psalmist names the depths of the earth, in which the developing body received its 'motley' (*rqm* piel). This is the reflection of an archaic view according to which man 'sprouted from the earth like corn'.[18] The way the land animals issue from the earth in Gen. 1.24 is reminiscent of this idea (cf. vv. 12f.). More clearly still, Job (1.21) sees his mother's womb and the womb of the earth as, for man, belonging together:

> Naked I came from my mother's womb,
>   and naked shall I return there.

'There' undoubtedly means the hidden places in the womb of the earth, in analogy to the mother's womb. The ancient oriental form of burial in a squatting position may be a reminder of the position of the embryo.[19] In Ps. 139 the idea that man proceeds from the 'depths of the earth' serves (in parallel to the secret hiding place in the mother's womb) to prove the psalmist's awareness of Yahweh's inescapable knowledge of man's secret places since the primal beginnings of his existence.

4. *Man's birth according to Job 10*

We can find a similar personal confession of creation with yet other new, still more precise ideas of conception and birth, in Job 10.8–12. It is supported by the tortured questionings of the suffering Job (10.3):

> Is it of value to thee to oppress,
> to despise the work of thy hands?

The way in which this precious piece of workmanship came into being – the work which Yahweh might one day long for (14.15) – is expressed in 10.8ff.:

> Thy hand fashioned and made me;
> 'and now thou dost turn about'[20] and destroy me.
> 9 Remember that thou hast made me as of clay;
> and now thou turnest me to dust again.
> 10 Didst thou not pour me out like milk,
> and curdle me like cheese?
> 11 Thou didst clothe me with skin and flesh,
> and knit me together with bones and sinews.
> 12 Thou has granted me life and grace;
> and thy care has preserved my breath.

The forming of man out of clay and his decaying to dust (vv. 8f.) still reminds us of Gen. 2.7 and 3.19. We saw a similar image of the 'clothing' with skin and flesh, and above all the weaving and knitting together (*skk* v. 11) of bones and sinews, in Ps. 139.13, 15.[21] But what is quite new and unique is the idea in v. 10 of the poured-out milk that curdles like cheese. As an analogy, it helps us to understand the pouring out of the milky seminal fluid into the female organism and the development of a firm embryonic body that follows insemination. This ancient physiology knows as yet nothing of the entry of the masculine spermatozoa into the female ovum as the decisive procedure, and one which eludes human option. It is all the more important that, in its own way, it does not trace the proceeding that leads to birth back to the will of father or mother, or both, but says: 'Didst *thou* not pour me out like milk . . . ?'

Not only the creation of mankind as a whole but also the evolution of the individual – indeed of one's own life – is traced back to Yahweh as being a work of art fashioned by his hands. No man can completely understand himself if he does not remain conscious that he derives from a process in which he had 'no say'.[22] Such insight also leads to the dialogue of man with his God, a dialogue which in Job's case takes on the bitterest edge. Whether man disputes with God as in Job 10 or whether, under attack, he tests himself and sees himself tested, as in Ps. 139, it helps him to relate the general belief in creation (Gen. 1–2) to his own birth. The extreme diversity of the natural philosophies underlying Gen. 2, Gen. 1, Ps. 139 and Job 10 suggests to modern man that he should transpose into the appropriate state of biological knowledge the fundamental assurance that both mankind and the individual originated in the will of God; and that he should not neglect the chance of being called to the dialogue of man with his Creator.

XII

Life and Death[1]

The time of man is limited time. Created in mortal form as he is (Gen. 3.19, 22), it is his opportunity for living between birth and death. If we think in terms of life's duration, the question of what man is finds as its answer: he is a perishable being, a mere breath (Pss. 39.5, 11; 49.12, 20; 82.7; 89.47f.). The beginning of his life is appointed by Yahweh, but dark and mysterious questions arise at its end.

1. *The words of the dying*

It is in the words of the dying that we first observe the consciousness of Old Testament man that in death something happens to him that is not in any way unusual. 'I am about to go the way of all the earth' – that is the way in which Joshua (23.14) and David (I Kings 2.2) are able to begin their last words in the Deuteronomic history.[2] Death draws even the greatest in Israel into a shared and universal destiny. But before that, the voice of the dying is important for the living. Throughout, the biblical narrators report men's departing words with much more attention than the act of dying.

According to one of the earlier strata of the Pentateuch, perhaps the Elohist, the dying Jacob or Israel is told that his son Joseph has come to see him, with his two grandsons, Manasseh and Ephraim. 'Then Israel summoned his strength, and sat up in bed' (Gen. 48.1f.). Almost blind, he blesses his grandsons, contrary to Joseph's expectations, 'crossing his hands' (v. 14) – that is, the younger will be the mightier (v. 19). Then he says to Joseph (v. 21): 'Behold, I am about to die, but God will be with you, and will bring you again to the land of your fathers.' The man who is dying in weakness sees the changes that are to come. In his experience of his own limitations he becomes the witness of the divine promises. He revolutionizes human legality, whereby the elder son takes precedence over the younger one. The dying man teaches us to reckon with alterations in the meaning of the promise. Similarly, even though its content is completely different, the blessing of the dying Moses contains, according to Deut. 33, 'creative words which are able to shape the future'.[3]

Deut. 31.1–6 shows Moses calling Israel to fearlessness after his great admonition to his people, with its blessing and its curse (v.6):

> For it is Yahweh your God who goes with you;
> he will not fail you or forsake you.

The dying man discovers in the fullness of experience both the limitations of all that is human and the power of the promises (v.4):

> Yahweh will do with your enemies
> as he did to Sihon and Og, the kings of the Amorites.

Joshua reminds his hearers even more strongly of the totality of experience, as he is 'about to go the way of all the earth' (Josh. 23.14):

> All has come to pass for you,
> not one promise has failed.

Consequently Israel ought to fear the threatening words which are linked with a breach of the covenant (vv. 15f.). Concentration on God's promise also opens up to the dying man the vision of all the promises that have already been fulfilled, as well as the changes that are still to come in the future.

The Deuteronomic history also shows from the words of the dying Samuel (I Sam. 12) and David (I Kings 2.1ff.) how man in his frailty becomes a witness of authority when he stands at the threshhold of death. This great historical work itself came into being on Israel's deathbed, in the period of the Babylonian exile. The temple, the state and the country had all been taken from her. Could she visualize any future other than death? In this situation Israel's spokesman recognizes the truth for the men of the future. The dying words of the great – of Moses, Joshua, Samuel and David – are to be understood in the light of Israel's dying hour as well.[4]

The voices of the dying in the Old Testament are a prelude to the fundamental importance of the words of the dying Jesus in the gospels, from the borrowing from Ps. 22 in Mark 15.34 to the *tetelestai* ('it is finished') in John 19.30. The authentic gospel is summed up in the tersest and clearest way in those departing cries which, in the hour of complete alienation from God, manifest the breakthrough of salvation.

2. *The grave*

The dying person has much of importance to say, but his grave has little significance. Certainly, burials and mourning ceremonies for the dead can occasionally be described in detail – indeed in ponderous detail, as Jacob's is in Gen. 50. But why? Is the long road taken by all Jacob's sons, with their vast accompanying train (vv.7–9), to the grave which Jacob had hewn out for himself in Canaan (v. 5) anything but a promise-laden prelude to the confirmation of the pledge that the people should inherit the land? The indication of the site of the burial place can vary in the various strata of the story. Besides the 'threshing floor in East Jordan' (10f.), which belongs to one of the older accounts, the Priestly document (v. 13) names the cave of the field at Machpelah to the east of Mamre, which Abraham had acquired as a burial place for Sarah. This points back to Gen.23, where an 'indirect prophetic aspect' is also unmistakable.[5] Thus the varying information about the place of the grave underlines the continuity of the promise. The grave itself has only subordinate importance.

Certainly some notable graves were still known to tradition, such as the oak of weeping near Bethel, under which Deborah, Rebecca's nurse, was buried (Gen.35.8). According to I Sam.25.1 Samuel was buried 'in his house at Ramah'.[6] On the other hand it is expressly noted that the great Moses was buried in the land of Moab, but that no one knows where his grave is (Deut.34.6). Bearing the sins of the murmuring people (Deut. 1.37; 4.1),[7] he was not destined to enter into the Promised Land (Deut. 3.23–29). It is not Moses' grave that is to be revered; it is Yahweh's word, proclaimed through him, that is to be obeyed and to find adherents. That is why we are told immediately after the account of Moses' death (Deut. 34.9):

And Joshua the son of Nun was full of the spirit of wisdom, for Moses had laid his hands upon him; so the people of Israel obeyed him, and did as Yahweh had commanded Moses.

David's grave is only referred to briefly and relatively vaguely, after the extensive account of his last will (I Kings 2.1–9); the note runs (v. 10): 'Then David slept with his fathers and was buried in the city of David.' Cf. the corresponding note about Rehoboam (I Kings 14.31), Asa (I Kings 15.24 and elsewhere) and in Samaria about Ahab (I Kings 22.40 and elsewhere). It is terrible for a man to find no proper burial place, as Saul's death shows (cf. I Sam. 31.10–13 with II Sam. 21.1–14).

Yet the places of the dead are anything but holy. The tithing regulation in Deut.26.14 is significant; according to this the Israelite, when yielding up his tithe to Yahweh, is to confess:

I have not eaten of the tithe when I was mourning, . . . or offered any of it to the dead.

The idea is that part of the tithe might be put in a grave as food for the dead; this would be sacrilege in Yahweh's eyes, just as it would be sacrilege if part had been eaten during the period of mourning.[8] Nothing is to come into contact, even remotely, with the sphere of death. The environment of death is not holy; it is defiled to a dangerous degree.

According to Isa. 65.4 it is one of the characteristics of a people who is rebellious against Yahweh (cf. v. 2) to 'sit in tombs', whether they do so in order to bewail the dead, or to honour them, or to question them.[9] The grave as the domain of death is not to be honoured. Later, Jesus cries woe to the hypocrites who, being the sons of those who murdered the prophets, build the prophets' tombs (i.e., chapels at their burial places) and adorn the monuments of the righteous (Matt. 23.29). The angel's saying in Luke 24.5f. wards off from the outset the contingency that Jesus' tomb might become a place of pilgrimage:

> Why do you seek the living among the dead?
> He is not here.

3. *The demythologizing of death*

Israel showed itself to be concerned with the demythologizing of death, which (in view of the country's neighbours), appeared both difficult and essential for the believer in Yahweh. In general the Old Testament sees death in all its hideousness. It is surrounded by no halo of any kind. No holiness whatever, let alone divinity, consecrates death, any more than the grave. If death is ever given any title of honour at all in poetry, it is the cynical one of 'the king of terrors' (Job 18.14). Mythical concepts are still relatively prominent in the Old Testament picture of the world of the dead, as we can see from the mocking song about the king of Babylon in Isa. 14.4ff.:

> How the oppressor has ceased,
>   and ceased his insolent claim!
> 5   Yahweh has broken the staff of the wicked,
>   the sceptre of rulers.
>
>   . . .
>
> 9   The underworld is stirred up
>   to meet you when you come.
>   It rouses the shades to greet you,
>   all who were princes on earth;
>   it causes to rise from their thrones
>   all who were kings of the nations.
> 10 All of them rise and say to you:
>   You too have become as weak as we!
>   you have become like us!
> 11 . . .

Maggots are the bed beneath you,
and worms are your covering.

. . .

13   You planned in your heart,
'I will ascend to heaven'.

. . .

15   But you are brought down to the underworld,
to the depths of the depths.

Just as among Israel's neighbours (as we see from the Gilgamesh epic, for example), the world of the dead (*šeʾōl*) is here (v. 15) thought of as a great subterranean collecting ground,[10] where the dead rise up as shades and talk. But *šeʾōl* also appears as a ruler, who startles the kings who are already reposing powerlessly beside him into excited expectation of the great Babylonian king (v. 9). This underworld drama is only described in order to make drastically clear the consequences of Yahweh's judgment on the tyrant who enslaved Israel (14.3f.). The kingdom of shades has no might or dignity of its own. Its reality is utter weakness (v. 10). Maggots and worms are the true sovereigns (v. 11).

Such poetic acceptance of mythical ideas cannot give even remote credence to the idea that the rule of death was being glorified, let alone deified. On the contrary, the ancient East's widely developed notions of the realm of the dead (such as those evidenced in the great underworld myth of Ishtar's descent into hell,[11] for example) shrink together into relatively rare and brief allusions. And the dead – even the greatest and most devout men in Israel – are not in any way adorned with a halo. In Egypt we come across frequent euphemisms – 'he goes living to his rest', 'the fairest of destinies has come to pass', 'he enters into his horizon, departs to heaven, and is united with the sun through the mingling of his divine body with his maker.'[12] In the Old Testament anything similar is unthinkable.[13] Usually talk about the descent into *šeʾōl* as the world of the dead means no more than an indication of burial as the end of life (Gen. 42.38; 44.29, 31; Isa. 38.10, 17; Pss. 9.15, 17; 16.10; 49.9, 15; 88.3–6, 11f.; Prov. 1.12).[14]

At the same time, Israel was seduced by its environment into ascribing a particular power to death or the dead. The fight put up by the prophets proves this most clearly. Thus Isaiah warns his hearers against the conjuring up of the dead (8.19f.):

When they say to you,
'Consult the spirits of the dead and the soothsayers
who whisper and mutter!'

> Should not a people consult their God?
> Should they consult the dead instead of the living?

Isaiah calls the people who have been led astray 'to the teaching and to testimony' (v. 20), as he himself proclaims it and as he has passed it on to his group of pupils (v. 16). Such an admonition has political consequences. In 28.15ff. Isaiah quotes Jerusalem diplomats who are proud of having made a pact with Egypt and say:

> We have made a covenant with death
> and with the world of the dead we have an agreement.

In ironical terms the prophet goes on to put words into the mouths of the politicians who are speculating on the Egyptian cult of the dead:

> We have made lies our refuge,
> and in falsehood we have taken shelter.

But Yahweh, on the contrary, says:

> I am laying in Zion a foundation . . .
> He who believes will not waver.

Hail will destroy the refuge of lies. The 'covenant with death' and the 'agreement with the world of the dead' will be declared null and void (vv. 16–18).

The Old Testament itself is able to report a successful case of conjuring up the dead; but in its very success it strikingly demonstrates the absurdity of the undertaking. It is part of King Saul's madness that, having already been repudiated by God, he disguises himself and, in the face of his own prohibition (I Sam. 28.3), begs the woman of Endor who is a medium to call up the dead Samuel; for God's silence in the face of the Philistine threat has left him completely at a loss (I Sam. 28.4ff.). Samuel does actually rise up in ghost-like form. But what does he say? He censures Saul for disturbing his peace and reminds him of what he had told him earlier: that Yahweh has turned away from him and has given the kingdom to David (vv. 15ff.). Thus this story of the conjuring up of the dead, which is unique in the Old Testament, shows that nothing is to be expected from the spirits of the dead beyond what has been witnessed to by living messengers. On exactly the same lines, Dives' request is rejected in Jesus' parable, when he asks that Lazarus might be sent from the realm of the dead to his brothers who are still alive. 'They have Moses and the prophets; let them hear them' (Luke 16.27ff.).

In Deuteronomy and the Law of Holiness all the customs and practices are already forbidden which reckon in any way at all with the return or with the power of the dead: Deut. 14.1f.; 18.11; Lev. 19.27f., 31; 20.6, 27.

As far as we can see, the Yahweh religion showed itself particularly intolerant towards the cult of the dead in all its forms. It would be 'quite wrong on the one hand to set too little store on the temptation which emanated from this sphere or, on the other, to underestimate the power of self-restraint which Israel had to call into being in order to renounce all sacral communion with her dead'.[15] For Israel's neighbours cultivated such communion, as the cults of the dying and resurrected godheads show. Ezekiel finds women who bewail Tammuz (the Mesopotamian God of the dying summer vegetation) even in Jerusalem (8.14).[16] Yahweh is in contrast testified to exclusively as 'the living God', especially in polemics against foreign gods: Josh. 3.10; II Kings 19.4; Hos. 2.1.[17] More frequently still, he is the one who gives and preserves life: Deut. 30.15, 19; Pss. 64.1; 103.4; 133.3; and frequently elsewhere.[18]

The zeal with which the Old Testament laws term everything that has any connection at all with death as 'unclean' (*ṭāmē'*) in Yahweh's eyes corresponds to this. Num. 19.11 declares in general terms: 'He who touches the dead body of any person shall be unclean seven days.' Verse 16 extends the regulation to 'whoever in the open field touches one who is slain with a sword, or a dead body, or a bone of a man, or a grave'. The uncleanness which emanates from human – or even animal – bodies has an unusually infectious power. Even the things that come into contact with it are unclean, for example vessels used for food or drink, or pieces of clothing (Lev. 11.32–35). 'An oven or stove shall be broken in pieces' when a carcass has fallen on it (v. 35). The fact that the dead are 'unclean' and make other things 'unclean' disqualifies them cultically to the strongest possible degree.

Lustrations of the usual kind are no help against the impurity caused by death. A particular purificatory water has to be prepared from the ashes of an unblemished red heifer (Num. 19.1ff., 17ff.). Can we guess 'the hard defensive warfare which Israel waged, aided by these very cultic prescriptions'? They show 'a radical demythologizing and desacralizing of death.'[19] Every euphemism is decisively rejected, and even more every numinous veiling – let alone deification – of the dead and the power of the dead; and this rejection meant a total lack of acceptance of a cult of the dead in Israel's life of faith. Anyone who belongs to Yahweh may not therefore clip his hair and beard or inflict cuts on his body because someone has died (Lev. 19.27f.; 21.5; Deut. 14.1f.; cf. Jer. 41.5). Such apotropaic rites, practised by Israel's neighbours, reckon with the power of the world of the dead; they are designed to make the mourners unrecognizable and hence undiscoverable. Such respect for death is impossible in Yahweh's presence.[20]

4. *The definition of death*

If this is the view of death taken by the Old Testament, how is the state of death to be *defined*? Perhaps Ps. 88 suggests an approach to a precise definition. The author of this lament is on the very fringe of life (v. 3):

> My soul is surfeited with trouble
> and my life draws near to the realm of the dead.

He already knows that he has been 'dismissed among the dead' (v. 5), whom he characterizes, in his appeal to God, as

> those whom thou dost remember no more,
> for they are cut off from thy hand.

This defines the dead as beings who have been expelled from Yahweh's sphere of influence.[21] Correspondingly, Job knows that there is a 'too late' even for God (7.21):

> Now I shall lie in the earth;
> shouldst thou seek me, I shall be no longer there.

In a series of rhetorical questions Ps. 88 makes clear what it means for the dead to be cut off from Yahweh (vv. 10–12):

> Dost thou work wonders for the dead?
> Do the shades rise up to praise thee?
> Is thy steadfast love declared in the grave,
> or thy faithfulness in the realm of the dead?
> Are thy wonders known in the darkness,
> or thy saving help in the land of forgetfulness?

For the psalmist the bitter 'no' is a certainty. In the world of the dead, Yahweh's work, Yahweh's proclamation and Yahweh's praise no longer have any place. This view is frequently endorsed, for example in Ps. 115.17:

> The dead do not praise Yahweh,
> nor do any that go down into silence.

Or in Hezekiah's prayer in Isa. 38.18f.:

> For the underworld cannot thank thee,
> and death – does it still praise thee?
> Those who go down to the pit cannot hope
> for thy faithfulness.
> Only the living, the living, he thanks thee,
> as I do this day.

This contrasts the definition of the dead (one who is cut off from the praise of God) with a characterization of the living, as the man who can praise Yahweh's works and word.[22] 'In the Old Testament life therefore means:

to have relationship. Above all: to have a relationship with God.' 'Death . . . means lack of relationship.'[23]

This definition of death in the Old Testament is of fundamental importance for the understanding of the death of Jesus in the New. Jesus dies a completely and utterly untransfigured – indeed a radically profaned – death. Here too every nimbus is completely missing. He dies man's most horrible death and is thus present for man in the midst of complete alienation from God.[24]

But a long road still has to be travelled from the Old Testament definitions of death as we have seen them up to now down to the New Testament understanding. First of all a difficult problem arises within the Old Testament itself. Death is on the one hand described as a sphere of pitiless alienation from God – an area where Yahweh can no longer exert any influence; any human attempt to set up even the least connection between the world of the dead and Yahweh is sharply checked. But on the other hand death is denied any independent power of its own over against Yahweh; it is unthinkable that an independent sovereign should rule in the world of the dead.[25]

5. *Yahweh and the vacuum of death*

How do the witnesses of the Yahweh religion cope with this remarkable theological vacuum? We can observe a groping into the nothingness.

The first step is taken by all petitioners in the Old Testament. When they are in danger of death there is for them only one possibility – to turn to Yahweh; for he is after all the 'fountain of life' (Ps. 36.7–9); it is in his holy place that the promise of life is surely to be expected.[26] Thus even Ps. 88 cries to Yahweh (2,13f.):

> Let my prayer come before thee,
>   incline thy ear to my cry!
>
> . . .
>
> O Yahweh, I cry to thee;
>   in the morning my prayer comes before thee.
> O Yahweh, why dost thou cast me off?
> Why dost thou hide thy face from me?

Who if not Yahweh could offer a refuge, even in the face of the underworld, where his hand has no efficacy (v. 5)? For only he controls entry into the realm of the dead (v. 6):

> Thou castest me into the bottomless grave,
>   into the darkness, the depths of the depths.

It is the petitioner's elemental assurance that only Yahweh can ordain or hinder the entrance to death, at least. Just as at the beginning of Israel's history Yahweh decided that the helpless foundling, weltering in its own blood, should remain alive (Ezek. 16.6f.), so in every individual case he determines over a person's death. This is the certainty standing behind the scene described in Amos 6.9f.:

> And if ten men remain in one house, they shall die. Someone finds their kinsman, and compels him to bring the bodies out of the house. If he says to him who is in the furthest corner of the house, 'Is there still anyone with you?' he says 'No'; and he says 'Hush! For we must not mention the name of Yahweh.'

The word of God thrusts further forward in Amos' fifth vision (9.2); the passage says, about those who want to escape the judgment,

> Though they press forward into the world of the dead,
> from there shall my hand take them.

Here Yahweh is not the one who delivers men up to the kingdom of the dead. The presupposition is rather that men flee there of their own accord, simply to be safe from Yahweh's grasp (see also Ps. 88.5, 10–12). But here we also hear the new message that Yahweh's hand also reaches into the world of the dead. Ps. 139.8 arrives at a similar certainty:

> If I make my bed in the world of the dead,
> thou are there.

If Yahweh alone is God, the recognition cannot be wanting that even death cannot secure any sphere of sovereignty into which Yahweh is incapable of penetrating. It not only gives universal validity to the threat that from Yahweh there is simply no escape; it then also becomes the assurance of salvation that we find celebrated in hymns of praise, e.g., I Sam. 2.6:

> Yahweh kills and brings to life,
> he brings down to the world of the dead and raises up.

In the Song of Moses a corresponding certainty is expressly associated with the proclamation of the uniqueness of Yahweh's divine lordship (Deut. 32. 39):

> See now that I, even I, am he,
>   and there is no God beside me;
> I kill and I make alive;
>   I wound and it is I that heal.

The expectation that Yahweh has the complete disposal of death and life creates for Job a new possibility of hope (14.13-17):

> O that thou wouldest hide me in the land of the dead,
> that thou wouldest conceal me until thy wrath be past.
>
> . . .
>
> All the days of my service I would wait,
> till my release should come.
> Thou wouldest call, and I would answer thee,
> thou wouldest long for the work of thy hands.
> For then thou wouldest number my steps,
> no longer wouldest thou keep watch over my sin.

In a quite different way Ps. 63.3 suggests how Yahweh's divine clemency transcends life: 'Thy steadfast love is better than life.' The overcoming of death's agony is not manifested in any elaborate hope of the beyond, but in the calm certainty that the community with Yahweh cannot be ended by death, because of his faithfulness.[27]

The idea that a man can be 'snatched away' (*lqḥ*, Ps. 49.15) is a further comment on this viewpoint:

> God ransoms my soul,
> yea, he snatches me away from the power of the underworld.

The idea is a familiar one from the traditions about Enoch and Elijah (Gen. 5.24; II Kings 2.3, 5). Before Yahweh, according to this notion, there is not only the alternative between this life and the shadow existence in the world of the dead; there is a third possibility – a permanent, living fellowship with him. The worshipper of Ps. 73 talks most clearly about this (vv. 23f.):

> I am continually with thee;
> thou dost hold me with thy right hand.
> Thou dost guide me according to thy counsel,
> and afterwards thou wilt snatch me away to glory.

The idea of snatching away expresses an expectation of a bond with Yahweh which even physical death cannot interrupt (v. 26):

> My flesh and my heart may fail,
> but God is my portion for ever.

The word 'portion' (*ḥēleq*) is the decisive word demanding interpretation. Originally meaning a portion of ground (Deut. 10.9; Num. 18.20), when it is related to Yahweh it takes on the general meaning of the basis of life, life's subsistence (Ps. 16.5).[28] Life cannot end in death for the man for whom God himself has become the subsistence of life (Ps. 73.27f.):

> For lo, those who are far from thee shall perish.
> . . .
> But I have made Yahweh my refuge.

So, contrary to the thesis about the prosperity of the godless, the truth comes to light at the end of this psalmist's life – though this may be in the first place only the uprush of an individual hope on the part of the devout Levite.

Basically and generally, the driving power behind apocalyptic thinking is the certainty of God. 'If God is all in all, there can in apocalyptic be no more death, consistently speaking.'[29] Isa.25.8 brings us the fundamental assertion:

> He swallows up death for ever.
> And the Lord Yahweh wipes away tears from all faces,
> and the reproach of his people he takes away from all the earth.

Here the universal vision is primarily elucidated as hope for Israel. So also in the first promise of the resurrection in Isa.26.19: 'Thy dead shall live, their bodies shall rise.' Daniel 12.2 takes the final step and no longer limits the expectation to the devout who belong to the people of God:

> Many of those who sleep in the dust of the earth
>   shall awake,
>   some to everlasting life
>   and some to everlasting shame.

This is a fundamental denial that God's rule permits a man to decay, or to vanish, in death. Here there is now also a glorification of 'the wise' and those 'who have turned many to righteousness', such as was unknown to Israel in the transition to the realm of the dead (Dan. 12.3).

Thus the knowledge of Yahweh, advancing in a series of waves, overcame the theological vacuum of death, though without abandoning the two principles which caused that vacuum: on the one hand death lies extremely far from God; and on the other, it does not represent an independent counterforce.

6. *Stages of dying*

Up to now we have only touched on the problem of the borderline between death and life. We read about Nabal's death – that it took place ten days after the death of his heart (I Sam.25.37f.);[30] so even in the Old Testament a man's death does not have to be identical with the death of a vital organ, and, as a corollary, man can also be survived by his body's organs.[31] From a biological point of view there are stages of dying. In order to define the borderline between life and death in any given case, we need to be able to define death and life. The Old Testament answer was that for the whole of man life passes into death at the precise moment when the praise of God falls silent.[32] This theological statement includes for modern man a psychological one, and it also implies very different stages of dying, biologically speaking.

In Psalm 88 we heard the voice of a man who has been 'close to death from his youth up' (v. 15), i.e., he is incurably ill. Although he was 'surfeited with trouble' (v. 3) we are not told that any organ is dead; and yet he knows himself to be so delivered up to the superior power of death that he is already 'reckoned among those who go down to the Pit, "dismissed"[33] among the dead' (4f.). Even when heart and breath are still active this man must already be viewed as someone encompassed by death. It is therefore possible for a dead man to be survived by all the organs of his body. That is why in Ps. 38 a man who is dumb in death can, paradoxically, speak (13f.):

> I am like a deaf man, I do not hear,
> like a dumb man who does not open his mouth.
> Yea, I am like a man who no longer hears,
> and in whose mouth there are no more answers.

In Ps. 55 the terrors of death (v. 4) have already fallen upon a man who is exposed to the persecutions of his enemies (vv. 3, 9f., 12f.). Ps. 116 is the hymn of thanksgiving of a man who has been exposed to injustice; looking back on the deception of the men he had been at the mercy of (vv. 10f.), he can say (v. 3):

> The cords of death encompassed me,
> the snares of the underworld had laid hold on me.

And, thinking of the liberation he has experienced (v. 16), he worships Yahweh (v. 8): 'Thou hast delivered my life from death.' Statements like this in the laments and songs of thanksgiving about the borderline between life and death are not meant pictorially. They exactly represent the recognition that when man is beyond the possibility of praising God, he is truly 'in death', 'in real objective fact'.[34] Thus the dangerously ill, the accused who face the court without any support, the persecuted who are helplessly delivered over to their enemies – all these already belong to the world of the dead. Here the '*pars pro toto* mode of thinking' comes into effect.[35]

Elihu can consequently teach in Job 33.29f. that a man crosses the frontier between life and death several times:

> Behold, God does all these things,
> twice, three times, with a man,

> to bring back his soul from the Pit,
> to lighten it with the light of life.

After that comes the death that is unalterable and has no return (II Sam. 12.23). It is only overcome through Yahweh's final victory over death itself, or through special living fellowship with him.[36]

The idea of crossing the frontier of death more than once always implies the notion of premature death. In great age, death finds a positive acceptance. It ends a life that has been fulfilled. Thus the Priestly document reports in Gen. 25.8:

> Abraham died in a good old age,
> an old man and full of years,
> and was gathered to his people.

This is the death that man is *allowed* to die, not the one that he *has* to die.[37] Isaac, David and Job also die full of days (Gen. 35.29; I Chron. 29.28; Job 42.17). Job had seen his children, his grandchildren and his great-grandchildren (42.16). In this way life is fulfilled. For 'full' does not mean satiated; it means satisfied.

Eliphaz shows that the dying of a man whom God has not corrected in vain is a high fulfilment (Job 5.26):

> He comes to his grave in ripe old age,
> as the ears of corn are gathered in their season.

In God's wounding and in his binding up he has experienced the fulfilment of the promise (vv. 17f., 24f.):

> Peace is thy tent.
> Thou wilt inspect thy pastures and miss nothing.

How completely and utterly un-Faustian this is – this affirmation that a fulfilled human life is a finite life! How different from Mephistopheles' utterance immediately after Faust's death:

> No lust contents him and no joy can sate him,
> And striving ever on towards protean forms,
> The last, the meanest, emptiest of his moments,
> Poor fool, he would hold fast.[38]

Old, yet not to have had enough of life – that would not be good. But the reverse is bad too – to have had enough of life, yet not to be old. It is only in extreme misery that a man can long for death. Where else than with Job (6.8–10)?

> That it would please God to crush me,
> that he would let loose his hand and cut me off!
> This would be my consolation.

And he curses the day of his birth (3.1ff.; cf. especially vv. 20–23). In deepest despair Jeremiah curses the man who told his father of his birth (20.14–18):

> O that my mother might have been my grave!
> And that her womb had been for ever great!
> Why must I come forth from the womb
> to see but toil and sorrow
> and but to end my days in shame?

It is only Jeremiah who broke down under the burden of the prophetic office in rebellion like this. Suicide is very rare in the Old Testament.[39]

But there is an 'enough' for everyone. Even in the era of salvation death comes at the last, although only when a man is more than a hundred years old (Isa. 65.20ff.). Later, belief in the resurrection increases the readiness to die: 'To live for longer than eighty years is a torment.'[40] Premature death, however, always manifests itself as the enemy of life. 'The earlier death comes, the greater the disaster.'[41] Thus King Hezekiah complains (Isa. 38.10, 12f.):

> In the noontide of my days I must depart,
> I must pass through the gates of the realm of the dead,
> robbed of the remainder of my years.
> . . .
> My dwelling is plucked up,
> and taken from me like a shepherd's tent.

Even more does a mother lament over her child, like Hagar in the wilderness (Gen. 21.16): 'Let me not look upon the death of the child.' As a father, David suffers unspeakably with his son, Bathsheba's dying child (II Sam. 12.16ff.). For a young person, death is shown to be a hopeless affair.[42] Numerous turns of phrase therefore describe it as 'a downfall' or as destruction, or as an entering into the country of no return, in which darkness, silence and forgetfulness reign, so that there is nothing more to see, nothing to hear, and nothing to remember (II Sam. 12.23; Job 7.9f.; 10.21f.; Pss. 94.17; 115.17). Here nothing is glossed over and nothing is glorified. It must be noted once more that Israel's God is, as a general rule, not to be sought in the realm of the dead, but only just on its very borders: he delivers men up to death, or snatches them away. He is ultimately recognized as the one who overcomes death.

7. *Passing and transitoriness*

The tension between God and death is inseparable from the connection between death and guilt. All sections of the Old Testament witness to

Israel's consciousness of this fact. Premature death, especially, frequently counts as death incurred through guilt. Eli is told that, as a punishment, no one among his kin would reach old age (I Sam. 2.31f.). According to Job 22.15f. wicked men are snatched away 'before their time'. Job 36.14 says of reprobates:

> They die in the flower of their youth,
> their life ends when they are but striplings.

The 'law of death' with its threat of the death penalty is intended to be a guard against this.[43] When it is summed up, the whole of the ancient divine law can be presented as follows (Deut. 30.15):

> See, I have set before you this day
> life and good, death and evil.

Cf. Lev. 18.5.

In the same way, in the midst of the harsh prophetic threat of death, Yahweh's call is to be heard (Amos 5.4): 'Seek me and live.' Cf. Ezek. 18.21, 28; 33.14f. Above all, wisdom interprets itself as the word of instruction in living (Prov. 13.14):

> The teaching of the wise is a fountain of life,
> that one may avoid the snares of death.

Cf. Prov. 3.1f. In the specific example of warning against the strange woman, this teaching runs as follows (Prov. 2.18f.):

> Her house sinks down to death,
> and her paths to the realm of the dead:
> none who go to her come back,
> nor do they regain the paths of life.

Such words presuppose that man can do something against death – in so far as God has summoned up something against it, and in favour of the life of man, namely, in the words of the law, in prophecy, and in the teachings of wisdom. By transgressing against the offer of life, man is delivering himself up to mortality.[44] For the sin that a man commits culpably leads to the destruction which he suffers culpably. That is why Solomon asks for 'a hearing heart' and not for long life (I Kings 3.11, 14).[45] In the face of the wrath of God, death becomes a call to prove oneself in life (Ps. 90.8ff.):

> Thous settest our iniquities before thee,
> our secret sins in the light of thy countenance.
> For all our days pass away under thy wrath.
> . . .

> Who considers the power of thy anger?
> Who fears the might of thy wrath?
> So teach us to number our days
>   that we may bring home a heart of wisdom.

This is a challenge to examine the death that a man brings upon himself, so that one may escape death's snares.

Enquiry into the reason for guilt seems indispensable in any concrete case, particularly enquiry by the person affected. But here too a man should be careful not to be over-zealous. Job's friends warn him in the strongest terms against the theological passion for looking for the pattern of guilt in others.

In the death that ultimately takes place in old age, the connection between offence and mortality usually remains concealed. Here the Old Testament reminds us rather that to die satisfied with life belongs to man's *nature as created being*. In the Yahwist's story of the Garden of Eden in Gen. 2–3, the fine distinction between the death that is culpably incurred and the death that belongs to the creature is already evident. The death penalty threatened in 2.17 for the grasp at the tree of knowledge is not carried out, although it is merited by the conversation with the serpent and the enjoyment of the forbidden fruit; instead it is changed into the decree of a life full of toil (3.16ff.). Death, when it finally occurs, is expressly explained by the reminiscence of man's creation (3.19):[46]

> . . . till you return to the ground,
>   for out of it you were taken;
> for you are dust
>   and to dust you shall return.

Here there is a precise reference to the very wording of the story of man's creation out of the dust of the earth in 2.7, and none at all to the death penalty decreed in 2.17. It is subsequently stressed in 3.22 that 'living for ever' is for God, not for man, and that it should not therefore become man's lot even through usurpation and robbery; hence access to the tree of life is denied to him through his expulsion from the garden. Thus the Yahwist saw man as a mortal creature, made out of dust.[47]

The later wisdom literature takes up this view and develops it further. In Job 30.23 death is called 'the house where all living things are gathered together'. Job complains:

> I know that thou wilt bring me to death
>   and to the house where all living things are gathered.

Ecclesiastes stresses that in this respect man is similar to the animals (3.19f.):

The fate of the sons of man and the fate of beasts is the same;
as one dies, so dies the other.
All go to one place;
all are from the dust;
and all return to dust again.

If there is here a clear reminiscence of the Yahwist's story of the Garden of Eden, in another passage the Preacher goes far beyond the older biblical statements; and also beyond the statements of the wisdom writings especially. He does not want the question of guilt to be so much as raised any more (9.2–4):

One fate comes to all,
to the righteous and the wicked,
to the clean and the unclean,
to him who sacrifices and to him who does not sacrifice.
As is the good man, so is the sinner;
and he who swears is as he who shuns an oath.
But he who is joined with all the living,
he has hope;
For a living dog is better than a dead lion.

Now the only important thing seems to be the contrast between death and life, whereas the difference between guilt and innocence disappears completely. Ecclesiastes enforces his view through his own observation (7.15–18):

In my vain life I have seen everything:
there are righteous men,
who perish in their righteousness,
and there are wicked men,
who prolong their life in evil-doing.
Be not righteous overmuch
and do not make yourself overwise;
for why will you destroy yourself with judgment?
Be not wicked overmuch,
neither be a fool!
Why should you die before your time?
It is good that you should hold this fast,
and from the other not withhold your hand.
Yea, he who fears God,
he can accomplish both.

It is true that for this preacher too the fear of God and length of life belong together in a general way; but exceptions are well known. Hence every attempt to extend life through excessive demands on the self, as well as every threat to one's own life through excessive wickedness, is rejected. Essentially, the mortality of all life appears to be the characteristic of the created being. So the gift of creaturely existence is also to be fully enjoyed within the temporal limits assigned to it (9.7ff.).[48]

8. *The death of the one and the death of the many*

We still have to direct our attention to two Old Testament borderline texts, in which an extraneous individual destiny influences those who have fallen victims to death.

In Psalm 22,[49] in the complaint of an individual (vv. 1–21), experiences of suffering are first accumulated and heightened into the experience of a comprehensive primal suffering; then, in the song of thanksgiving (vv. 22–31), the salvation of this suffering person becomes the pledge of the break-through of the royal rule of God (vv. 24, 28), for all who also gratefully celebrate this salvation. The whole present world of the nations (vv. 27f.) is included; but those who already 'go down to the dust' are also reached; astonishingly, they too will worship (v. 29), though this was previously completely unthinkable.[50] It is proclaimed even to the coming generations of those as yet unborn that 'he has wrought it' (v. 31). With this the apocalyptic recognition of the complete conquest of death[51] has found a new form in a song of thanksgiving that surmounts all previous limitations. Such thanks are taken up in the New Testament's representation and realization of the death of Jesus in the Lord's Supper. Because Jesus died the death of one alienated from God, those who have been cast out into death's alienation from him are brought back into the thanksgiving of the saved.

Isaiah 53 talks about the unprecedented, revolting suffering of the Servant of God. But why did he suffer?

> Yahweh let the iniquity of us all fall on him.
> Through his suffering my servant shall make many to be
> accounted righteous

(vv. 6b, 11). Not only is all suffering life therefore included in the death of this Servant; the life that has fallen a victim to guilt is not excluded. Together with him, it too will be led into liberty. The New Testament church also drew upon this great text for the better understanding of the death of Jesus and his resurrection. In the fate of Jesus a living fellowship with God has opened up in a new way – a fellowship, moreover, which does not end in the failing of flesh and heart. Psalm 73[52] can now be understood afresh: the Lord is the foundation of my life (Rom. 4.25; II Cor. 5.21; Mark 10.45).

New Testament witnesses took up the small number of texts about death which were interpreted as promise (such as Ps. 22 and Isa. 53), using them as types, in order to grasp more acutely the meaning of Jesus' death. For man today, the complete demythologizing of death, through which the Old Testament stripped away every trace of halo from it, is important. Jesus died a death in which horror swallowed up the praise of God and the proclamation of his acts down to the last note. It was from this barren vacuum – a vacuum which today gapes more widely than ever – that he took away the power.

XIII

To be Young and to Grow Old[1]

Man goes through various phases in his time, until old age takes the place of youth.

1. *Expectation of life*

The Hebrew word for length of life (*ḥeled*) is linked with the complaint about its brevity (Pss. 39.5; 89.47; cf. Job 11.17). How high was the expectation of life in the Old Testament? We have the Chronicles of the kings of Judah to thank for the only exact and historically reliable statements of age spanning several centuries; and these details apply to the Davidic kings themselves. The chronology has been pretty reliably investigated, to the extent that we can more or less determine the age reached by the fourteen kings who belonged to the House of David between 926 and 597 BC.[2] According to this reckoning, they were the following ages when they died:

Rehoboam	56 years old	Jotham	40 years old
Jehoshaphat	55	Ahaz	35
Jehoram	38	Hezekiah	56
Ahaziah	21	Manasseh	66
Joash	45	Amon	22
Amaziah	38	Josiah	38
Azariah	66	Jehoiakim	35

The degree of accuracy can vary in each case by one or two years; in addition the information given for the period from Amaziah to Hezekiah (825–697?) is particularly uncertain. But for our purpose the possible errors average out, generally speaking. The remarkable thing is that the age reached varies between 66 and 21 years, the average being a bare 44.[3] When we remember that princes were particularly well looked after in infancy and childhood, and that adult kings were more carefully protected than most other members of the nation, we shall have to put the average expectation of life (particularly in view of the high rate of infant mortality) much lower.[4] When according to Ps. 90.10 a man reaches 70 years, and only 'by reason of strength' 80 years (*bigbūrōt*), unusually high figures are being given, for none of the 14 Davidic kings listed above reached even 70 years. Only David himself was 70 years old, according to II Sam. 5.4; but we have to reckon with a figure rounded off upwards, both for the age when he is said to have come to the throne (30 years old) and for the length of his reign (40 years). According to I Chron. 29.28, a life of 70 years counts as being 'a good old age'. When Deut. 34.7 gives Moses' age as 120, this, like the information about the patriarchs belonging to Israel's primeval period, conforms to the hoped-for era of salvation, in which according to Isa. 65.20 the youngest will die at the age of 100. In post-Mosaic times, the only people who are said to have been more than a hundred years old were Joshua (110, according to Josh. 24.29), Job (140, according to Job 42.16) and the High Priest Jehoida (130, according to II Chron. 24.15). In Gen. 6.3 length of life was limited to 120 years after man had transgressed his limits (cf. Gen. 5). Here mythical and not historical standards hold good.[5]

2. The seasons of life

Generally speaking, at least three phases of life are distinguished from one another: children (*yōnēq*, the sucking child, Deut. 32.25; *naʿar*, the boy, Ps. 148.12; *tap*, pattering, not capable of walking, Ezek. 9.6); young but fully grown men and grown-up girls (*bāḥūr* and *bᵉtūlā*, Deut. 32.25; Ezek. 9.6 and Ps. 148.12); and mature, elderly men and women (*zāqēn*, who wear a beard, Ezek. 9.6; Ps. 148.12; *ʾīš śēbā*, the grey-haired man, Deut. 32.25; *ʾiššā*, Ezek. 9.6). Jer. 51.22 sees life as divided into four divisions; after children (*naʿar*) and youth (*bāḥūr* and *bᵉtūlā*), a distinction is made between younger married adults (*ʾīš* and *ʾiššā*) and the elderly (*zāqēn*). Jer. 6.11, finally, names five stages of life: the small child (*ʿōlāl*), the youth (*bāḥūr*), man and woman (*ʾīš* and *ʾiššā*), the elderly man (*zāqēn*) and the aged (*mᵉlēʾ yāmīm*); here, therefore, the oldest group is subdivided.

What we discover by way of the statements of age given for these various phases of life conforms to the lower average expectation of life. According to Num. 4.23, a Levite only entered on his service at the sanctuary when he was 30 years old, and ended it as early as the age of 50. The particular requirements of this office demanded complete maturity, but also a man's full powers.[6] It is only a later amendment[7] that puts the taking over of the office as early as 25 years old, and this does not abolish the retiring age in principle, but merely allows those who are over 50 to take over auxiliary services only (Num. 8.24–26). Lack of new applicants will no doubt have elicited this extension of the Levite's term of service, as well as the still later lowering of the commencement age to 20 years old (I Chron. 23.24, 27; Ezra 3.8).

Although full maturity for special tasks connected with worship was only reached at 30,[8] in general the 20-year-old counted as being completely responsible (Num. 14.29; 32.11), and as being liable for military service (Num. 1.3, 18; 26.2; II Chron. 25.5) and for taxation (Ex. 30.14). At 60 a marked falling off of the working capacity was expected (Lev. 27.7). In the early years of life, still other divisions are observed: after the first month of life the danger of death in infancy diminishes considerably (Lev. 27.6); children are not infrequently born 'for calamity' (Isa. 65.23). The child was weaned in its third year (II Chron. 31.16; II Macc. 7.27; I Sam. 1.21–28; cf. also Isa. 28.9; Lam. 4.3f.).[9] From the fifth year of life onwards, the child's working capacity could be reckoned with (Lev. 27.5). Physical maturity was reached with the 13th year (Gen. 17.25).[10]

In Lev. 27.1–8 an interesting list offers us insight into the value set upon the different stages of life; it represents an appendix to the Law of Holiness and dates from a time in which people themselves were no longer brought to the sanctuary as consecrated gifts, as Samuel once was, for instance (I Sam. 1.11, 24ff.); now a sum of money was offered, corresponding in value to their working capacity:[11]

age	male	female
in the first month	–	–
1 month to 5 years old	5 shekels	3 shekels
5–20 years old	20 shekels	10 shekels
20–60 years old	50 shekels	30 shekels
more than 60 years old	15 shekels	10 shekels

In the first month, therefore, it was a matter of waiting to see whether the child was capable of living. After that, up to the age of five, expectation of later usefulness is valued at a tenth of the full working power. At the age of five, the value is already three or four times as much; from this age onwards, the child, like the youth, counts as productive. A person's full value is only expected between the ages of 20 and 60. After that it drops rapidly, more for the old man (by 35 shekels) than for the old woman (by 20 shekels), who is useful as grandmother in the family group. While a girl has only half the value of a boy, an old woman has, relatively, her highest value, two-thirds of an old man's, whereas in her maturity she is only valued at three-fifths.

3. Characteristics of youth
The mark of the growing youth is his entering into the grown-up world.

We hear very little about children playing. Ishmael played with Isaac, much to Sarah's displeasure (Gen. 21.9). According to Zech. 8.5 it is a sign of the age of salvation when boys and girls play in the streets of Jerusalem. Isa. 11.8 presupposes that children like to play in the streets and that crevices excite their curiosity, without their being afraid of snake bites. The 'sucking child' crawls about and grabs at earth and stones (ﬠﬡﬥ=paddling about, playing KBL) and does not see the danger lurking at the 'adder's hole'; the rather older 'weaned child' 'stretches out his hand to the place where the adder is hidden' and wants to investigate it; it is only in the days of the Messiah that the danger to which they are exposed will be overcome. Girls enjoy playing with (tied up) birds (Job 41.5). Growing boys may have practised shooting arrows at a target (Job 16.11f.; Lam. 3.12).

In the young girl, it is above all her beauty that is to be praised (Gen. 24.16; S. of S. 4.1–7; 7.1–5 and passim).[12] An old man can find warmth beside her, as the ageing David did beside Abishag the Shunammite (I Kings 1.1–4), who was 'very beautiful . . . but the king knew her not'. The appearance of young men can be praised too, as it is with David and Absalom.[13] But primarily 'the glory of young men is their strength' (Prov. 20.29a). When the flower of the nation's youth falls in war, that is particularly serious for the people's future (Hos. 9.12f.; Jer. 48.15; Ps. 78.31). The period of youth ought to be the time of joy and of ardently devoted love (Eccles. 11.9; Jer. 2.2; Ezek. 16.43).

Typical of youth is a hesitant lack of decision (Judg. 8.20) and a shrinking from the tasks before it (Jer. 1.6); this is based mainly on youth's consciousness of its lack of experience (I Kings 3.7ff.; I Sam. 17.33).[14] But equally marked, on the other hand, is an ill-considered severity, mingled with cynical harshness, such as is shown by Rehoboam's youthful advisers (I Kings 12.8ff.). By acting in this way they are cutting across the advice of the older men (vv. 6ff., 13f.) – and indeed to despise the old is the most obvious temptation of the young. It is part of the chaos with which Isaiah (3.4f.) threatens Jerusalem, as the judgment of Yahweh, that 'babes shall be the servants of the state' and that 'youth will be insolent to the old'. That is why the wisdom writings warn youth against a false assessment of age (Prov. 23.22): 'Do not despise your mother when she is old.' The Law of Holiness says (Lev. 19.32):

> You shall stand up before the hoary head,
> and honour the face of an old man,
> and you shall fear your God:
> I am Yahweh.

Cf. Deut. 5.16. Behind the commandment concerning parents in the Decalogue, we can descry real problems about the care of the old.

4. *Characteristics of age*

For the essential mark of increasing age is increasing weakness. Beside the playing children, 'old men and old women shall again sit in the streets of Jerusalem, each with staff in hand for very age' (Zech. 8.4). The ornament of old age is grey hair, whereas the adornment of youth is its strength (Prov. 20.29; cf. Hos. 7.9; Gen. 42.38). In the one psalm of lament which is clearly the prayer of an old man (Ps. 71), diminishing strength (v. 9) and many heavy troubles (v. 20) are named; the ageing man fears that he will be cast aside and that he will be lonely (9ff.). There is often talk about the failing, blind eyes of the old – in the case of Isaac (Gen. 27.21), Jacob (Gen. 48.10) and Eli (I Sam. 3.2). Exceptions, like that of Moses, are deserving of special mention (Deut. 34.7): 'His eye was not dim, nor his natural force abated.' Women suffer under their final incapacity to bear children (Gen. 18.13). The ills of old age are summed up in a unique allegory in Eccles. 12.1–7, which is now introduced as an admonition to the young to rejoice over their youth in remembrance of their creator, and to be mindful of the process of growing old. The allegory was probably originally composed in the form of a riddle.[15]

> Remember your Creator in the days of your youth,
>   before the evil days come,
> and the years draw nigh, when you will say,
>   'I have no pleasure in them';
> 2 before the sun and the light
>   and the moon and the stars are darkened
> and only the clouds return after the rain;[16]
> 3 in the days when the keepers of the house tremble,[17]
>   and the strong men are bent,[18]
> and the grinders cease because they are few,[19]
>   and those that look through the windows are dimmed,[20]
> 4 and the doors on the street are shut;[21]
>   the sound of the grinding is low,[22]
> and the voice of the bird 'grows still'[23]
>   and every song is quenched.[24]
> 5 They are afraid also of what is high,
>   and terrors are in the way;
> then the almond tree blossoms,[25]
>   the grasshopper drags itself along,[26]
>   and the caper bursts asunder.[27]

> Yea, man goes to his secluded house,
>   and the mourners go about the streets;
> 6   Before the silver cord is snapped,[28]
>   and the golden bowl is broken,[29]
>   and pitcher is broken at the fountain,
>   and the wheel broken at the cistern,
> 7   and the dust returns[30] to the earth as it was,
>   and the breath returns to God, who gave it.

This is a sober analysis of how with increasing age the powers, the senses and all the manifestations of life become weaker and weaker.

Ought not a person to become old quite consciously, recognizing his limitations in good time? II Sam. 19.31–37 draws us a splendid picture of the aged, eighty-year-old Barzillai. A wealthy man, he had provided David with food when he was fleeing from Absalom. Now, as thanks, David wants to take him back to Jerusalem and to provide royally for him there. But Barzillai answers the king (vv. 34ff.):

> How many years have I still to live, that I should go up with the king to Jerusalem? I am this day eighty years old; can I discern what is pleasant and what is not? Can your servant taste what he eats or what he drinks? Can I still listen to the voice of singing men and singing women? Why then should your servant be an added burden to my lord the king? . . . Pray let your servant return, that I may die in my own city, near the grave of my father and my mother.

Then he suggests that a younger man should go with the king instead. Thus a man who quite soberly observes his increasing weakness and does not want to be a burden to the other, follows his path to the end, modestly and well satisfied with life. But just as beauty and strength are only aspects of youth, so weakness and modesty are only one side of age. For Barzillai shows wisdom.[31] In general it ought to be true that

> Wisdom is with the aged,
>   and understanding in length of days (Job 12.12).

The older generation has to pronounce judgment at the gates of the city (Deut. 21.2–6, 19f.; 22.15–18; 25.7–9; Ruth 4.2, 4, 9, 11; Jer. 26.17). The 'elders' ($z^e q\bar{e}n\hat{i}m$) are the men with beards ($z\bar{a}q\bar{a}n$) – men of mature age who form the juridical assembly. The ageing man in Ps. 71 wants to proclaim God's power and righteousness, which God himself has taught him from his youth up, to a future generation (vv. 17–19). Rehoboam should have listened to the kindly and wise advice of the elders when they advised him to lighten the burden of the Israelites (I Kings 12.6ff.), instead of letting himself be goaded on to severity by the young men with their crude vigour. The account shows lively interest (cf. vv. 6, 8, 10, 13f.) in contrasting the older generation (Solomon's contemporaries, v. 6) with the younger (the contemporaries of Rehoboam, who was also already 41 years old: v. 8, cf. 14.21): the old are cautious, and prepared to acquiesce in the demands of the harassed people (cf. v. 4 with v. 7); the younger men are hard, swaggering and obscene ('My little one is thicker than my father's loins', v. 10b, is probably a covert hint at the penis, not the little finger!). They are utterly unreasonable, which is why the narrator continually calls them *yᵉlādîm*, 'childish fools' (vv. 8, 10, 14). But age is not always wise, just and clement. Job sees that transgressors grow old too, and are vigorous and healthy into the bargain (Job. 21.7). Prov. 16.31 teaches that grey hair as a crown of honour is to be found along the paths of righteousness.

Thus general experience shows that both youth and age have their specific dangers and burdens, as well as their typical gifts and capabilities.

5. *The overthrow of biological rules*

But biblical anthropology is marked by the fact that Yahweh sets these human norms aside. No biological rule is without exceptions. In important sections of the biblical tradition dating from different periods, Yahweh's choice falls on a young man, while the older ones are disregarded or even repudiated – Joseph, over against his elder brothers, for example, or Samuel over against old Eli, or the young David over against Saul. Numerous individual stories from the most varied periods expressly stress the precedence of the younger. In Gen. 48.17–19 (E) Jacob, in spite of Joseph's protest, sets aside Manasseh, the first-born, in favour of Ephraim: 'His younger brother shall be greater than he.' In Judg. 6.15 Gideon, after his call, first tries to cast doubt on his capacity for warding off the Midianites: 'I am the least in my family.' In the story of Samuel's birth consecration and call in the sanctuary at Shiloh, it is stressed again and again how young he is, in spite of his call (I Sam. 1.24; 2.21, 26; 3.1, 7, 19). The tension in the relatively late story of David's anointing (I Sam. 16.1–13) is directed entirely towards the point that Yahweh has chosen the youngest son, who is at first missing completely, being with the sheep. In the duel with the mighty Philistine, David conquers although Saul holds him to be incapable because of his youth (I Sam. 17.33) and the Philistine himself despises him for the same reason (v. 42). Here, as in the related stories, the intention is not that youth as such, or that the youngest, let alone the smallest, is preferred on principle, as is the case in the corresponding fairy-tale motifs. Rather the choice of the boy as inexperienced and immature makes clear Yahweh's liberty and sole efficaciousness in the historical process.[32] In the last story, the young David himself then pits only the name of Yahweh against Goliath's heavy weapons (v. 45). The theme appears in altered form in classical prophecy as well. When Jeremiah resists Yahweh's commission because he is young and inexperienced, the voice contradicts him (1.6f.):

> Do not say 'I am only a youth';
>> for to all to whom I send you you shall go,
>> and whatever I command you you shall speak.

The wisdom writings bring the motif in their own way. In the book of Job, the young Elihu respectfully but definitely raises the claim to be heard within the circle of the elder teachers of wisdom (Job 32.6–10):

> I am young in years,
>> and you are aged;
> therefore I was timid and afraid
>> to declare my opinion to you.
> I said, 'Let days speak,
>> and many years teach wisdom'.
> But it is the spirit in a man,
>> the breath of the Almighty,
>> that makes him understand.
> The old are not always wise,
>> nor do the aged always understand what is right.
> Therefore I dare to say: Listen to me!
> Let me also declare my opinion!

Thus Yahweh's spirit can, contrary to what is usually expected, make young people the teachers of the old and experienced. Cf. Luke 2.46–50.

Yet on the other hand Yahweh also, when he wishes, calls a halt to the laws governing age. Ps. 92 lauds the righteous who flourish like a palm tree and grow up like the cedars of Lebanon (v. 14f.):

> They still bring forth fruit in old age,
>> they are ever full of sap and green,
> to show that Yahweh is upright;
>> he is my rock, and there is no unrighteousness in him.

The primal image is the aged Moses, according to Deut. 34.7, whose 'freshness'[33] had not abated. Deutero-Isaiah shows how important man's relation to his God is in consequence; trust in Yahweh can bring about the reversal of the natural state of affairs (Isa. 40.30f.):

> Even youths shall faint and be weary,
>> and young warriors shall fall exhausted.
> But they who hope in Yahweh shall renew their strength.
>> They mount up with wings like eagles,
> they run and are not weary,
>> they walk and do not faint.

This is what man is like: the norms about the ages of life can in general be read by all; but the Incomparable One is free to bring about the unusual in any individual. Ecclesiastes sums up this possible reversal of the norm in the maxim (4.13):

> Better a young man, poor but wise,
>> than an old and foolish king,
>>> who no longer has the sense to take advice.

XIV

Waking and Working[1]

The time of man is also his time for working. Man would undoubtedly be misunderstanding and misusing his time if he were to devote it exclusively to work. He need only be reminded of Ecclesiastes, according to whom there are not only times for planting and pulling up, for pulling down and building up; there are also times for weeping and for laughter, for embracing and for dancing. But none the less work unquestionably plays an important part.

1. *Work in the Yahwist's account*

The Yahwist's story of the Garden of Eden points out in three exemplary passages that work belongs to the basic commission of the Creator to his creation.

In Gen. 2.5 we are told what was missing before the beginning of creation; apart from the vegetation of the steppes and the cultivated lands, it was above all rain – and man. Rain is enough for growth on the steppes; but the plants of the cultivated lands need man as well.[2] For his task here is named: it is to till (*'bd*) the ground. It is important to see that here labour appears as the only definition of man's proper significance, and that it is in this way seen simply in the context of creation. The same is true in the Priestly document; in Gen. 1.26, when God resolves to create mankind, the only purpose given is that man should rule over the beasts. In the words of blessing in v. 28 the subjection of the earth is named in addition; this is what man is capable of, and this is the task before him.[3]

That labour is already a matter for man as created being is stressed by the Yahwist in 2.15. Immediately after man's creation and the planting of the paradisal garden, Yahweh leads him into that garden, so that he may cultivate it and protect it. When at this point the Yahwist mentions both the serving of the earth through labour (*'bd*) and the protective watching over it (*šmr*), he is indicating the two aspects of all man's activity in his various callings. The context of the passage brings out the divine working and giving as the premise of all human activity; when the gifts of creation are made over to man, the care and protection of these gifts is also given him as the task of his life.[4]

Curiously enough, in 3.23 the destiny of man – that he should till the ground – is picked up in the very wording of 2.5, but now this is not the meaning and purpose of man's creation; it is the intention behind his expulsion from the garden, which results from his mistrust of his maker. It is only the immediately preceding passage[5] which talks about the cursing of the ground (3.17) and about the farmer's toil and trouble (vv. 18f.). But it is now clear from the context that the curse does not consist of labour as such, but merely of the associated trials and vexations which the thorns and thistles in the fields bring with them.

As he goes on with his account, the Yahwist shows how abundantly man's work branches out: the tiller of the soil is joined by the breeder of sheep and goats (Gen. 4.2); towns grow up beside the Bedouin tent-dweller (4.17, 20); professional groups of musicians (lyre and pipe players, 4.21) and technicians (workers in bronze and iron, 4.22) come into existence. Then vine-growing develops (9.20f.), and new building materials make huge buildings possible (11.3). It is in this working world, with its many facets, that the task of creation unfolds itself to men. Blessing is followed by progress. But *hubris* encounters 'thorns and thistles' everywhere.

2. *Industry and sloth in proverbial wisdom*

From the time of Solomon the wisdom teachers of Israel developed scientific and scholarly studies: a theory of education for all walks of life, beginning with the education of princes and civil servants; the art of statesmanship; the wisdom reposing in law and natural history (I Kings 3.8ff., 16ff.; 4.32f.); and also historiography. But it was above all the problems of work and its outcome that exercised the teachers of wisdom. They first of all establish an extensive natural law, according to which hard work is granted success, whereas laziness is followed by poverty. Prov. 10.4;

> A slack hand causes poverty,
> but the hand of the diligent makes rich.

Riches are not seen as something 'given', but as something that can grow in the hands of the responsible man.[6] The social contrasts between poor and rich should also be interrogated, at least, as to the part played by industry and slackness, if human reality is not to be ignored. Prov. 13.4:

> The soul of the sluggard craves, but in vain,[7]
> while the strivings of the diligent are satisfied.

Even freedom and slavery, ascendancy and oppression, also derive from the work invested (Prov. 12.24):

> The hand of the diligent will rule,
> while the slothful will be put to forced labour.

Numerous other sayings establish similar rules: Prov. 11.16b; 12.27; 14.23; 21.5. Cf. also Eccles. 10.18:

> Through sloth[8] the roof sinks in,
> and through indolence the house leaks.

Since Israel's teachers know what man is like, they try their best to ward off laziness. This is the motive underlying Prov. 24.30–34, where a personal experience is being described:

> I passed by the field of a sluggard,
> by the vineyard of a man without sense;
> and lo, it was all overgrown with thorns;
> the ground was covered with nettles,
> and its stone wall was broken down.
> Then I saw and considered it;
> I looked and received instruction.
> 'A little sleep, a little slumber,
> a little folding of the hands to rest,' –
> and poverty will come upon you like a robber,
> and want like a beggar.

Observation teaches that laziness deprives a man of Yahweh's gifts. The evil is rooted in lack of resolution to make a prompt beginning. Somnolence is the companion of laziness (Prov. 19.15):

> Slothfulness casts into a deep sleep,
> and an idle person will suffer hunger.

The counsel in Prov. 6.6–11 sees the same danger:

> Go to the ant, O sluggard;
> consider her ways, and be wise.
> Without having any chief,
> officer or ruler,
> She prepares her food in summer,
> and gathers her sustenance in harvest.
> How long will you lie there, O sluggard?
> When will you arise from your sleep?
> 'A little sleep, a little slumber,
> a little folding of the hands to rest,' –
> and poverty will come upon you like a robber,
> and want like a beggar.

To work sensibly also means to recognize the favourable hour – not to miss the right moment. The reasonable man should go promptly to work, without anyone to goad him on, and should not let himself be put to shame by an animal (cf. Jer. 8.7). The wise man has studied the characteristics of laziness exactly. They are listed in Prov. 26.13–16:

> The sluggard says, 'There is a lion in the road!
> There is a lion in the streets!'
> 14 As a door turns on its hinges,
> so does a sluggard on his bed.
> 15 The sluggard buries his hand in the dish;
> it wears him out to bring it back to his mouth.
> 16 The sluggard is wiser in his own eyes
> than seven men who can answer discreetly.

According to this the essential tokens of laziness are: feeble evasions and invented excuses (cf. 22.13), excessive sleep (cf. 6.9f.; 19.15; 24.33), indolence, even in eating (cf. 19.24), and an unduly high opinion of oneself. By allowing himself to be driven by the pleasure of the moment, the lazy man contributes to his own downfall (Prov. 21.25). Thus he misses the proper hour and the opportunities that are granted to him. Work brings the blessing provided by the Creator (Prov. 14.23):

> In all toil there is profit,
> but mere talk tends only to want.

Thus man is faced with two possibilities: to win, or to let the chance slip, to accept the offer of the soil, or to disregard it (Prov. 20.4):

> The sluggard does not plough in the autumn,
> he will seek at harvest and have nothing.

In this way the teachers of wisdom develop what the Yahwist began to teach. Since man is called to work, he should take up his Creator's offer. In addition the wisdom writings lay down what they have found by experience – that work brings profit, whereas indolence leads to want.

3. *The questionable success of labour*

But this empirical rule is not a law. Anyone who wants to see human reality as it is must learn to reckon with the free intervention of Yahweh. Otherwise he fails to recognize the facts that human industry in itself does not lead to success, and that riches as such do not represent an unequivocal value. The ambiguity of phenomena and events has to be borne in mind.[9]

The self-assured thinking which believes that it can deduce an imperative connection between industry and success, is categorically countered by the maxim (Prov. 10.22):

> The blessing of Yahweh alone makes rich,
>   and man's own toil adds nothing to it.

The general expectation that labour brings profit is never realized in concrete terms unless Yahweh decides to add his blessing. Yahweh is also at work in the discrepancy between what a man desires and what he achieves (Prov. 16.1):

> The plans of the will belong to man,
>   but the answer of the tongue is from Yahweh.

All unsanctioned over-eagerness can meet with a cold 'in vain' (Ps. 127.1f.):

> Unless Yahweh builds the house,
>   those who build it labour in vain.
> Unless Yahweh watches over the city,
>   the watchman stays awake in vain.
> It is in vain that you rise up before day
>   and go late to rest,
> eating the bread of anxious toil;
>   for to his beloved he gives it in sleep.

Here too it is the wisdom of experience speaking. It knows that limits are set to man's independence and self-will. Anyone who does not remember the possible 'in vain' misconstrues man as man.

But it is not only unremitting industry that remains questionable; riches and success are also ambiguous. Poverty and privation can be more valuable than riches (Prov. 15.16):

> Better is a little with the fear of Yahweh
>   than great treasure and trouble with it.

Just as diligence cannot bring results without Yahweh's blessing, so riches without the readiness for obedience and trust towards Yahweh[10] are null and void (Prov. 11.4):

> Riches do not profit in the day of wrath,
>   but righteousness delivers from death.

Riches easily lead to lack of integrity (Prov. 19.1) or to quarrelling (17.1):

> Better is a dry morsel with quiet
>   than a house full of feasting with strife.

Prov. 15.17 is afraid of hate:

> Better is a dinner of herbs where love is
>   than a fatted ox and hatred with it.

Above all, however, success lures men to false confidence (Prov. 11.28):

> He who trusts in his riches will wither,
> but the righteous will flourish like a green leaf.

Thus Israel's wisdom teaches a right understanding of work. Man has to accept the rules; but above all he has to recognize the Lord of the rules. Then he will be kept from falling lower than the animals (the ant, for example!) through his laziness; or from usurping the place of God in his self-deception.

XV

Sleep and Rest[1]

The time of man is above all time conferred on him. His work is useless and meaningless when he forgets this. The Old Testament wisdom indeed plainly calls man from laziness; but it warns in still stronger terms against the misunderstanding that man receives the gifts he has only through his own works.[2]

1. *Sleep and rest*

Sleep can be praised provocatively as being the opportunity through which Yahweh supplies his friends with the bread (Ps. 127.2b) which the over-zealous only enjoy with a great deal of trouble, without reaching their aims in spite of many self-torturing extra hours of work (vv. 1–2a).[3] The poetry of the proverbs describes more factually the value of wisdom in life, wisdom which is to be found, among other things, in the refreshing sleep of those who live with her; Prov. 3.24 addresses the man who has found wisdom:

> If you sit[4] down, you will not be afraid;
>> when you lie down, your sleep will be sweet.

Ecclesiastes (5.12) stresses that sleep is pleasant when it stands in the right relationship to work:

> Sweet is the sleep of a labourer,
>> whether he eats little or much;
> But the surfeit of the rich
>> will not let him sleep.

Surfeit takes away rest just like excessive zeal (Eccles. 2.23). Good sleep becomes the mark of the man who lives in the rhythm of Yahweh's giving and calling. Rest manifests the art of living, that is to say the wisdom whose crowning characteristic is the fear of Yahweh.[5] It knows that the 'all for nothing' which answers the fruitless efforts of the fanatically industrious man is finally replaced by the 'all for nothing' of Yahweh's gift which he gives in sleep (Ps. 127.1f.).[6]

In prophecy, Isaiah stresses rest (*šqt*) as an essential mark of faith. When in 7.4 he admonishes King Ahaz to rest during the threat to Jerusalem, he is offering him the attitude of mind that expects and observes the acts of divine salvation which have been proclaimed, and so becomes fearless (vv. 5–9). It is the same attitude to which Moses summons the Israelites in the hour of their pursuit by the Egyptians at the Reed Sea (Ex. 14.13f.). Such rest is indissolubly bound up with trust, which the whole of Israel ought to find anew through conversion (Isa. 30.15; cf. 32.17). The nation should let political consequences ripen in a policy of strict neutrality on Jerusalem's part. Peace follows from the certainty that Yahweh acts.[7]

Deuteronomy and the Deuteronomic history make rest into a theme of its own (*menūḥā*) as the great saving benefit promised to God's people.[8] It means both rest after the unsettled period of wandering, and rest from all their enemies round about (Deut. 12.9f.; 25.19; Josh. 21.43ff.; II Sam. 7.1, 11; I Kings 8.56). Ps. 95.7–11 sees the gift of rest for the individual as having to do with his willingness to listen to the voice of Yahweh (Heb. 3.7ff.).

In multifarious ways, accordingly, the various strata of the Old Testament, each in a different language, testify to the fact that man's rest is a treasure and a capacity which is not a matter of course but is deeply bound up with trust in Yahweh.

2. *The sabbath*

With this as starting point, it is not surprising to find that in the Old Testament the commandment about the observance of the sabbath, as the decree of a day of rest, plays a considerable role. There is a wider testimony to this than to any other commandment, and it occupies the most space in the decalogue. It is found in different forms in what is known as the Yahwistic decalogue in Ex. 34 and in the best known version of the decalogue in Ex. 20, in the Book of the Covenant, and in the Priestly document. Prophets as different as Amos and Hosea, Jeremiah and Ezekiel all have something to say about the sabbath. Finally, the day of rest appears in numerous narratives, from the first account of the creation and the manna story to Nehemiah's 'memoirs'. Statistics underline the wide distribution: when days are particularized, 'the seventh day' occurs much the most often.[9]

What has the Old Testament to say about the observance of the sabbath? What may be the oldest form of the commandment in Ex. 34.21a runs:

> Six days you can work,
>> but on the seventh day you shall rest.

The Hebrew takes the form of two rhyming triplets:

šēšet yāmīm taʿᵃbōd
ūbayyōm haššᵉbiʾī tišbōt.

This offers the keyword that gives the day of rest in the Old Testament its name: *šbt*=to cease working, to stop what one is doing.[10] According to this the sabbath is to be observed by resting from work.

But does not the commandment about the sabbath take on positive form in the decalogue? In Ex. 20.8 it runs:

Remember the sabbath day, to keep it holy.

Deut. 5.12 deviates only slightly, and expands to:

Observe the sabbath day, to keep it holy,
as Yahweh your God commanded you.[11]

Moreover the seventh day is now expressly called in both texts 'a sabbath to Yahweh your God' (Ex. 20.10; Deut. 5.14). But if we go on to ask what form the 'remembering', the 'observing' and the 'keeping holy' is to take on 'a sabbath to Yahweh', the answer is clear and exclusive: 'You shall do no work!' So it is completely possible, and indeed probable, that the positive Decalogue form goes back to a categorical statement of prohibition, such as is authenticated in the Book of the Covenant (Ex. 23.12) and in the Law of Holiness (Lev. 19.3), as well as in Ex. 34.21a. The hallowing of the seventh day is to take the form of a demonstrative laying aside of all work.

Only quite late and poorly authenticated sacrificial regulations for the daily morning and evening sacrifice mark the sabbath cultically; a double (Num. 28.9f.) or treble (Ezek. 46.4f.; cf. Num. 28.3) number of lambs are to be brought, together with the appropriate offerings of food and drink. In so far as these link up with the everyday regulations, they practically confirm that the sabbath as a rule enjoyed no qualitatively special cultic distinction.

> The sabbath . . . was from its origin characterized only by the prohibition of all work, and at the earliest period of Israelite history . . . had nothing to do with the positive cult of Yahweh.[12]

At the end of every six days all business was to be interrupted for a whole day.

Was the day of rest perhaps supposed to be significant of the Yahweh religion precisely in this very way? Was this regular strike against all compulsion to work, a demonstration of principle for Yahweh, Israel's God? In order to clarify the question let us look at the different versions of the sabbath commandment.

(*a*) Let us begin with the *Deuteronomic* version. Deut. 5.15 links up the sabbath commandment with the ancient Israelite tradition of the Exodus:

> Remember that you were a servant in the land of Egypt, and Yahweh your God brought you out thence with a mighty hand and an out-stretched arm; therefore Yahweh your God commanded you to keep the sabbath day.

With this the day of rest finds its justification in what was for Israel the absolutely basic acknowledgment of its liberation from Egypt through Yahweh. Every seventh day is to remind Israel that God is a liberator, who dealt with brutal slave owners and who will be a match for all those rulers who still seek to afflict his people. Was it not precisely this that early Christianity grasped when it associated the day of rest with the resurrection of Jesus Christ? No power, not even the power of death, can conquer the liberator of man any longer. Because of Jesus' work of redemption, no pressure to produce results is now to torment man, no transgressions are to rise up to accuse him, not even the imperfections and incompletions of a past week.

According to the Deuteronomic view, therefore, the basic meaning of the rest from labour on the seventh day is to remind men of the liberty conferred on them. It is what God has done for man that we have to remember, not cultic duties. In ancient Israel it was no doubt parents who had the duty of teaching this in the first instance. Perhaps that is why the command to honour one's parents is linked together with the sabbath commandment in the Law of Holiness (Lev. 19.3) and follows it immediately in the Decalogue. Mother and father (so the order in Lev. 19.3) are the first who pass on salvation history to the next generation and in this capacity they deserve the attentiveness of their children. The Deuteronomic preachers will not have been the first to point this out; cf. Deut. 6.20ff.

The sabbath commandment is a shining example of the fact that the basic commandments given to Israel are all benefits. They are not really demands; they are a liberation from demands. They are permissive, not oppressive. The sabbath makes the gift of free time plain. The institution of a sabbatical year for the soil, according to Lev. 25.1–7, can make these facts clear to us. By abstaining from working the fields in every seventh year, according to the edict, the farmer shows that the land is Yahweh's gift. It is to be compared with the 'fallow time of the seventh day'.[13] In so far as the commandment of the day of rest is a rejection of 'the greedy snatching at the whole of time' and guides us towards 'a renunciation of revenue', it is a testimony that Yahweh is the lord and giver of all other days. The observance of this time of leisure is an example and a reminder of the truth that all Israel's time derives from the event of liberation. The

Deuteronomic version of the commandment brings this out most clearly of all.

(*b*) The second main reason for the commandment about the sabbath is bound up with the thinking of the *Priestly document*. In Ex.20.11 the command to lay down work is motivated as follows:

> for in six days Yahweh made heaven and earth, the sea and all that is in them, and rested on the seventh day; therefore Yahweh blessed the sabbath day and hallowed it.

According to this the purpose of the day of rest is to point out to man that he was set in a world richly equipped with everything that is necessary and with much that is beautiful. The wording reminds us of the first account of the creation (Gen.2.1–3), which describes in its archaic fashion how man's first day was the great day of rest. God had six days of labour behind him. Now a completed work is ready. Man's first working day will begin only after God's day of rest, with its contemplation of the fullness of creation. Early Christianity showed theological wisdom in decreeing that the first day of the week was to be the day of rest instead of the seventh. For liberated man, man who is the receiver of God's gifts, the week does not end with the day of rest; it begins with it.[14] The working days can then take on rather more of the character of play – even the character of protest against the principle of judging performance by results and against the demand for those results. What can man do more in his work than to see to it that what the Creator has prepared for him is rightly harvested and rightly used – is not spoiled, but is protected from being ruined by man's misuse? Without the focus on the work that God has already completed, man cannot find a right relationship either to his own work or to rest.

Ex.20.11 emphasizes expressly that on the seventh day 'God rested'. In Ex.31.17 to *šābat* is added *wayyinnāpaš*: he 'took breath'. This divine rest probably means two things: God *can* rest, for his whole work, everything that man needs, is finished. The extension, he 'took breath', he 'recovered himself', suggests in addition, with some slight anthropomorphism, that he *had* to rest; he was exhausted by his work of creation. This only becomes completely comprehensible through the 'exhaustion' of the one who was crucified: *tetelestai*, 'it is finished' (John 19.30). The God of the Bible has given man everything in the utter giving of himself.

'Therefore Yahweh blessed the sabbath day', Ex.20.11 goes on, thus picking up Gen.2.3. Before, in Gen.1.22, 28, God blessed the fish, the birds and men, and the blessing brings with it the power to be fruitful and to multiply.[15] Now the day of rest is blessed; it too, therefore, is equipped with enlivening power, so that man's time can receive refreshment and can be made fruitful. That is why God 'hallowed' the day of rest – that is to say separated it from the working days. This division between the day of rest and the working days is to prove itself as much of a benefit to man as the division of light from darkness.

(*c*) In the *Book of the Covenant*, Ex.23.12 presents one of the oldest versions of the sabbath commandment:

> Six days you shall do your work, but on the seventh day you shall rest; that your ox and your ass may have rest, and the son of your bondmaid, and the alien, take breath.[16]

What this passage states as being the sole purpose of the day of rest is highly suggestive: working dependents are to find recreation. The moving factor is care for the hard-driven beasts, who are mentioned first. But what are listed next are not any random dependents but 'the son of your bondmaid (slave) and the alien'. These are people who are particularly without redress against any orders given to them. Though a master might not dare to exact work on the sabbath from his adult woman slave, or from his male Israelite slave, he was much more easily able to exert pressure on her son or on the foreign worker, who was all too easily viewed as being outside the sphere of liberty set by Yahweh's commandment. This version of the sabbath commandment therefore picks up borderline cases: the sabbath has been instituted for the sake of all those who are especially hard driven and especially dependent.

Incidentally, immediately beforehand in the Book of the Covenant (Ex.23.10f.), the reason given for the lying fallow of the fields, vineyards and olive orchards in the sabbatical year (which involved a complete relinquishment of the harvest) is that the yield should benefit the poor and that the remainder should provide food for the wild animals.

The major versions of the commandment about the day of rest in the decalogue series take up the idea about dependents and develop it further. Ex.20.10 runs:

> In it you shall not do any work, you, or your son, or your daughter, your manservant, or your maidservant, or your cattle, or the sojourner who is within your gates.

Deut.5.14 adds significantly, in the parallel version:

> that your manservant and your maidservant may rest as well as you.

kāmōkā – 'just like you'! Thus the commandment about the day of rest inaugurates a position of equality for all men before God. On this day at least parents should stop giving orders to their sons and daughters, let alone their subordinates.

The idea that the day of rest ought to benefit the weaker members of society above all, is taken up by the New Testament. In one of the few passages in which it mentions the first day of the week (I Cor. 16.2), we are told that the day is to serve the purpose of collecting and saving money for those in Jerusalem needing help. Jesus emphasized that the sabbath is made for (needy) man, and not man for the sabbath (Mark 2.27).

(*d*) *Prophetic* voices systematically repudiate the doing of business on the sabbath. The prophet Amos condemns the corn dealers who cannot wait for the end of the sabbath because they want to sell corn again and to cheat their customers with poor wares, false weights and unduly high prices (8.5). It may be noted that this same prophet, who attacks the whole business of pilgrimages and other cultic activities in connection with the sacrifices and prayer of the sanctuary (cf. 4.4f.; 5.21ff.), insists that the sabbath is to be observed. In his sight too it is apparently a powerful testimony to the fact that man does not live from his own works; he lives from the acts of Yahweh. A Deuteronomic saying revised by Jeremiah (17.21ff.) cries warningly:

> Take heed for the sake of your lives,
> and do not bear a burden on the sabbath day.

The saying may be said to be already pointing in the direction of a later casuistry, but it is still primarily determined by joy in the free life which Yahweh has conferred on Israel, but which she is gambling away through her own worries. A saying of Trito-Isaiah (Isa. 58.13f.) shows this most clearly:

> If you turn back your foot from the sabbath, from doing your business on my holy day, and call the sabbath a delight[17] and the holy day of Yahweh honourable; if you honour it, not going your own ways, or pursuing your own callings, or talking idly; then you shall take delight in Yahweh, and I will make you ride upon the heights of the earth; I will feed you with the heritage of Jacob your father; for the mouth of Yahweh has spoken.

These concrete admonitions do not derive their force from the fear of punishment but from the desire for joy. The prophetic words resist all the inclination of the natural man to secure, or even to intensify, life through unceasing labour.

An extension to the short early text of the commandment in Ex. 34.21b already combats this error.[18] The wording of the text in the emphatic form in which it has come down to us runs (v. 21a): 'Six days you can work, but on the seventh day you shall rest.' To this the text adds (21b): ' – even in ploughing time and in harvest!' The short ancient version may perhaps go back to nomadic times.[19] But the addition clarifies it in the light of circumstances in the cultivated lands, by drawing attention to the seasons in a farmer's life when work piles up and is particularly pressing. It is just then that man needs the day of rest.

The story of the manna in Ex. 16 criticizes restless and undue zeal in an almost humorous way. The Yahwist fragments that are incorporated are already familiar with the sabbath rest and introduce it as if it were a long-familiar observance.[20] The main threads of the Priestly document's account link the manna story with the sabbath motif in detail. God allows fresh bread to fall every day and, since yesterday's stinks, it has to be gathered afresh each time. But on the sixth day the double amount of manna falls. The manna destined for the seventh day 'did not become foul, and there were no worms in it' (vv. 22–24). Even so, some people were unable to refrain from going out to gather manna on the seventh day; 'but – they found none,' says the narrator (v. 27), not without gentle mockery. Officious industry on the sabbath is simply derided as being in vain. It is a disdaining of God's providing care. Now, as always, man lives not from his own untiring zeal but from the activity of God.

This is the gospel which Nehemiah also wanted to drive home in his way; cf. Neh. 13.15ff. He saw people on the sabbath treading wine presses, loading grain, selling wine, figs and other foodstuffs, Tyrians bringing fish to market; and he chides those responsible:

> What is this evil thing which you are doing! . . .
> So have your fathers increased God's wrath.

After this he has all the city gates in Jerusalem closed every sabbath. Many people will undoubtedly have considered this as being injurious to their economic success. Others reproach those who keep the sabbath with laziness – a reproach that Tacitus already levied against the Jews (*Hist.* V. 4). But

> the meaning of human life is higher than the struggle for existence. Every sabbath gives anew to those who stand under the royal rule of God the liberty of God's children; it may at first be only to a limited degree, yet it always holds the renewed promise of perfect fulfilment.[21]

(*e*) It is a New Testament premise that the day of rest brings a prelude – a first hint of the ultimate and utter freedom. According to the epistle to the

Colossians (2.17f.) the sabbaths are to be understood as being 'shadows of what is to come' – the future that has taken bodily form in Christ. In the Old Testament this meaning of the sabbath – its significance for the future – finds its preparation in the period of the exile. There it is no longer a token of Israel's religion, like the circumcision; it is a pledge of the perpetual divine covenant. Ezekiel first pointed out that the transgression against the sabbath commandment particularly was the reason for the present judgment of the exile (Ezek. 20.13, 16, 24; 22.8, 26; 23.38). But he also emphasizes the sabbath's symbolic meaning (20.12, 20): 'Hallow my sabbaths that they may be a sign between me and you, that you may know that I Yahweh am your God.' The Priestly document takes up the sabbath ordinance even more clearly and urgently along the same line (Ex. 31.12–17). Here the first noticeable thing is that those who profane the sabbath are threatened with the death penalty (v. 14; cf. 35.2). Num. 15.32–36 reports that the death penalty was actually enforced. At the same time we should note that the Priestly document too does not require that the sabbath should be hallowed by even the smallest piece of active service. It is to be hallowed precisely by doing nothing whatsoever – by resting completely. For it is through this very thing that the Israelite proclaims Yahweh's intervention on his behalf. The sabbath counts as the 'sign' of a 'perpetual convenant' (Ex. 31.13, 16f.).[22] What the sign of the rainbow meant for Noah (Gen. 9) and the sign of the circumcision meant for Abraham (Gen. 17), the sign of the sabbath means for Israel: a *berit* (Ex. 31.16), that is to say, Yahweh's everlasting obligation towards Israel,[23] a promise which is, it is emphasized, a promise 'for ever', 'throughout your generations' (vv. 13, 16). This gives Israel freedom in hope, a freedom which every Israelite can already realize provisionally in his acceptance of God's concrete offer of an order for day-to-day life. Anyone who does not accept Yahweh's promise and is not able to rest on the seventh day at least, is surrendering himself up to death.[24]

Even in the Old Testament, therefore, the sabbath becomes an eschatological event in the midst of man's provisional world. Even within the flux of time man can partake of the rest which lies with God.[25] Early Christianity celebrated the day of rest on the first day of the week, as being the day of Jesus' resurrection (Matt. 28.1; Rev. 1.10). It is on this recollection that Christians base their hope for the new world promised to man (Rev. 21.4). Unless it points in this direction, the seventh day is not being completely comprehended in its basic significance for man's understanding of time.

XVI

Sickness and Healing[1]

The time of man is also threatened and endangered time. It can always be conferred anew through deliverance and liberation. Deliverance through healing corresponds to the danger brought by sickness.

1. *Sicknesses*

Israel suffered from sicknesses in plenty. The most important and frequent root uses in their designation is *ḥlh*.[2] This almost always[3] designates a state of weakness – of slackness and exhaustion; that is to say, vital power that, has somehow been snapped. In this connection injury through accident can also be meant, as well as the usual illnesses (II Kings 1.2); a disease of the foot caused by age (I Kings 15.23) as well as an abnormal mental condition (S. of S. 2.5; 5.8, 'sick with love'). The root *dwh* also occurs (Isa. 1.5; Deut. 7.15) and this reflects the mental effects of weakness – anxiety and a feeling of indisposition, such as are typical of a woman's menstrual periods (Lev. 12.2; Ps. 41.3). In addition a number of expressions are used for wounds (*makkāh*, literally 'stroke', root *nkh*, I Kings 22.35; II Kings 8.29; Isa. 1.6) and for contagious diseases (*maggēpā* II Sam. 24.21, 25; *negep* Num. 16.46f.; both substantive formations from *ngp*=to strike; *nagaʿ*=touch, Deut. 24.8, most frequently *deber* for bubonic plague, Ex. 5.3, about 50 times).

A wide variety of *skin diseases* of every kind were apparently the most widespread – leprosy, ulcers, inflammation, suppurating eczemas and scabies. In the lists of curses in Deut. 28.22, 27 these are mentioned first in each case. Well-known stories about individual illnesses are always telling of tormenting and dangerous ulcers which attack the whole body. This was true of Job (2.7), Hezekiah (II Kings 20.7=Isa. 38.21) and Naaman (II Kings 5.1, 6f.) and, in the New Testament, of Lazarus in the parable (Luke 16.20f.).[4] When they are infectious, skin diseases crop up in epidemic form (Lev. 26.25; Deut. 28.21; II Sam. 24.13). Since they generally end in death, they are (like *deber*) often mentioned in lists after the sword (e.g., Ex. 5.3; Jer. 14.12; Ezek. 5.17). Zechariah announces a mass epidemic in particularly frightful terms (14.12):

> His flesh shall rot while he is still on his feet, his eyes shall rot in their sockets, and his tongue shall rot in 'his'[5] mouth.

Diseases of the eye were also very common. The Old Testament definitely mentions blindness about 30 times (*'iwwēr*, *'iwwārōn*, *'awweret*), but in addition it often talks about 'not being able to see any more' (e.g., Gen. 48.10), or about the growing dim of the eyes (e.g., Gen. 27.1), or about their wasting away (e.g., Lev. 26.16). The list of curses threatens blindness (Deut. 28.28f.) – in Lev. 26.16 as a result of consumption and fever, which are mentioned separately in Deut. 28.22.

Apart from blindness, *mental illness* is mentioned in Deut. 28.28 under the heading of madness and confusion of mind.[6] Isa. 1.5 talks about the sick *head* and, at the same time, about the faint *heart*. II Kings 4.18ff. (cf. Ps. 121.6) gives an account of a headache resulting from a sunstroke which ends in death. Jer. 4.19f.[7] describes a heart attack, and I Sam. 25.37 paralysis following 'the death of the heart' (a stroke[8]).

> Like a lame man's legs, which hang useless,
> is a proverb in the mouth of fools,

says Prov. 26.7. Accidents also cause paralysis (II Sam. 4.4) as well as broken bones (Lev. 21.19) and wounds (I Kings 22.35, in war).

Lev. 21.18–20 sums up the bodily infirmities which make a man unfit for priestly office:

> No one . . . blind or lame, or one who has a limb too short or too long, or a man who has an injured foot or an injured hand, or a hunchback, or a consumptive, or a man with a defect in his sight, or an itching disease, or scabs, or crushed testicles, may approach the sacrificial service of the sanctuary.

Psalm 38, which is a psalm of lament, lists a multiplicity of complaints: no health in flesh and bones (v. 3), festering wounds (v. 5), lassitude and exhaustion, pain in the heart (v. 8), a throbbing heart, weakness, flickering eyes (v. 10), deafness and speechlessness (vv. 13f.). Psalm 88[9] complains of lifelong disease 'from youth up' (v. 15) and the danger of death, which is now acute (vv. 3ff.). Sufferings which deform a person physically make him appear 'inhuman' and can lead to his complete isolation through the aversion or contempt of others, or even through banishment (cf. Isa. 52.14; 53.2f.). Groaning and weeping are not only an expression of the emotions; the tears that stream forth from the inner springs take the body's power with them, and with the rattle in the throat life vanishes entirely (Pss. 6.6; 31.10; 42.3; 116.8; 126.5; Lam. 2.11).[10]

2. *Physicians and medicine*

What possibilities of healing sickness by human means are known to the Old Testament? As far as we can see these are confined largely to wounds. The *rōpe'*, then, is the man skilled in healing, but also solely as a surgeon for external wounds. The word's stem, *rp'*, now generally used in the sense 'to heal', originally means to patch, to sew together, to unite.[11] Wounds are 'squeezed out', oil is dropped into them,[12] or they are anointed[13] with balm and bound up (Isa. 1.6; Jer. 8.22). A broken arm is bandaged as well (*ḥbš* Ezek. 30.21; 34.4). Thus the *ḥōbēš* like the *rōpe'* is the surgeon for external wounds (Isa. 3.7; Hos. 6.1). In general the function of the man versed in healing was to bring back strength to the person who had been weakened through sickness (*ḥzq* piel, Ezek. 30.21; 34.4).

Other illnesses are within the competence of the priest, especially the common skin diseases. Lev. 13f. gives the regulations in detail. But here the purpose is not to heal; it is to determine whether the sick man is clean or unclean, i.e., whether he is capable of joining in the worship of the community or whether he has to be kept apart. The isolation can be provisional, for seven or fourteen days, or it can be permanent, according to the symptoms (cf. Deut. 24.8 and Luke 17.12–24). When Job is plagued with malignant ulcers from the soles of his feet to the crown of his head, he can only sit in the ashes, scratch himself with a potsherd and accept the evil at the hands of God, as he did the good that preceded it (Job 2.8–10). Medical treatment was apparently only applied in exceptional cases, by charismatics. Thus the prophet Elisha makes the leprous Aramaean general Naaman bathe seven times in the Jordan; 'and his flesh was restored like the flesh of a little child' (II Kings 5.14).[14] When King Hezekiah is plagued with ulcers, Isaiah prescribes poultices of fig cakes (II Kings 20.7=Isa. 38.21).

The sick bed is mentioned in Ps. 41.3 and Ex. 21.18, but it is also presupposed in the case of the sick Hezekiah (cf. II Kings 20.2=Isa. 38.2 with I Kings 21.4). Saul's mental illness, in which depression and envy lead to violent outbreaks of rage, is to be improved by David's playing of the lyre; music helps the therapy (I Sam. 16.14–23; 18.7–9, 10f.; 19.8–10).[15] When passionate love becomes a mental 'sickness', raisin cakes and apples are coveted as 'medicine'[16] (S. of S. 2.5); the beloved who is exhausted by the first experience of love needs such strengthening and refreshing measures.[17]

In the case of the wounded, damages are regulated when liability exists. Ex. 21.18f. presupposes that in the course of a quarrel one man was so badly injured by another through a stone or pickaxe that he had to stay in bed. The guilty person has then to offer material compensation for the time when the other man is unable to leave his house and cannot work; and he is also liable for the medical costs.

There is no clear evidence in the Old Testament for the existence of an actual professional group of doctors in Israel.[18] But in the second century BC we find the book of Ecclesiasticus (38.1–15) concerning itself in some detail with the doctor and the chemist:

1 Honour the physician with the honour due to him, according
                  to your need of him,
   for God has given to him, too, his lot;[19]
2 for healing comes from the Most High,
   and he will receive a gift from the king.
3 The skill of the physician lifts up his head,
   and in the presence of great men he is admired.
4 The Lord created medicines from the earth,
   and a sensible man will not despise them.
   . . .
7 By them he heals and takes away pain;
8   the pharmacist makes of them a compound.
   . . .
9 My son, when you are sick do not be negligent,
   but pray to the Lord, and he will heal you.
10 Give up your faults and direct your hands aright,
   and cleanse your heart from all sin.
11 Offer a sweet-smelling sacrifice, and a memorial portion of
                    fine flour,
   and pour oil on your offering, as much as you can afford.
12 And give the physician his place, for the Lord created him;
   let him not leave you, for there is need of him.
13 There is a time when success lies in the hands of physicians,
   for they too will pray to the Lord
   that he should grant them success in diagnosis
   and in healing, for the sake of preserving life.
15 He who sins before his Maker,
   may he fall into the care of a physician.

Here the medical profession is viewed with sober realism. The doctor has his wisdom and his skill from God, just as medicines are gifts of the Creator from the earth. He can arrive at the right diagnosis, can relieve pain and perhaps preserve life. But his gifts have their limitations and he does not always have them at his disposal. So he himself, like the sick person, is dependent on prayer. Moreover it can be a punishment to fall into the hands of a doctor. God and the physician are therefore seen in conjunction with one another in curious and multifarious ways.

3. *The Lord of sickness*

Yahweh alone is the lord of sickness and of healing. That is the unbroken biblical assurance. Natural and miraculous healings are not distinguished from one another fundamentally. Whether human prescriptions and applications also help or not, what is always essential is that the invalid in his sickness and the convalescent in his recovery should encounter the God who indirectly or directly sends both sickness and healing.[20] Whereas even Asclepius, the supreme god of healing, has to endure the rivalry of Apollo, and Apollo has to tolerate the competition of Machaon and Podalirius (Asclepius' two sons),[21] for Israel dealing with sickness is Yahweh's exclusive prerogative. He himself never falls sick and is never wounded, unlike gods such as the Egyptian Horus, whom Thoth has to cure after he has been stung by a scorpion.[22]

According to his own unfettered will, he wards off sickness, or sends it (Job 5.18; Deut. 7.15). Even when the leprous Naaman or King Hezekiah have to do with Elisha or Isaiah as physicians, in the process – and from the very outset – the essential dialogue is with God, as in the case of Job. Naaman confesses at the end: 'Behold I know that there is no God in all the earth but in Israel' (II Kings 5.15) and he puts measures in train for Yahweh's lasting honour (vv. 17ff.); and Hezekiah acknowledges:

> He himself has done it.
> I will praise thee all my years. . . .

(Isa. 38.15). But even without this personal acknowledgment the processes surrounding sickness and healing can never be detached from Yahweh's activity. It is a matter for the person involved whether he comes through this particular experience with Yahweh and absorbs it permanently into his life.[23]

This coming face to face with Yahweh begins with the prayer in sickness, the prayer that Ecclesiasticus recommends (38.9); we meet it frequently in the psalms of lamentation (Ps. 6.2):

> Be gracious to me, O Yahweh, for I am languishing away,
> Heal me, for my bones are troubled.

Cf. 38.1ff.; 88.1ff. Physical distress is often the occasion of self-examination. It constantly gives Job's dialogue with God renewed impetus, although in this case the question of guilt does not solve the riddle; Yahweh himself has finally to give him the answer. As a rule a sufferer discovers his preceding acts of commission and omission (Pss. 38.4; 39.8, 11; 41.4; and frequently elsewhere); his suppression and concealment of his transgressions preys on his strength until he finally manages to speak of them (Pss. 32.3–5; 107.17–19). Yahweh's forgiving consolation is also the first step in his recovery (Pss. 32.5b; 107.20; cf. Mark 2.5–12).

Just as it can lead to an examination of what is past, sickness can also lead to meditation on what is to come; in Elihu's discourses, for example, illness acquires a warning and educative function (Job 33.19ff.). In Num. 21.4–9 (E) healing is bound up with a test of the people's trust in Yahweh's decrees: Yahweh has let loose fiery serpents among the murmuring people in the wilderness. They bite the people, whereupon they confess their sins and beg Moses to intercede for them. After this Yahweh orders a bronze serpent to be set up (v. 8): 'If a serpent bit any man, he would look at the bronze serpent and live.' Now everyone who has been bitten is healed of the deadly poison if he trusts Yahweh's injunctions.

A brief early passage in Ex. 15.23–25 tells how, on Yahweh's instructions, Moses makes the undrinkable water at Marah sweet. To this note a Deuteronomist has appended a conditional sentence (v. 26), teaching the stringent connection between obedience and recovery:

> If you will diligently hearken to the voice of Yahweh your God, and do that which is right in his eyes, and give heed to his commandments and keep all his statutes, I will put none of the diseases upon you which I put upon the Egyptians; for I am Yahweh your healer.

The final sentence about Yahweh the healer sounds both programmatic and polemical.[24] It proclaims that human life with all its derangements finds its unity before God, and it rejects the notion that the future is to be won other than in dialogue with him. To remain closed up within oneself in a monologue, or to seek other healers *in place of* Yahweh (II Chron. 16.12), where they ought at most, according to Ecclesiasticus, to be consulted *because* of Yahweh,[25] shows a hopeless misunderstanding of man.

The texts indicate the multifarious ways in which Israel saw itself to be drawn into dialogue with Yahweh through sickness and healing. Everyone touched by either had to listen anew. When the goal of recovery is reached, it is above all the praise of Yahweh that can be heard, signalizing life and health. Such praise covers a wide spectrum, including healing and forgiveness (Ps. 30.2, 5, 11f.; 32.1–11; 103.3; cf. Isa. 53.4).[26] A prophetic voice leads its hearers towards a future Zion of which it is said (Isa. 33.24):

> No inhabitant will say, 'I am sick';
> for the people who dwell there will be forgiven their iniquity.

XVII

The Hope of Man[1]

Since Yahweh allots man his times, the eye of man can expect the future, but cannot anticipate what that future will be. The decision between fearing and hoping does not find its sufficient foundation either in man himself or in circumstances, but in the promise of the God who brings the future to pass.

1. *The expectation of the future*

It is part of man's nature to anticipate the future, since he is, as created being, entrusted with tasks that give the future form.[2] Even the words of punishment addressed to man after his transgression do not close the door on the future, for they deal with the birth of children (Gen. 3.16), man's future work and sustenance (vv. 17–19), God's promise of protection against the dreaded vendetta (4.14f.), and the ceaseless alternation of seed-time and harvest (8.21f.). Thus the Yahwist already recognized man *per se* (even the men who lived before Israel, as well as those outside her borders) as the being who can consciously direct his life towards the future. In the covenant with Noah, the Priestly document proclaimed the rainbow in the clouds as a sign that man cannot overlook – a token that in spite of all his threats, the destruction of life is not God's final intention (Gen. 9.14–16).

The late book of Ecclesiastes brings us a corresponding reflection on the human subject (3.11): 'Also he has put remotest time into man's mind.'[3] The Preacher teaches, therefore, that to ponder over the future is man's inescapable fate, although he cannot survey and comprehend God's work in its totality from beginning to end. Because the component parts of the future are also endangered, hope is, generally speaking, accompanied by fear. 'Only who is joined with all the living has hope.' says Eccles. 9.4. That is why man awaits the future with strained expectation.

The most important Hebrew words for man's attitude to the future bring this out. The root *qwh* is most frequently found in the sense of the expectation of the future (piel 39 times, qal 6 times, *tiqwāh* 32 times, *miqweh* 5 times; 82 times in all). The special nuance of meaning is brought out by the related noun *qaw*, the term for the measuring cord when it is stretched to its full extent (II Kings 21.13; Isa. 34.17), as well as *qawqaw*, for tension, which only occurs in Isa. 18.2, 7. Accordingly *qiwwāh* means hope as strained expectation (cf. Isa. 5.2, 4, 7). Thus Isaiah with strained expectation hopes in Yahweh, who has hidden his face from the house of Jacob (8.17b). The saying expresses in intensified form the attitude which is described by *ḥkh* piel in the first part of the Isaiah saying (v. 17a). This word (qal once, piel 13 times, no substantive form) means rather a hesitating 'tarrying' or lingering (II Kings 9.3), or a patient (Dan. 12.12) waiting for something (Isa. 64.4). *yḥl* appears more often (piel 24 times, hiphil 15 times, niphal twice, *tōḥelet* 6 times, *yāḥīl* once; 48 times in all); this word interprets hope as an enduring and confident waiting; Gen. 8.10, 12 is a typical example, where Noah 'waited another seven days' each time before he sent the dove forth from the ark again. Finally we must mention *śbr* (piel six times, noun *śeber* twice). Here there is an echo of the aspect of testing in watching expectancy; *śbr* qal (Neh. 2.13, 15) then means to inspect, to prove, while in Ps. 145.15 it is the eyes that are the author of hope of this kind:

> The eyes of all look to thee,
> and thou givest them their food in due season.

Thus the linguistic possibilities of the Hebrew already bring out a number of modified attitudes towards the future: hope expresses itself as strained expectation (*qwh*), as patient waiting for someone or something (*ḥkh*), as watching for (*śbr*) or as enduring and hopeful waiting (*yḥl*).[4] Man *per se* therefore differs greatly in his attitude to the future, and his success is equally varied (Prov. 10.28):

> The hope of the righteous ends in gladness,
> but the expectation of the wicked will be short.

Here the attitude of the righteous is described as *tōḥelet*, that is to say, an enduring, hopeful waiting; whereas that of the wicked is *tiqwāh*, i.e., strained (self-assured, or fearful and importunately impatient[5]) expectation. Cf. Prov. 11.23. In his own way, every man hopes as long as he lives.

2. *The hidden nature of the future*

Man undoubtedly lives in anticipation and is called to mould the future with 'foresight'; but, equally, he does not have the future at his disposal. He plans indeed, and must do so – differing from the beast in this respect.[6] But he can never be certain that his plans will find fulfilment.

> The horse is made ready for the day of battle,
>> but the victory belongs to Yahweh (Prov. 21.31);
>
> A man's mind plans his way,
>> but Yahweh directs his steps (Prov. 16.9).

The prudent man, especially, calculates on the incalculable difference between his plans for the future and their historical realization. Anyone who is not quite consciously alive to the difference between these two things is in danger of misunderstanding the human nature of man and of putting man himself in God's place. He does not remain truly secular man, confined to this world, but stabilizes the rule of disbelief through his faith in some ideology or other. Ecclesiastes' scepticism resists most vigorously of all the certainty that man has the future within his power. This is impossible for two reasons. In the first place he cannot be sure what the circumstances of the future will be (Eccles. 8.7):

> He does not know what is to be,
>> for who can tell him how it will be?

Only the fool wastes many words about it (10.14):

> Though no man knows what is to be,
>> for who can tell him what will be after him?

In the second place – and this is the main point – he does not even know what his own future is to be (8.8):

> No man has power over the breath of life (. . .),
>> or authority over the day of death;
> there is no discharge from war,
>> nor do riches[7] save the man who owns them.

No planner has his own condition in his own hands at the hour when his plans find their fulfilment (9.1b): 'Whether it will be love or hate man does not know.' Job emphasizes that it is above all God himself who will foil the self-assurance of human expectation (14.19f.). Before the negative sentence just quoted (9.1b) Ecclesiastes states in positive terms (9.1a): 'The righteous and the wise and their deeds are in the hand of God.'

3. *Yahweh, man's hope*

From this it follows for the whole of the Old Testament that, basically and pre-eminently, Yahweh is man's hope. Even the statistics show that, of everything that man can hope for, it is much the most frequently Yahweh himself towards whom expectation in Israel is directed or should be directed. *qiwwāh* is applied 26 times to Yahweh and only 19 times to anything else, *yḥl* piel and hiphil 27 times to Yahweh and 15 times to other things.[8] If we ask the reason for these personal bearings of hope, we must not only investigate the occurrence of the main terms used for the expectation, but must discover the reasons behind them. Israel understands its beginnings and its continuing history largely as being the fulfilment of Yahweh's promises: the rise of the nation, the gift of the promised land, Israel's mission among the nations, the kingdom and the continuance of the house of David, the catastrophes of the period of the judges and the kings, and then especially the Babylonian exile, the return home from exile, the new beginning in Jerusalem and, above all, the fulfilment of the promises in Israel's new covenant, in the incorporation of the world of the nations and in complete world-wide renewal. The hopes of the individual too only have their basis, continuance and power in as much as they are included in these promises to Israel and the nations. The expectations of all these transformations, however, are founded solely on Yahweh's word, which became known to Israel as promise to the patriarchs and then primarily as the proclamation of judgment and the pledge of salvation through the prophets.[9] On the basis of the experience of generations, the Deuteronomists brought out 'how the word of Yahweh functioned in history.'[10]

Thus it is understandable that hope that is well-founded is primarily expectation based on Yahweh himself. The very explanation of his name in Ex. 3.14 emphasizes him as 'he who proves himself'.[11] But it is not only the faithfulness of Yahweh as such that is the reason for hope but, more precisely, the reliability of his promise.

In this light we can understand why the explicit assertions of hope made by the individual in Israel have their real 'Sitz im Leben' – their setting in life – in the personal psalms of lament[12] and, more precisely, in the assertion of trust which forms one of their elements (Ps. 39.7):

> And now, Lord, for what do I wait?
> My hope is in thee.

Cf. Isa. 8.17; Micah 7.7; Ps. 69.3; Isa. 64.4. Psalm 33.20 makes clear why Yahweh is the foundation of hope:

> Our soul waits for Yahweh;
> he is our help and shield.

Psalm 130.5f. stresses that this assurance is based on the promise and on its realization:

> I wait for Yahweh, I wait with longing,[13]
> I wait for his word.
> My longing[13] is for Yahweh
> more than the watchman's is for the morning.

(Cf. Ps. 119.81.) The admonition in Ps. 130.7 links on to this:

> O Israel, hope in Yahweh!
> For with Yahweh there is steadfast love,
> and with him is plenteous redemption.

Neither here nor elsewhere does the admonition fail to give its foundation, which lies in Yahweh's steadfastness. Cf. the psalmist's self-exhortation in Ps. 42.5, 11; 43.5. Wisdom therefore also advises waiting on Yahweh, because that is a correction to one's own plans and in so far issues from the fear of God (Prov. 20.22):

> Do not say 'I will repay evil'.
> Hope in Yahweh! He will save you.

The way in which the fear of God and hope in Yahweh can be parallel and mutually supporting concepts is shown by Ps. 147.11:

> Yahweh takes pleasure in those who fear him,
> in those who hope in his steadfast love.

Thus the man who hopes appears at the same time as the receiver of Yahweh's new pledge. Isa. 40.31 promises that waiting on Yahweh is in the end more than a man's natural expectations of life.[14] A man whose hope was already completely exhausted (Lam. 3.8) takes home the consolation to himself (v. 25):

> Yahweh is good to those who wait for him,
> to the soul that seeks him.

Hope in Yahweh like this spreads to the furthest islands and ends of the earth, according to Deutero-Isaiah (Isa. 42.4; 51.5).

It is characteristic of this hope founded on Yahweh that it first of all takes the place of the statements of trust in the songs of lament (and that not merely in a form-critical respect);[15] and that the noun for trust (*bṭḥ*) can be used parallel to the words 'to wait for' (*yḥl*) (e.g., Ps. 33.20, 21) and 'to hope' (*qwh*) (e.g., Pss. 40.1, 3f.; 52.8, 9); just as *ḥsh* (to seek refuge) can also be parallel to *qwh* (Ps. 25.20, 21). When LXX rendered *bṭḥ* 47 times and *ḥsh* 20 times by *elpizein*,[16] it was because it grasped the approach to synonymity of the two words.

Thus hope is not a subsidiary theme in the Old Testament. On the contrary, it is indissolubly linked with Yahweh as the God of the patriarchs and prophets, the God of the threats and promises that he has proclaimed, the God of great changes and of final salvation; but equally with the God of all who pray and with the God of the wise. Just as hearing and speaking are man's specific characteristics,[17] so the expectation of the future is the distinctive mark of human life in time. In so far as it is a well-founded hope, the expectation of the future is for the Old Testament inseparable from obedience to the God who has promised himself to Israel and to the nations.

4. *The gift of specific hopes*

Inasmuch as Yahweh himself is the hope, particular hopes are Yahweh's gift. In fact certain expectations about the future are also bound up with Yahweh's promises. We need only remind ourselves here of the expectations which, starting from particular experiences on the part of Israel, spread out into universal significance, absorbing into themselves people from all nations. The first of these to be named must be the promise to Abraham in the Yahwist's account, which tells us that in Abraham-Israel all the tribes of the world are to find blessing (Gen. 12.3b). Through models drawn from the behaviour of the patriarchs towards strangers, this blessing is elucidated as meaning intervention on behalf of those ripe for destruction (Gen. 18.17ff.); as readiness to come to an understanding with arch-enemies (Gen. 26.28ff.); and as economic help for those in need (Gen. 39.5; 41.49, 57).[18] Isa. 19.23–25 shows how Israel, as third power, is to become the mediator of blessing to the great powers Assyria and Egypt. Paul testifies in Gal. 3.8 that in the light of Jesus the blessing to Abraham will actually reach the nations. Prophecy takes up the promise of peace particularly. What Isa. 9.5f. expects from a new Davidic king is first of all a 'peace without end'. According to Isa. 2.2–4 this is not to be confined to Israel. A pilgrimage of the nations to Zion has as its purpose that all strangers should receive Yahweh's guidance and should refashion all their war potential into instruments of service for life, abandoning all their warlike manoeuvres. Yahweh himself breaks the weapons, according to Hos. 1.4; 2.18; Jer. 49.35; Micah 5.10–14; Zech. 9.10. That is why Israel praises the God who breaks bows, shatters spears, and burns chariots with fire (Ps. 46.9).[19] Justice and help for all the oppressed are not the least among the blessings of the new and universal empire of peace; and it is these that are expected from the messianic ruler (Ps. 72, cf. Isa. 11.2ff.). Changes such as these which bring about the truly all-embracing salvation, in which all unsatisfied need, all violent dissension and all oppressive injustice is overcome, never come about without the activity of the God of Israel; just as later, in the New Testament, they are indissolubly bound up with the mission of Jesus (Rev. 21).

This leads to certain conclusions for anthropology. The man who abandons the God of hope (*Deus spei*) as the founder of specific hopes in the history of Israel, its fathers, its prophets and Jesus of Nazareth and pays allegiance to the idol hope (*Deus spes*), which embraces what is human as independent content,[20] either makes excessive and inhuman demands on men, or he relativizes the expectation of the new world to a lamentable degree. The hope towards which the Bible moves promises a new creation that radically transcends man's own possibilities. But in promising this it also encourages him to take the steps that are within his power in the direction of this goal, and to refrain from steps leading in the opposite direction. Anyone who wants to reach the new world across the sea will start off for the port of departure on his own feet and with the means of transport at his disposal in this old world, even though he realizes that very different forces will be needed before he can land in the new world and become its citizen. The promise of the God of hope is fighting strength to meet a double disappointment: some tell people to put their trust in the next world, and disappoint them by declaring that the present is hopelessly unalterable; others claim that they can realize the heaven of total salvation by their own strength, and disappoint because they ruin the present in a completely inhuman way.[21] On the other hand man, who is of his very nature orientated towards the future, can – trusting in the word of promise – remain radically hopeful within the relativity of 'a step at a time'. He neither reduces what is totally new to the trivial level of paltry innovations, nor does he burden men intolerably with what only the One who is incomparable can achieve. Only the man of confidence, as the hearer of the promise, already experiences the foretaste of the new world. And it is a foretaste that he can extend to others.

PART THREE

THE WORLD OF MAN
Sociological anthropology

XVIII

God's Image – The Steward of the World[1]

The world of man is God's whole creation. This is the testimony of the two accounts of the creation in Genesis,[2] and of related assertions, such as Ps. 8. The Priestly document reduces the special position of man in the world to the concise formula that he is created and protected as 'God's image' (*ṣelem 'elōhīm*; Gen. 1.26f.; 9.6). What does this definition mean?

1. Man as the image of God

In what sense is man 'the image of God'? Taken by itself, the phrase points first and fundamentally to a correspondence between man and God. The unique nature of man in creation is to be understood in the light of his special relationship to God. In the context it would be still better to speak of God's relationship to man as the presupposition for man's self-understanding. For the definition appears first when God deliberates with himself and comes to a decision in 1.26:

> Let us make man in our image,
> after our likeness.

But how are we to understand this relation of correspondence between God and man more precisely?

(*a*) According to this word of personal decision, man proceeds from God's *address*. We must not view this in the purely formal sense, especially since the address in which God blesses man in 1.28 is similar to the words spoken to the fish and the birds in 1.22. What is unique is the continuation of the words addressed to man. This confers on man the office that distinguishes him. Psalm 8.5 understands it as a 'crowning with glory and honour'. According to the Yahwist too, when the Creator gave created beings over to man, he also gave him responsible tasks (2.15–17)[3] and powers of decision (2.18–23) within creation. God's personal decision to give man a help corresponding to him (2.18) is matched by the human words which name the animals and by the bridegroom's exultation (2.19f., 23). The assigning of the trees in the garden in 2.16f. not only provided the theme for the first discussion among created beings (Gen. 3.1ff.); it also led to the first dialogue between God and man. The different features of the Yahwist's narrative make the implications of Gen. 1.26–28 graphically evident. According to this the relation of correspondence to which the phrase 'the image of God' points is to be seen first of all in that man, in hearing and then also in obeying and in answering, corresponds to the word of God's address.

(*b*) The purpose of the divine personal decision to create an 'image of God' is from the outset so ordained that man is set in a particular relationship to the living beings that have been created previously (1.26b):

> so that[4] they may have dominion over the fish of the sea, and over the birds of the air, and over the cattle, and over all the animals on the earth[5] and over every creeping thing that creeps upon the earth.

Moreover, according to Ps. 8.6 man is put in possession of the works of God's hands. In the Yahwist they are given to him for his work, as sustenance or as helps (2.15, 16, 19). It is always God's creatures with whom man is put in contact. When man enters into relationship to the things of the world, whether in his day's work, or in his meals, or in his discoveries, he also enters objectively into relationship with God, as their Creator, who has apportioned these things to him. Accordingly the relation of correspondence, to which his destiny as 'God's image' points, is also to be seen in the fact that man has to cope in the world with the very things that God has created.

(*c*) But why is this relationship of correspondence described as being God's *image*? Here we have to notice that special relationship to the rest of creation in which God sets man, according to the Priestly document, when he deliberately makes 'an image of God'; it is the *dominating* relationship (1.26b; *weyirdu*). In the blessing in 1.28, before man is commanded to rule over the animals, he is ordered to subdue the earth generally. Similarly, the meaning of man's 'crowning' in Ps. 8.5f. is seen in his 'ruling' (*mšl*) over the world of divine creative power[6] and in the fact that 'all things are put under his feet'. It is precisely in his function as ruler that he is God's image. In the ancient East the setting up of the king's statue was the equivalent to the proclamation of his domination over the sphere in which the statue was erected (cf. Dan. 3.1, 5f.). When in the thirteenth century BC the Pharaoh Ramesses II had his image hewn out of rock at the mouth of the *nahr el-kelb*, on the Mediterranean north of Beirut, the image meant that he was the ruler of this area. Accordingly man is set in the midst of creation as God's statue. He is evidence that God is the Lord of creation; but as God's steward he also exerts his rule, fulfilling his task not in arbitrary despotism but as a responsible agent. His rule and his duty to rule are not autonomous; they are copies.

Apart from the talk about 'God's image' in 1.26, there is also a mention of man's 'likeness' (*kidmūtēnū*; cf. 5.1). This is perhaps intended to guard against the misunderstanding that correspondence indicates identity only, and not differentiation within the similarity as well. But it could also emphasize the nearness and relationship, just as the double expression in Gen. 5.3 (though the order is reversed compared with 1.26) says that Adam begot a son who was 'in his own likeness, after his image'; this underlines the close relationship between the two.[7] In the task of governing the world, therefore, we ought not to forget the special nearness of God to man, which comes to expression pre-eminently in the bond existing through the word. Yet we must not forget that, according to the specific meaning of the ruler's image in the context of the statements in 1.26a, b, the relationship of correspondence is to be seen in man's function as the ruler of the rest of creation.

2. *Man and mankind*

In what sense is man, as the image of God, the steward of the world? It is quite clear in Gen. 1 that it is not any outstanding individual that is meant, such as perhaps the king of Egypt; for instance it was possible to say to King Rahotep (Seventeenth Dynasty): 'He has appointed thee as his image.'[8] But when we read, in 1.26a, 'Let us make '*ādām* in our image,' how is '*ādām* to be understood?

(*a*) The context makes it clear that no individual at all is meant. The continuation in 1.26b '(Let us make '*ādām*) so that *they* may have dominion . . .' points to a plural. Thus '*ādām* is unquestionably to be understood in a collective sense; God wants to create *mankind*. Dominion over the world is not to be made over to great individuals, but to the community. Psalm 8 says that man is crowned to rule over all creation, surprising though it at first seems (v. 4) that it should just be man, in view of the mighty works of the Creator which are to be seen in the heavens (v. 3):

> What is man that thou art mindful of him,
> and the son of man that thou dost care for him?

It is precisely man in his littleness[9] that God has cared for and has called to be his plenipotentiary. No member of mankind is to be excluded from this authority.

(*b*) But Gen. 1.27 gives an even more precise answer to the question, in what sense mankind is to be a steward commissioned by God:

> So God created man in his own image,
> in the image of God he created him;
> male and female he created him.

An explanation is added to the double account of the carrying out of God's resolve – an explanation of how mankind, created in God's image, is to be fashioned: it is to take the form of two sexes. Karl Barth has called the expansion in v. 27b a 'definitive explanation'[10] of the text of v. 27a. Men are to be allowed to complement themselves in love. That they live together in this way and not in warfare is an essential presupposition for the success of the stewardship of the world entrusted to them. They are the image of God in that together they are one. But this interpretation is not undisputed, particularly if it is put forward with moral implications, which demand insight into man's mutual dependence. It will at most be permissible to cling to the fact that men can only fulfil the commission as the image of God given to them in their creation by turning towards one another and by complementing one another, like man and wife.

(c) What is incontrovertible, however, is the interpretation which follows with the charge to multiply in 1.28:

> Be fruitful and multiply,
> and fill the earth and subdue it.

This addition makes it clear why men as God's image are created male and female: they are to be able to generate children and thus to increase mankind. The increase of mankind and dominion over the earth and the beasts are directly linked together. The stewardship over the world is therefore entrusted to the great company of mankind with the multitude of its members; and this presupposes that they all partake in the dominion over creation.

3. *Rule over creation*

How does mankind as God's image exercise this dominion?

(a) The *presupposition* is a demythologized world, such as the creation account displays in general, and to some extent polemically, in its countering of the myths of the surrounding world. All and everything that is to be found in the world is revealed as being God's creation; consequently, for the man who has grasped this, there is neither a divine earth, nor divine beasts, nor divine constellations, nor any other divine spheres basically inaccessible to man. The whole demythologized world can become man's environment, his space for living, something which he can mould.[11]

For us, but for the ancient world as well, one thing seems paradoxical: the more consistently the world is viewed as creation, the more consistently one can speak of its 'worldliness'.[12]

(*b*) The *nature* of the universal human stewardship is absolute dominance. This is dazzlingly illuminated through the word of command in 1.28. *kibšuhā* opens the way for a complete subjection of the earth; *kbš* can otherwise mean the subjection of a country through war (Num. 32.22, 29), the subjugation of peoples (II Sam. 8.1) and of slaves particularly (Neh. 5.5); but it can also be used for the raping of women (Esth. 7.8). It always means an action in which man reduces something to his use through the application of force (Josh. 18.1). Thus mankind as God's image is equipped with certain capacities and authorized to have the world at his disposal. The other imperative, *rᵉdū*, takes up the opening keyword from 1.26b. *rdh* is applied to a king's rule in Ps. 72.8; 110.2; Isa. 14.6; Ezek. 34.4. But here the dignity of absolute royal rule is granted to the multitude of all men. The meaning 'to rule' has perhaps developed out of the meaning 'to tread', which may be found for *rdh* in Joel 4.13, describing the treading of the wine-press. This points in the direction of a re-fashioning activity, such as takes place in the wine-press when the grapes are turned into wine. Man is empowered to make comparable useful alterations.

(*c*) As the *object* of rule, first of all the earth is named as a whole, and then the animals in particular. Why are they singled out? Only they can be considered possible rivals to man. To make plants yield food (v. 29) is child's play beside mastery over animals. For the ancients, control over the world was displayed first and most impressively in their training and discipline. Perhaps Gen. 1 is not thinking of killing, since the world of vegetation is expressly assigned as food to man and beast alike (vv. 29f.). This changes in 9.1ff.

Psalm 8 also includes the chase. Here the order of beasts listed differs from that in Gen. 1. The growing wonderment over the sovereignty of little man finds its climax in vv. 7f.: 'First the poet names the tame animals, then, more comprehensively, all the beasts of the field. Birds and fish follow the land animals; these too, although they belong to the heavens and the no less mysterious element of the seas, are caught by men with traps and nets. In order to underline the remarkable aspect of this fact, v. 8b gives a closer description of the fish; it is almost divine for man to dominate what passes through these mysterious "paths of the sea".'[13] Thus in principle everything is 'put under man's feet' (Ps. 8.5b). Only man himself is not to be the object of subjection (Gen. 9.6), all men having the joint task of administering and moulding creation and of having it at their disposal.[14]

Ludwig Köhler,[15] taking Gen. 1.28 as his starting point, has finely described the task given to man as it was in former times and as it is down to the present day:

This is the commission to establish civilization. It applies to all men, and it embraces every age. There is no human activity which is not covered by it. The man who found himself with his family on an unprotected plain exposed to ice-cold wind and first laid a few stones one upon another and invented the wall, the basis of all architecture, was fulfilling this command. The woman who first pierced a hole in a hard thorn or a fishbone and threaded a piece of animal sinew through it in order to be able to join together a few shreds of skin, and so invented the needle, sewing, the beginning of all the art of clothing, was also fulfilling this command. Down to the present day, all the instructing of children, every kind of school, every script, every book, all our technology, research, science and teaching, with their methods and instruments and institutions, are nothing other than the fulfilment of this command. The whole of history, all human endeavour, comes under this sign, this biblical phrase.

That is its objective aspect. But there is also a subjective side to it. It belongs inescapably to the nature of every man that he should come to terms with life. He must seek to come to terms inwardly with everything which he encounters, whether it be a speck of dust in his eye, or a flood which threatens the life of himself and his family. . . . The nature of a man is recognizable from the way in which he comes to terms inwardly with things.

Unquestionably, the commission to man has not as yet found its goal. But man as God's image is in danger because his domination threatens to escape from him because he misunderstands his tasks as ruler.[16] The reason for the prohibition of the shedding of human blood, with its indication of man's creation as the image of God, already points fundamentally to such limitations. Today two concrete instances, at least, should be noticed. First, the subjection of the world must not lead to such an endangering of man as is taking on threatening proportions in the pollution of the environment; the lordship of man over man is a falsification of the image of God. Secondly, the subjection of the world must not lead to man's being dominated by a myth of technology, which produces the technically possible simply because it *is* possible, and therefore subjects man to technological and economic compulsions.

The epistle to the Colossians, which called Jesus Christ 'the image of the invisible God' (1.15; cf. II Cor. 4.4) sees the necessity of putting on the new man, 'which is being renewed in knowledge after the image of its creator' (3.10; cf. II Cor. 4.1–6). Through Matt. 28.18f. Gen. 1.28 receives 'a completely new, eschatological interpretation'[17] in the words of the exalted Christ: 'All authority in heaven and on earth has been given to me. Go therefore and make all nations into my disciples.' We ought to consider how, through the mode of sovereignty of the One who was crucified, mankind's stewardship over the world is snatched back from self-destruction, and the image of God once more emerges in all its freedom.

XIX

Man and Woman[1]

The Priestly document defined 'God's image' in the world as being mankind in its bi-sexual nature (Gen. 1.27).[2] What does the Old Testament
have to say in detail about the relationship between man and woman? We
shall enquire into the external order of that relationship, into its inner fire,
and into the disorders affecting it.

1. The main features of the law of marriage

Anyone who looks into the basic features of the law of marriage in the Old
Testament is first of all surprised to find that it has no common word of its
own for the institution of marriage. This is significant. For as a rule man
and wife find their place in the grouping of the family (*bēt 'āb*=the family
group), to which four generations generally belong.[3] The idea is to secure
the continuance of 'the father's house'. As a rule the woman enters the
family community of the man (e.g., Gen. 24.5–8, 58f.); but other arrange-
ments were evidently possible (Gen. 31.26–43; 2.24).[4]

Legally, man counts as being the 'owner' of his wife (*ba'al 'iššā*, Ex. 21.3,
22; Deut. 24.4; II Sam. 11.26), and the wife is considered as her husband's
'possession' (*be'ūlat ba'al*, Gen. 20.3; Deut. 22.22). How was this legal
situation arrived at? The man who wanted to win a wife for himself had as
a rule to pay a 'marriage gift' (*mōhar*) to the bride's father (Gen. 34.12;
Ex. 22.16; I Sam. 18.25). Its amount was as a rule fixed and generally
known; the regulations in Deut. 22.29 fix the sum at 50 silver shekels. The
subject of this particular passage is a punishment levied on a marriage of
compulsion, after the violation of a girl who was not betrothed. In such a
case the man can also leave it to the family affected to fix the amount of the
marriage gift (Gen. 34.11ff.). In Lev. 27.4f. a woman's value is generally
30 shekels if she is over 20 years old, 10 shekels if she is younger.[5] Service
in the house of a man's father-in-law can replace the money payment
(Gen. 29.15–30). Cases are reported in which the demands are stepped up
as time goes on. Jacob complains to Rachel and Leah (Gen. 31.7): 'Your
father has changed the price ten times!' King Saul demands warlike

services from David in return for his daughter Michal, namely the delivery
of one hundred Philistine foreskins (I Sam. 18.25). Just like the young man
himself, a father can also take the initiative on his son's behalf, in order to
win a wife for him (Judg. 14.1–3; cf. Ex. 21.9) and a father can also seek a
husband for his daughter (Jer. 29.6; cf. II Cor. 11.2, following I Cor. 4.15).
With the delivery of the marriage gift, the 'betrothal' is sealed and the
bridegroom's legal claim comes into force. The Hebrew *'rś* piel, which is
generally translated as 'to betroth', therefore actually means 'to win
legally for one's own'.[6]

The next act in the 'marriage' is clearly distinguished from the 'betrothal': it is the bringing home of the bride (cf. Deut. 20.7; 28.30), the
'taking' (*lqḥ* Ex. 21.10; Lev. 21.7; Deut. 20.7; 22.13; Hos. 1.2; also I
Sam. 25.43a, cf. Gen. 4.19; 6.2), or 'the taking possession' (*b'l* Deut. 21.13;
24.1) of the woman (cf. also *bw'* Gen. 29.21). On the woman's side,
marrying means 'being assigned to her husband' (*hāyetā le'iš*, Num. 30.7)
or 'becoming his wife' (*hāyetā lō l'eiššā*, I Sam. 25.43b). All these phrases
suggest that the wife is one of the man's possessions. But the possibility of
a partner-like relationship is already reflected in the replacement of the
form of address 'my lord' (*ba'lī*) by 'my husband' (*'išī*) in Hos. 2.16; cf.
Gen. 2.23.[7] We only have evidence for a marriage feast quite late on, with
the word *ḥatunnā* (S. of S. 3.11), and then it applies to court circles:

> Go forth, O daughters of Zion, and behold King Solomon, with the
> crown with which his mother crowned him on the day of his wedding,
> on the day of the gladness of his heart.

Occasionally the union of man and woman is called a *berīt*: in Mal. 2.14
the 'wife of your youth' to whom the man has been unfaithful, is termed
his 'companion' (*ḥaberet*) and the wife of his covenant (promise) (*'ēset
berīteka*). Yahweh is introduced as witness to the bond of marriage. Here
we must remember that *berīt* can also mean any firm covenant of friendship
(I Sam. 18.3). Ezek. 16.8 describes in allegorical form the story of the love
and marriage between Yahweh and Israel:

> Behold, you were at the age for love; and I spread my skirt over you,
> and covered your nakedness; yea, I plighted my troth to you and entered
> into a covenant (*berīt*) with you, says Yahweh, and you became mine.

The spreading out of the skirt (cf. Ruth 3.9) represents the opposite pole to
the exposure of the adulteress (Hos. 2.3). The idea of the covenant fixes
the relationship between people in the form of a valid contract. Prov. 2.17
talks about the loose woman

> who forsakes the companion of her youth
> and forgets the covenant of her God.

Probably *bᵉrīt ʾᵉlōhehā* does not mean the marriage contracted before God but the commitment to conjugal faithfulness on the basis of the divine law proclaimed in Israel.[8]

After marriage the man is free for a year from military service and similar obligations, according to Deut. 24.5; he is to be able to devote himself to his household and to taking 'pleasure in his wife'. Generally speaking, it is expected that the bond between 'the wife of a man's youth' (Prov. 5.18; Isa. 54.6; Mal. 2.14f.) and 'the husband of a woman's youth' (Joel 1.8⁹) will be observed in a monogamous marriage, as the basic form. We find evidence of concubines (*pileges*) and the introduction of slaves through the chief wife for the patriarchal period particularly. Gen. 25.6 talks about Abraham's concubines, Hagar and Keturah probably being meant. According to Gen. 16.1f. (J) Hagar was brought to Abraham by Sarah; as his chief wife she gave him her slave with the words (v. 2): 'Behold now, Yahweh has prevented me from bearing children; go in to my maid; it may be that I shall obtain children by her.' Similarly, Rachel says to Jacob (Gen. 30.3 J): 'Here is my maid Bilhah; go in to her, that she may bear upon my knees, and even I may have children through her.' The story goes on: 'So she gave him her maid Bilhah as a wife (*lᵉʾiššā*).' Judg. 8.30f. justifies the number of Gideon's sons (seventy) by saying 'for he had many wives'. Judg. 19.1ff., 24ff.; 20.4ff. gives a detailed account of the dramatic love story of a Levite and his concubine. According to II Sam. 5.13 David had several concubines, and Solomon possessed three hundred of them, as well as seven hundred 'official wives' (I Kings 11.3); here we are dealing with round figures, and perhaps with an estimate of all the women who had gone through the king's harem in the course of his forty years' reign.[10] The great number belonged to the royal status. We hardly hear anything of several wives in the case of ordinary people in the period of the kings. Elkanah in I Sam. 1.2 had two wives, Hannah (who was at first childless) and Peninnah.

According to Ex. 21.7–11 a man could sell his daughter as slave for the purpose of conjugal intercourse. But the purchaser was not allowed to sell her again as slave. In this way she was protected from being bought and sold like any other wares. If the owner assigned her to his son, he had to treat her like a daughter. If he himself took another slave in addition to the first one, he was not allowed to reduce her 'food, clothing and accommodation'. If he could not afford to comply with this, she was allowed to go away freely.[11]

For the large-scale family, conjugal intercourse was regulated with extreme care, as Lev. 18 shows.[12] The levirate marriage (which makes it a duty for the brothers of a man who has died without male issue to continue the marriage with his widow; Deut. 25.5–10) presupposes that the brothers live together, that is to say, that the family group exists and that it should go on existing, whereby the consolidation of the family property through the exclusion of an 'outsider' as husband may have played a not unimportant part.

In general, apart from the regular, main marriage, there were apparently various ways in which wives might be assigned to husbands. In assessing the early Israelite sociology of marriage, we should note

> that it was originally better, in the close contacts of life, for every marriageable woman to be in proper relationship to some man, rather than that improper relationships should arise in which the children would suffer because no one would be responsible for them.[13]

When we look at the Old Testament regulations we are bound to see that here the problems of unmarried women, of childless marriages and also of the man who may be occasionally unsatisfied in his marriage – all agonizing problems in modern times – were solved. On the other hand, for many women jealousy of another woman – or of several other women and their children – must have been a torment (e.g., I Sam. 1); the relations and right of inheritance of the various children could also bring about difficult problems, if two women were loved to a different degree by their husband, as was no doubt generally the case (that is the premise of the regulation in Deut. 21.15–17). Finally, many women must have missed the permanent security which a strictly monogamous marriage can give. (And it is in this light that the conflict in Ex. 21.7–11 must be understood.)

2. *The relationship of love*

The love relationship between man and woman plays by no means an unimportant role even in the legal texts; on the contrary, it provoked them to a considerable extent, as we can see from the slave's claim to love in Ex. 21.7–11, or from the precaution against giving precedence to the children of a beloved wife over those of a woman who has been set aside (Deut. 21.15–17). Nor is there any lack of stirring descriptions of ardent love. Jacob loved Rachel far more than Leah (Gen. 29.16–18, 20): 'So Jacob served seven years for Rachel, and they seemed to him but a few days because of the love he had for her.' Elkanah (I Sam. 1.5) tries to comfort his wife Hannah, who (unlike Peninnah) was childless (v. 8): 'Hannah, why is your heart sad? Am I not more to you than ten sons?' Incidentally it can be seen here that the meaning of marriage was by no means viewed as lying merely in the birth of children.

Love could undoubtedly proceed from the woman's side, too. One

thread in the story of the rise of David shows this dramatically. It begins in
I Sam. 18.20 with the remark:

> Now Saul's daughter Michal loved David.

Cunningly, Saul will only give her to him in return for a hundred Philistine foreskins (vv. 21–25). Later, out of hatred for the fleeing David,
Saul deliberately gives this daughter to a certain Paltiel (I Sam. 25.44).
When David becomes king after Saul's death, he demands Michal from
Saul's son Ish-bosheth for himself; for she has been legally given to him
and still loves him hotly. II Sam. 3.15 goes on: 'And Ish-bosheth sent, and
took her from her husband Paltiel.' Now, on the other side, there is a
moving love scene with Paltiel; II Sam. 3.16 writes: 'But her husband
went with her, weeping after her all the way to Bahurim. Then Abner said
to him, "Take yourself off!"; and he returned.' A man whose wife has been
taken from him is eaten up with love; and a woman who is deeply in love
with a man finds her way back to him at last, after her father's hate has
separated them and she has become bound by another man's love. The
humanism of early Israel was well able to capture human interest like this.
Since marriage was not infrequently determined by the father, love
frequently only developed after marriage. Isaac's relationship to Rebecca,
who has been brought to him from afar, is an example (Gen. 24.67): 'Isaac
brought her into the tent, and took Rebekah, and she became his wife; and
he loved her. So Isaac was comforted after his mother's death.' The ancient
Israelite order, then, which envisaged a marriage of love, tended much
more strongly towards a monogamous marriage as a legal institution. The
collections of maxims show this. Prov. 5.18–20:

> Let your fountain be blessed,
>   and rejoice in the wife of your youth,
> the lovely hind, the graceful doe.
>   Let her breasts fill you at all times with delight,
>   continue to be drunk with her love.
>   Why should you be infatuated, my son, with a loose
>   woman,
> and embrace the bosom of another?

What an endless distance sentences like these are from any damning of
sexuality! And how clearly, at the same time, they indicate the senselessness of changing partners. To grow old with the beloved of the days of
one's youth – it is this alone that brings truly increasing pleasure in ever
new ways and ever new circumstances. Prov. 31.10–31, the great hymn to
the good wife, grasps this constantly increasing treasure feature by feature;
we shall pick out only a few sentences:

10 A good wife who can find?
   she is far more precious than corals.
12 She does him good, and not harm,
   all the days of her life.
14 She is like the ships of the merchant,
   she brings her food from afar.
20 She opens her hand to the poor,
   and reaches out her arms to the needy.
23 Her husband is known in the gates,
   when he sits among the elders of the land.
26 She opens her mouth with wisdom,
   and the teaching of kindness is on her tongue.
30 Charm is deceitful and beauty is vain,
   it is the wise woman who is to be praised.

Long after fleeting youth, the spirit and goodness of the experienced woman has its effects on a man's life. She can acquire prime and fundamental importance in their duality. She concerns herself in a self-reliant way with hidden needs, but she also contributes to her husband's public stature. Even Ecclesiastes, who sees through the frailty of all things, does not push aside the mutual pleasure of being together for the time that may still be at one's disposal. He even wakes understanding for such pleasures (9.9):

   Enjoy life with the wife whom you love,
     all the days of your fleeting life
       which he has given you under the sun.

The premise of the Yahwist's story about the Garden of Eden is also a love relationship between man and woman which is crowned with happiness. This aspect can be shown as a continuous thread running right through the whole. (1) The state of being alone is expressly stated by Yahweh as not being good for man (2.18a). (2) From the very beginning man's partner is defined as the help fit for him (v. 18b); this presupposes the social character of the difference between the sexes.[14] (3) Help of this kind is not to be found in the animal world; man is distinguished from that world by his superiority in possessing language (the naming of the beasts); and he remains lonely in the midst of it (vv. 19f.). (4) The partner who really corresponds to man is not created out of the earth, like the first man (v. 7) and the animals (v. 19); she comes from the rib of man himself; thus man and woman belong together qualitatively in a completely different degree from the way in which they belong to other created beings; it is only man and woman together who represent the whole man (cf.

v.24b *bāśār 'eḥād*[15]). (5) Unique though their solidarity is, man and woman none the less stand in genuine contrast to one another. The woman is formed during man's deep sleep (v.21) and is only brought to man when she is a complete, independent person (on *bw'* in v.22b as the end of the leading home of the bride cf. Judg.12.9[16]). (6) Whereas man only gives the animals names (v.20), in the discovery of his wife he arrives at a true expression of himself; with his bridegroom's exultation the Yahwist quotes man's speech for the first time; next to the formula of relationship[17] stands the derivation of the name *'iśśā* ('woman') from *'iś* ('man'), which brings out both the unity of nature and the difference in sex.[18] The note of exultation – 'this at last!' – announces the fulfilment of a long desired happiness. (7) Love is essentially marked by the personal yearning for one another; even the powerful bonds of the family group are burst apart (v.24a) and in man's 'cleaving' to his wife the original physical unity is realized anew (v.24b). (8) Shame in the form of embarrassment and inhibition only penetrates the duality of man and woman as the result of their mistrust towards God and their disobedience towards his word (cf. v.25b with 3.7–11).[19]

The love songs of the Song of Solomon celebrate the unparalleled nature of the love relationship. The uniqueness of love corresponds to the uniqueness of the beloved (S. of S.6.9):

> My dove, my perfect one, is only one,
>   the unrivalled one of her mother.

Thus the one belongs to the other in mutual and exclusive interrelation (S. of S.6.3): 'I am my beloved's and my beloved is mine.' The mutual character of love is also expressed by the fact that in the Song of Solomon we have, as well as two songs describing young girls, one in which the woman describes her beloved: 5.10–16.[20] The erotic vitality of these poems, their pleasure in sensual beauty and in the enjoyment of love, is illustrated by the song of desire in 8.1–4:

> O that you were like a brother to me,
>   that nursed at my mother's breast!
> If I met you outside, I could kiss you,
>   and none would take it amiss.
> I would lead you and bring you
>   into the house of my mother.
> You would teach me,
>   I would give you spiced wine to drink,
>   the juice of my pomegranates.

> His left hand is under my head,
>   and his right hand embraces me.
> I adjure you, O daughters of Jerusalem,
>   that you stir not up nor awaken love
>   until it please.

No moralizing must dim the warmth of feeling like this. Like the enjoyment of bread and wine, the joys of love also belong to God's gifts in this incalculable world, says Ecclesiastes (9.7–9).

3. *The disorders of love*

Israel was not blind to the dangerous disorders of the love relationship either, however. The Old Testament saw them more clearly than its neighbours. There the sexual life, like death,[21] had undergone a comprehensive mythologization. Through this the things of love were drawn deep into the cultic world. The opening of the womb took place in the sacred grove in intercourse with priests or strangers (Hos.4.13f.); numerous lovers courted the beloved (Hos.2.2–13).[22] For Israel these goings on were adultery and whoredom. The uniqueness of Yahweh's love relationship to Israel meant a fundamental prohibition of adultery (Ex.20.3, 14). The stories of the patriarchs already showed Israel that it ought to differ from its neighbours in its sexual ethics (cf. Gen.12.10–20; 19.1–11; 26.7–11; 34.1–12).[23] The wisdom writings also warn emphatically against the loose woman (Prov.5.2–5):

> (Pay no attention to a bad woman)[24]
> For the lips of a loose woman drip honey,
>   and her speech is smoother than oil;
> but in the end she is bitter as wormwood,
>   sharp as a two-edged sword.
> Her feet go down to death;
>   her steps strive towards the underworld.

In Prov.7.4–27 the mention of offering and vows (v.14) shows on the one hand the connection between what Israel called *lewdness,* and cultic practices; on the other hand the psychological processes that take place in the person who is seduced are sharply observed (vv.21f.):

> With much seductive speech she persuades him;
>   with her smooth talk she leads him astray.
> He follows her in a daze,
>   as an ox goes to the slaughter.

The sign of seduction is shame. We saw it in Gen. 3.7, 11 (following 2.25), set off by mistrust, which led Adam and Eve to make aprons of fig-leaves and to hide themselves. In a world of mistrust, will shame be able to ward off the capricious and overbearing desire of the one for the other (cf. 3.16)? Prov. 11.22, for example, presupposes that shame could be a protection against the break up of the whole person, if he is in danger of surrendering to the 'disturbance of our ego beneath the navel':[25]

> Like a gold ring in a swine's snout
> is a woman who is beautiful but shameless.

sārat ṭāʿam would be more literally translated, not by 'shameless', but by 'removed from the finer feelings'; thus man is defenceless against decked-out lust. Ham-Canaan, who uncovered the nakedness of his father Noah, is cursed because of his violation of shame (Gen. 9.22–25). The priests who go up to the altar are to wear linen trousers, according to Ex. 28.42 (cf. Ezek. 44.18); this was probably 'in view of the danger to the priests that could emanate from the peculiar holiness of the altar to that part of the body which is surrounded by uncanny powers'.[26] This uncanny atmosphere must also find an anthropological explanation. A sight of the genitals could give rise to wrong desires at the wrong moment and at the wrong place, and could promote a cleavage in the person's mind.

II Sam. 13.1–15 can show how shame ought to hinder violence from breaking out. David's son Amnon is morbidly in love with his half-sister Tamar. His improper desire first gives rise to a double lie. He pretends to be ill and wants his sister to bring him food. When he is finally alone with her, he lays hold of her and expects her to sleep with him (v. 11). She answers (v. 12):

> 'Such a thing is not done in Israel; do not do this wanton folly!'. . . .
> But he would not listen to her; and being stronger than she, he forced
> her, and lay with her. Then Amnon hated her with very great hatred; so
> that the hatred with which he hated her was greater than the love with
> which he had loved her. And Amnon said to her, 'Get out!'.

The swing over from unbridled lust to revulsion is described in masterly fashion. 'There can hardly be found a deeper expression of psychological insight into the nature and instability of merely sensual desire.'[27] In unbridled lust desire and revulsion lie directly side by side. The revulsion lays bare the false desire for what it is. This is what happens when love lacks completeness, when only something in the man and something in the woman become one, and not the man himself and the woman herself – when there is lack of the complete partnership which is in its very nature always exclusive. 'Coitus without co-existence is daemonic.'[28] In the Canaanite cult this daemonism was institutionalized.

The Old Testament legal order reckons with division in the person and therefore in marriage as well (Lev. 18.7ff.; 20.10ff.). In the relationship of the sexes to one another, the law protecting the person takes absolute priority over the rights of property; the weaker members of society particularly need protection against masculine tyranny (Amos 2.7). If in a weak moment a man has seduced a girl who is not betrothed to him, he must then also be prepared to take her as his wife for life (Ex. 22.16); according to Deut. 22.28f. he is not allowed to divorce her as long as he lives. In other circumstances Deut. 24.1–4 envisages a writ of divorce on the man's side. Conditions that are to be put down to human failure and which have become unbearable should not be given permanence. On the other hand a capricious to-ing and fro-ing is resisted. If the divorced woman has meanwhile entered into a new marriage, return to her first husband is afterwards impossible. Caprice which could have devastating consequences is given its precautionary limits so that human unhappiness cannot go on perpetuating itself without restriction. Troubled and disappointed love brings indescribable grief. Once we see a Levite running after the wife who has left him in anger, appealing to her and trying to persuade her to remain with him after all (Judg. 19.1ff.). So the admonition to be constant in love turns into a blessing for the healing of human divisions (Mal. 2.15). Let none be faithless to the wife of his youth.

A priest should not take a divorced woman for his wife, any more than he should marry a whore or a girl who is no longer a virgin (Lev. 21.7).

Not to be married is a disgrace, because it means that man is prevented from realizing a complete life. Thus according to Isa. 4.1, in the days of judgment, when men are killed in war in their hordes (3.25), seven women shall cling to one man, saying:

> We will eat our own bread and wear our own clothes, only let us be called by your name; take away our reproach.

To be scorned by a man is shattering and deranging for a woman – a shock which continues to make itself felt even if she marries later; such a person counts as being just as unbearable as a slave who becomes king, or a fool when he lives in luxury (Prov. 30.21–23). When Jeremiah has to remain unmarried as a sign for Israel, he is signalizing the disturbed relationship between Yahweh and Israel, which is threatening Israel's life (Jer. 16.1ff.; cf. 15.17).

Abnormal sexual practices are also warned against because they mean the cleavage of the whole person. Lev. 20.13 says of homosexuality: 'If a man lies with a male as with a woman, both of them have committed an abomination.' Cf. Lev. 18.22. Homosexuality is a failure to recognize the difference of the sexes, and with it the basic way of arriving at a fruitful life through the overcoming of self-love. Sodomy is resisted in the same way (Lev. 18.23): 'You shall not lie with any beast and defile yourself with it, neither shall any woman give herself to a beast to lie with it; it is perversion.' Since the affirmation of one's own sex is not always a matter of course, a word is directed against transvestism (Deut. 22.5): 'A woman shall not wear anything that pertains to a man, nor shall a man put on a woman's garment.' Homosexual relations are not to be surreptitiously enjoyed in this way.

Thus the Old Testament is perfectly frank about the varied disorders and threats to man in his status as created being, and to the love relationship founded on that status. It describes these disturbances as clearly as it describes the rapture of the whole union of love. It is always a disturbance in the relationship to God which shows itself – in different ways – in the disturbances within the common life of man and woman. In the exclusiveness of the love that is required of them, nothing less is at stake than the wholeness of the love conferred on them at their creation.

XX

Parents and Children[1]

In ancient Israel the most important components of the social structure are the family group, kindred and the tribe. Consequently the relations between parents and children take on fundamental importance. Problems between the generations go on to call in question the reality of man, and also the future of Israel.

1. *Yahweh's gift*

That children are to be viewed as Yahweh's gift is an essential premise for the understanding of the diverse relations between fathers and mothers on the one hand, and sons and daughters on the other. The relationship of man and wife certainly does not find its sole meaning in the conception of children,[2] but this is none the less an essential part of that relationship. According to the Priestly document, mankind can only fulfil its civilizing task on earth if it multiplies.[3] According to the Yahwist, after Abraham is promised that he will become a great nation, a goal is set: that in him all the tribes of the earth shall be blessed (Gen. 12.2f.; cf. 28.14). Here as there, the multiplying of man is a result of Yahweh's blessing (Gen. 1.28; 12.2). From that time on Israel hopes to be as numerous as the stars in the heavens and the sand of the sea (Gen. 15.5; 26.4; 22.17; Hos. 1.10). Rebecca is sent away from her parents' house with the wish: 'Our sister, be the mother of thousands of ten thousands!' (Gen. 24.60).

But human planning does not make the transition to realization as a mere matter of course and without friction; and we are shown that there is considerable tension between the will to have a child and its materialization in the child's birth. Man is not in control of the difference between the wish to multiply and its fulfilment. The stories of the patriarchs are an extreme testimony to the fact that Israel can grasp its genesis as a nation only in the light of Yahweh, as the Lord of this difference. The mothers of Israel counted as being unfruitful. Sarah, who had already given Abraham her slave because she was childless (Gen. 16.1f.), finally, in her old age, laughs over the promise of a son (Gen. 18.9ff.). Rebecca's barrenness is only ended after Isaac's special prayer (Gen. 25.21). Jacob's beloved Rachel also despairs at first because of her childlessness: 'Give me children, or I shall die,' she cries (Gen. 30.1). Jacob's answer is significant (v. 2): 'Am I in the place of God, who has withheld from you the fruit of the womb?' Later the decimated generation of the exile sees its descendents issue once more from the power of Yahweh's promise (Isa. 54.1):

> Sing, O barren one, who did not bear;
> break forth into singing and cry aloud,
> you who have not been in travail!
> For the children of the desolate one
> will be more than the children of her that is
> married, says Yahweh.

Thus in Ps. 127.3 sons generally are Yahweh's gift, as a heritage; and in Ps. 128 they are called a blessing springing from the fear of Yahweh. Ps. 113 praises Yahweh, who grants the childless joy over their children (v. 9; cf. Ps. 144.12f.). For their parents, children are honour and pride (Ps. 144), joy (Ps. 128) and a noticeable help (Ps. 127.4f.). Male descendants particularly are highly valued (Jer. 20.15; I Sam. 4.20; Gen. 30.2); their capacity for work counts as being more valuable[4] and they remain in their father's family group and increase it. But for Ecclesiastes, even a throng of children has no value in itself (6.3):

> If a man begets a hundred children . . . but he is not satisfied with life's good things, I say that a still-born child is better off than he.

2. *Upbringing*

Upbringing is the task of mother and father. The educative effect of both is called in Hebrew *ysr* piel (Deut. 8.5; Prov. 31.1), which means both instruction (Job 4.3) and discipline (I Kings 12.11). In the first years of a child's life it is primarily the mother who undertakes the upbringing. The small child is entrusted to her. Moses loses his mother when he is three months old, according to Ex. 2.3–9, but by means of a trick he gets her back as his nurse. Until the baby is weaned, which may not be until its third year,[5] the mother usually provides for it entirely (cf. I Sam. 1.21–28). After that time she devotes herself especially to the daughter. Disposition and upbringing lead to the proverbial observation (Ezek. 16.44): 'Like mother, like daughter'. The son too is well advised to observe the teachings of his mother as well as those of his father (Prov. 1.8f.; 6.20). Lemuel, king of Massa, passes on the admonitory words of his mother especially; she had particular things to say about relations with women, the dangers and uses of alcohol, and how to treat those in need (Prov. 31.1–9). The excellent wife who can give good advice is praised not least by her sons

(Prov. 31.26, 28). The king's mother exercises a strong influence as 'mistress' (*gᵉbīrā*, I Kings 15.13) and 'adviser' (II Chron. 22.3).[6]

As a rule the father's role in upbringing grows in importance the older the child is. Normally the young man had to grow up to his father's profession. A boy's upbringing and his training for a profession lie in the same hands, whether the sons, as is usual, become farmers and cattle-breeders, or craftsmen, or priests and judges. When Gen. 4.20–22 names the 'father' of the tent dwellers, the 'father' of the zither and flute players, and the 'father' of the workers in bronze and iron, this points rather to 'family guilds', where a trade is passed on from father to son, rather than to professional corporations, as Egypt knew them. The two examples of the sons of Eli (I Sam. 2.12ff.) and Samuel (I Sam. 8.1ff.) show that in the higher professions of priest and judge particularly, a failure of upbringing could not by any means be excluded either. Eli's sons 'had no regard for Yahweh nor for that which was their duty as priests with regard to the people'; with great forks they fetched out what they wanted from the still-boiling sacrificial meat. And the sons of Samuel as judges 'turned aside after gain; they took bribes and perverted justice'. It is repeatedly stressed that David failed with his sons. True, Amnon's severe offence against Tamar[7] incensed him greatly, but he did not venture to offend his sons (II Sam. 13.21). And in spite of Adonijah's rebelliousness 'his father had never at any time displeased him by asking, "Why have you done thus and so?"' (I Kings 1.6).

The craftsman's cunning, to which a man is introduced by his father, cannot be distinguished from a man's dealings with things in the town and in the country, with animals, and above all with other men and with himself. The young person is to learn to live with good weather and bad, with the changing times and seasons, with the laws and with experiences of suffering, with life's unsolved riddle, and with his God. Most of the subjects of education of this kind are to be found in the collections of proverbs. Others are preserved in stories and in the Psalms. Here we are shown that a considerable part of education came through the accounts that fathers gave their children of their own experiences and the things that befell them (Pss. 44.1ff.; 78.3ff.; Judg. 6.13). The telling of these things could be triggered off by the questions of youth. They took fire from objects like the twelve stones set up at Gilgal on the River Jordan, which were reminders of the passing over Jordan and God's saving act at the Reed Sea (Josh. 4.20–24); or from the Passover ritual, which provoked the question 'What do you mean by this service?' (Ex. 12.24–27); or from other ordinances, where children's questions would stimulate their fathers to tell of God's most important acts in salvation history (Deut. 6.20–25;

Ex.13.14ff.). Of course instruction could be initiated on the father's side as well (Ex.13.8; Deut.4.9; Ps.71.18).

It is not by chance that 'father' comes to be the title of the teacher of wisdom also (Prov.4.1), while the teacher's disciple is called his son (Prov.13.1; 1.10, 15, and frequently elsewhere).[8] In the traditions about Elijah and Elisha, we also find the prophet addressed by his disciples (II Kings2.12) and by other people (6.21; 13.14) as 'my father'. The prophet's disciples are his 'sons' (I Kings20.35; II Kings2.3, 5, 7; 4.1, 38; 5.22; 6.1; 9.1). Job is admonished by Bildad (8.8f.):

> Inquire, I pray you, of bygone ages,
>   and consider what the fathers have found;
> for we are but of yesterday, and know nothing,
>   for our days on earth are but a shadow.

To show the consequences of an act is an essential instrument of education, as the structure of numerous proverbs shows, when they depict the connection between what a man does and what befalls him;[9] e.g., Prov.30.33:

> Pressing milk produces butter,
>   pressing the nose produces blood,
>   and pressing anger produces strife.

In this way insight is wakened. But there is foolishness, too, which is healed by physical correction (Prov.29.15):

> The rod and reproof give wisdom,
>   but a child left to himself brings shame to his mother.

Prov.23.13f.:

> Do not withhold discipline from a child;
>   if you beat him with a rod, he will not die.
> You beat him with the rod
>   but you save his life from the world of the dead.

(Cf. 13.24; 22.15.) The last thing that fathers can bestow on their children is the blessing which begs of God freedom and fruitfulness (Gen.27.27–29; 48.15f.; 9.27). Ecclus3.9:

> A father's blessing strengthens the houses of the children,
>   but a mother's curse uproots their foundations.

3. Tension

Tension between parents and children has various causes. They can be due to the 'sins of the fathers', about which the Old Testament talks with extraordinary frequency, above all from Jeremiah onwards[10] (2.5; 3.25;

11.10 and frequently). Hosea already demands that his sons should accuse their adulterous mother (2.2f.). The person who really educates Israel is Yahweh, as Hosea proclaims him, but also as Wisdom expounds him.[11] Because of the fact that parents are not the ultimate court of appeal but are subject to Yahweh's word, like their children, sons can even have the duty of disobedience towards the claims and customs of their fathers; this is brought out by Ezek. 20.18 in a saying of Yahweh's:

> I said to their children in the wilderness,
> Do not walk in the statutes of your fathers,
>   nor observe their ordinances,
>   nor defile yourselves with their idols.

The Old Testament knows the effects of the sins of the fathers on all four simultaneously living generations (Ex. 20.5f.; 34.6f.; Deut. 5.9f.). It sees the sons suffering under them, e.g., in exile (Lam. 5.7):

> Our fathers have sinned, but they are no more;
>   and we bear their iniquities.

A 'word of cynical protest'[12] goes the rounds among the people in the exilic period (Ezek. 18.2; Jer. 31.29):

> The fathers have eaten sour grapes,
>   and the children's teeth are set on edge.

But against this Ezekiel has a new message to proclaim. In the name of Yahweh he says (Ezek. 18.4): 'All life is mine; the life of the father as well as the life of the son. They are mine. Only the one that sins shall die.' According to this every generation is directly and immediately present to Yahweh in the freedom of the decision offered to it. 'The son shall not suffer for the iniquity of the father, nor the father suffer for the iniquity of the son' (18.20). The chance of a new life is offered to the new generation.

But the sins of the sons must not be forgotten either. Ezekiel hears Yahweh complain (20.21): 'The children rebelled against me.' Cf. Jer. 5.7. When we come to the individual family, the wisdom of Proverbs knows very well how a foolish son can grieve his mother and vex his father (Prov. 10.1; 15.20; 17.25; 19.13). Prov. 15.5, 32:

> A fool despises his father's instruction,
>   but he who heeds admonition is wise.
> He who throws warnings to the winds casts his life away,
>   but he who heeds admonition gains understanding.

Deuteronomy deals with an extreme case (Deut. 21.18–21): a son is so stubborn that he will listen neither to his father nor to his mother and does not cease his recalcitrance even after repeated rebukes. In this dispute the parents have no legal power beyond that of rebuke. The elders, as the local judges, have to take up the matter and both parents must put forward their case jointly. The power of disposal is taken from the parents. Their extremity and that of their son belongs to the 'evil' which affects 'all Israel' (v. 21).

Extreme tensions can therefore arise, both from the parents' side and from that of the children. The prophet Malachi expects the real end of this tension only from the return of the prophet Elijah, God's plenipotentiary (Mal. 4.6):[13] 'He will turn the hearts of fathers to their children and the hearts of children to their fathers, lest I come and smite the land with a curse.' Thinking of the presence of Christ in his word, the epistle to the Colossians already seeks to overcome the antagonism from both sides (3.20f.): 'Children, obey your parents in everything, for this pleases the Lord. Fathers, do not provoke your children, lest they become discouraged.' Such phraseology – 'in the Lord' – presupposes life which has been completely renewed out of gratitude for the forgiveness that has been experienced.

4. *Responsibility*

The Old Testament already points to the responsibility of the generations for one another in the overcoming of tension. The father's business is not only to answer his children's questions, but above all to offer a certain refuge in which they can, as a matter of course, find everything that they need for a secure life (Prov. 14.26):

> The man who fears Yahweh has strong confidence,
> and his children will have a refuge.

Orphans are therefore especially recommended to the protection of the community (Deut. 14.29; Job 31.17; Prov. 23.10). A foolish father cannot offer his sons any help either (Job 5.4). In the family the father is the chief person and the one who is responsible; that is why in Hebrew the family is called 'the father's house' (*bēt 'āb*) (Ex. 12.3; I Chron. 7.2). The father's authority has weight for his son (Mal. 1.6).

Such authority is not a matter of course for everyone at all times. The positive formulation of the commandment to honour parents in the Decalogue can be linked with the parents' task to tell of Yahweh's saving acts. Unlike the sabbath commandment, this commandment is not given a reason; it is furnished with a promise, which offers the prospect of long enjoyment of the land given by Yahweh (Ex. 20.12), to which Deut. 5.16 adds prosperity in that land. According to this, the behaviour which is enjoined towards parents is to take them seriously (*kabbēd*). In the Law of

Holiness (Lev. 19.3) there is a shorter version. It too can be linked with parental teaching in connection with the services of the sanctuary, since it stands at the head of a short series which further deals with the observance of the sabbath, and with the prohibition of strange gods and idols. Here obedience (*yr'*) is enjoined on the children. In this connection it is especially noticeable that the mother is mentioned *before* the father, not merely *beside* him, as in all the forms of the commandment about parents.

The sentences about capital offences in the Book of the Covenant make an archaic impression when they apply the death penalty (Ex. 21.15, 17) to anyone who strikes his father or mother, or in any other way treats them contemptuously, or as if they were accursed (*qallēl*). For anyone who despises his parents burdens himself with blood guiltiness (Lev. 20.9). In the dodecalogue of curses proclaimed at Shechem (Deut. 27.16) such a person is himself cursed. Apparently in these latter cases it is not only young people who are addressed, but grown-up children particularly, who live together in the family group together with their parents, who are now getting to the stage of needing help.

The wisdom of Proverbs shows more clearly how concrete problems of the care of the old[14] have to be solved through a person's behaviour to his parents (Prov. 23.22, 24f.):

> Hearken to your father who begot you,
>> and do not despise your mother because she is old.
> The father of the righteous can greatly rejoice;
>> he who begets a wise man will be glad in him.
> Let your father and mother be glad in you,
>> let her who bore you rejoice.

When parents get old, children are no longer asked first of all whether they are obedient or disobedient; the question is whether they are considerate towards their parents, or despise them, whether they are a joy or a sorrow to them (Prov. 10.1; 15.20):

> A wise son makes a glad father,
>> but a foolish son is a sorrow to his mother.

The proverbs face the fact that the old can become a burden. Against the wish to inherit prematurely, Prov. 19.26 says:

> He who does violence to his father and chases away his mother
>> is a shameful son who brings reproach.

More frequent is the temptation not to respect parents' property (Prov. 28.24):

> He who robs his father or his mother and says,
> 'That is not transgression',
> is the companion of a man who destroys.

Even a contemptuous glance thrown at the parents brings disaster to the children (Prov.30.17):

> The eye that mocks a father
> and scorns a mother when she is old
> will be picked out by the ravens at the brook
> and eaten by the young eagles.

The widow needs very special protection, as do children without any parents. The prophets and Deuteronomy plead emphatically on their behalf (cf. for example Ex.22.21; Deut.16.11; 27.19; Isa.1.17; Jer.7.6; Ezek.22.7; Zech.7.10). Life has become unbearable when

> the son treats the father with contempt, the daughter rises up against her mother, the daughter-in-law against her mother-in-law; and a man's enemies are the men of his own house (Micah 7.6).

These chaotic difficulties seem inescapable where men – whether the older or the younger generation – see themselves as the final court of appeal and put themselves in the place of God, instead of living with the goodness of his word. With the entry of Jesus Christ into human history and the offer of unconditional reconciliation which it means, every dissension is to be seen as at most the penultimate phase in the relationship of the generations; and it is as such that it should be treated.

XXI

Brothers, Friends and Enemies[1]

It is not only the different generations which have duties to one another and difficulties with one another; relationships between people of the same generation also have to be resolved. How does brother behave to brother (*'āḥ*) and sister (*'āḥōt*), how does a man behave to his neighbour and companion (*rēaʿ*),[2] to his friend (*'ōhēb*) and to his enemy (*'ōyēb*)? How, in fact, does the Old Testament view man as fellow-man?

1. *Brothers by blood*
Brothers by blood are defined in the story of Joseph as 'the sons of one man' (Gen. 42.13) or as 'sons of the same father' (v. 32). Deuteronomy, which expands the concept of brother in general, defines the brother by blood as 'the son of your mother' (13.6). Hate between brothers, based on jealousy, is one of the themes of the Joseph story (Gen. 37.3–11) and the narrative shows how such enmities can be led in the direction of forgiveness, on the basis of God's providence (50.15–21). Deuteronomy sees that the danger of being led to follow strange gods is greatest when it comes from the circle of a man's nearest relatives (Deut. 13.6–11). Brother and sister, like father and mother and son and daughter, belong to the group of a person's closest relatives. Consequently even a priest is allowed to 'defile himself' by preparing their bodies for burial (Lev. 21.2f.).[3]

In special circumstances (especially on the premature death of the father) forms of fratriarchy develop.[4] These show themselves in the naming of the brothers and sisters after their brother instead of after their father (e.g., Gen. 4.22; 36.22; I Chron. 24.25), but also in the role which Laban plays in marrying off his sister Rebecca in Gen. 24.29ff. (their father Bethuel is only named in conjunction with Laban in v. 50, and this is probably a secondary reference), and (less unambiguously) in Gen. 34.11f. in Shechem's negotiations over Dinah with her father and brothers. Isaac makes Jacob 'lord' over his brothers (Gen. 27.29; cf. v. 40 and 49.8). I Chron. 26.10 also shows that the father can appoint someone other than the first-born to be the head (*rōʾš*) of the family (see p. 214 below), especially when the first-born has died. Generally speaking, traces of fratriarchy have been incorporated into the patriarchy in the Old Testament.

The younger brothers' duty towards the older one is shown in the regulations about the levirate marriage[5] in Deut. 25.5–10. According to these, a widow without a son is to marry her brother or her brother-in-law (Hebr. *yābām*, Lat. *levir*=husband's brother). The first-born of this marriage will bear the name of the brother who has died. The story of Tamar, Judah's daughter-in-law (Gen. 38), offers us insight into the actual practice. According to this, the obligation is passed on to the next brother-in-law, if the marriage with the first brother-in-law also remains childless (cf. Matt. 22.24–27). Ruth, who had no brother-in-law left on the death of her husband, is married to their nearest relative (Ruth 1.11f.; 2.30; 3.12; 4.4f., 10, 17). In all other cases sexual intercourse with a sister-in-law is as strictly forbidden for a man (Lev. 18.16; 20.21) as intercourse with his own sister (Deut. 27.22; Lev. 18.9; 20.17).

In the law of inheritance the first-born brother is distinguished by being given the double share (Deut. 21.17). Otherwise brothers are not allowed to be treated differently from one another, even if the father gives one of his wives preference over the others (Deut. 21.15f.). In early times daughters only inherit if they have no brothers (Num. 27.1–8). If a man dies without children, then his brothers inherit (v. 9). If he has no brothers either, his father's brothers succeed, and after that other blood relations (vv. 10f.). That Job's daughters inherit as well as their brothers may perhaps reflect later law (Job 42.15).[6] According to Prov. 17.2 even a slave gifted with wisdom is counted among his master's sons in the inheritance and is included in the groups of brothers:

A slave who deals wisely will rule over a son who acts shamefully, and will share the inheritance as one of the brothers.

Thus it becomes evident even in the closest family circle that there are bonds which are stronger than brotherhood in the physical sense and more than blood relationship.[7]

2. *The brotherhood of God's people*

Israel learnt to interpret itself as being a brotherhood of God's people. It is true that in the ancient East the kings of different nations also addressed one another as 'brother' if they were allies – as Hiram, king of Tyre, did King Solomon (I Kings 9.13); and pacts between foreign states were called 'covenants of brotherhood' (Amos 1.9).[8] Israel viewed the Edomites in particular as a brother people (Num. 20.14; Deut. 2.4, 8; 23.8; Obad. 12), holding that the fathers of the tribes on both sides, Jacob and Esau, belonged together, since they were the sons of Isaac and hence brothers (Gen. 27f.). But the tribes of Israel knew that as Yahweh's people they were especially closely bound together, above all on the basis of their common salvation history and Yahweh's proclamation of his will (Josh. 24). As 'Israel's sons' they were a nation of brothers who traced their descent to twelve brothers as the fathers of their tribes (Gen. 29f.).[9] The word 'brotherhood' (*'aḥ*ᵃ*wā*) appears on one single occasion in the Old Testament (Zech. 11.14), for the threatened alliance of the two divided states of Judah and Israel.

Israel's basic understanding of itself as a nation of brothers had results for the mutual relationships of its individual members. The early collections of laws already provide evidence for this. But it is Deuteronomy that first teaches, superlatively and also with terminological precision, how an Israelite is to behave as brother of his fellows. It is noticeable that Deuteronomy does not take over older regulations from the Book of the Covenant without in each case expressly calling the fellow-Israel involved 'brother'.[10] Every creditor should see his debtor as his[11] brother and accordingly grant him remission of his debt in the seventh year (15.1ff.). With regard to the poor, the passage says: 'You shall not harden your heart or shut your hand against your poor brother' (v. 7).

The ancient prohibition of usury, which in the Book of the Covenant is formulated for the benefit of the poor, is enforced with a reference to the brotherhood of all who are fellow-countrymen (cf. Deut. 23.20f. with Ex. 22.24). This regulation appears in other strata of the Old Testament as well and sets Israel apart from its neighbours, who were familiar with sometimes very high rates of interest, up to a quarter or a third of the loan.[12] Among God's people, on the other hand, no one should enrich himself through another's need. Interest may only be charged to foreigners. What is particularly noteworthy, and had far-reaching consequences, is that even the people on the very outskirts of early Israelite society are included in this brotherhood. Thus Deuteronomy talks of slaves on the one hand, and on the other of the king as a brother among brothers. The slave law does not merely grant an empty title to the most dependent members of society; it enjoins truly brotherly behaviour (15.12–18).[13] On the other hand the king is not to 'lift up his heart above his brethren' (17.20).[14] From the king down to the slave 'all Israel' lives on the common 'heritage' of the land which Yahweh has given her (Deut. 12.9; 15.4; 19.10 and frequently elsewhere).[15] That is why one man is the other man's brother. The relationship founded on Yahweh takes precedence over physical brotherhood (Deut. 13.7ff.; cf. Ex. 32.29).

3. *Neighbourly love*

Other strata of the Old Testament draw our attention to brotherhood as a universal human phenomenon. The Yahwist focuses sharply on this in the story of Cain and Abel in Gen.4.1–16, where the word 'brother' is a *leitmotif* that occurs seven times[16] (vv.2, 8a, b, 9a, b, 10, 11). The universal problem of human co-existence is illustrated by the sons of the same mother who pass their lives in the two totally different occupations of farmer and sheep-breeder, and therefore also belong to two different social structures. The one who feels at a disadvantage becomes his brother's arch-enemy and murderer. He has to face the question of where his brother is; but he wards it off with the counter question, whether he is his brother's keeper. So he is sent away from the cultivated land from which his brother's blood cries aloud – sent away to a wandering life. But even as the murderer of his brother he is still shielded against uncontrolled vendetta by God's protective mark. The general human theme of the enemy brothers is continued through the stories of the patriarchs, acquiring new, rich variants in the stories of Esau and Jacob (Gen.27ff.) and in Joseph and his brothers (Gen.37.39ff.). Genesis makes it strikingly evident that morally Israel is no better than the rest of the world.

But it experiences a word that leads it further, and that sets up ripples extending beyond its own brothers. Lev.19.17f. runs:

> You shall not hate your brother in your heart. You can reason with your neighbour, but you shall not lay any transgression to his charge.[17] You shall not take vengeance or bear any grudge against the sons of your own people, but you shall love your neighbour as yourself: I am Yahweh.

And v.34 supplements:

> The stranger who sojourns with you shall be to you as the native among you, and you shall love him as yourself; for you were strangers in the land of Egypt: I am Yahweh your God.

Each of these sentences struggles with the Cain in every man, with Jacob and with Esau, with Joseph and with his brothers, with every budding hate, with every urge towards accusation, revenge or even the bearing of a grudge. The words thrust forward to the command to love one's neighbour which, in the form in which we have it here, had no parallel among Israel's neighbours[18] and which takes on central significance in the New Testament. Even here it already expressly includes, in a postscript, the non-Israelite, who lives as a protected citizen in Israel.[19] The reason is solely that Yahweh has manifested himself to Israel as the holy and gracious one, above all to its condition as stranger in Egypt.

In the culminating sentence:

You shall love your neighbour as yourself,

is the final word, *kāmōkā*, rightly translated? Modern Jewish interpretation would have liked to render it: '(You should love your neighbour), he is like you.'[20] But repeated studies have shown that the sentence does not mean to compare the stranger with the person addressed; it wants to compare love of one's neighbour with love of oneself.[21] Here self-love is not something as it were enjoined; it simply serves as a 'paraphrase of the measure of love';[22] recollection of a man's own wishes becomes the spur towards loving action towards the other, and thereby (in remembrance of Yahweh's act on behalf of Israel) to the overcoming of self-love.[23] Perhaps this 'as yourself' is contrary to self-love as a 'sinister power', 'as a dangerous temptation to faithlessness towards Yahweh'.[24] At least here all legalized regulation of the relations between man and man is surmounted and a personal brotherhood with near and far is established.

Besides the unique command to love one's neighbour in the Law of Holiness, we find in the sphere of proverbial wisdom a concrete struggle with the daily problems of living together. Among the kinds of behaviour that Yahweh hates is 'to sow discord among brothers' (Prov. 6.19), who have to live peaceably together in kinship if their life is to be successful under Yahweh's blessing (Ps. 133). But the impoverished brother is easily cast off (Prov. 19.7):

All a poor man's brothers hate him;
how much more do his friends go far from him!

The proverb still presupposes that brothers are nearer to a man than his other countrymen. But Prov. 27.10b takes a different view:

Better is a neighbour who is near
than a brother who is far away.

But even when the two are equally near, says Prov. 18.24b,

There is a friend who sticks closer than a brother.

Prov. 17.17 distinguishes more precisely:

A friend loves at all times,
but a brother is born for adversity.

Wisdom advises walking carefully, even with one's best friend and closest neighbour (Prov. 25.17):

Let your foot be seldom in your neighbour's house,
lest he become weary of you and hate you.

Neighbourliness and friendship can mean far more than physical brotherhood. The Old Testament paints the most beautiful picture on this theme in the friendship between David and Jonathan. One of them becomes as dear to the other 'as his own self' (I Sam. 18.1). They can weep together and be silent for one another, but in what they say Yahweh stands as witness between the two (I Sam. 20.41f.). At the end David laments the death of his friend (II Sam. 1.26):

> I am distressed for you, my brother Jonathan;
> > very pleasant have you been to me;
> your love to me was wonderful,
> > passing the love of women.

This is what perfect human brotherhood is like among men who are not sons of the same father.

4. *Love of one's enemy*

Does the Old Testament reach beyond the love of brother, neighbour and friend to love of one's enemy? Two texts, at least, deserve attention in this connection. The ancient Book of the Covenant already commands (Ex. 23.4f.):

> If you meet your enemy's ox or his ass going astray, you shall bring it back to him. If you see the ass of one who hates you lying under its burden, you shall refrain from leaving him with it, you must help him to lift it up.[25]

The man who is poor and helpless is the subject of the whole passage, and here it is the beast in need of help. But when the beast is in danger, its owner too is threatened with a considerable loss. The law of God wants every Israelite to be guided in what he does by the animal's need, and that this should be more important to him than the enmity of its owner. Under the misfortune threatening that owner, he should be reconciled to him. In practical ways such as this this Book of the Covenant overcomes hate and thoughts of revenge.

Prov. 25.21f. leads us one step further. Here the enemy himself is in need and requires direct help:

> If your enemy is hungry, give him bread to eat; and if he is thirsty, give him water to drink; for you will heap coals of fire on his head, and Yahweh will reward you.

Here the enemy's emergency becomes the chance to overcome enmity. It emerges from Egyptian texts that fiery coals really were heaped on a man's head in an atonement ritual, as a sign of shame and remorse on the part of someone who has been guilty of an offence.[26] Thus the wise man who begins to practise love of his enemy in his misfortune may expect that the man who hates him will also be sorry for the enmity, and that he will be ready for reconciliation. He can hope that Yahweh will 'complete' (*šlm* piel) the act for him.[27] Thus Paul can pick up the Old Testament word of wisdom exactly (Rom 12.17–21).

The Old Testament shows both clearly and forcibly the dissensions existing between men. Just as plainly, it also sees that men lose sight of one another and destroy themselves if they do not progress along the road that leads to the overcoming of hate; after all, Israel's God has begun the process and has promised its consummation. Only along this path – the path which God has chosen – will man in the confusion of his feelings and his encounters avoid losing his way. For man is the being who is called to brotherhood.

XXII

Masters and Slaves[1]

The Old Testament is alive to the full acrimony of the antithesis between ruler and ruled, exploiter and exploited. The rich, and especially kings, counted as being the owners, with complete power over their subordinates. Dependents, on the other hand, and above all slaves, often had practically the status of property; they counted as pure cash (Ex. 21.21) and they could be transferred by will at a man's death, like real estate (Lev. 25.46).

Israel lived in this antithesis as it lived in the air of its environment. Yet even in the early Old Testament traditions it is an antithesis that meets with severe criticism. This is heightened in classical prophecy and is carried further to a fundamental rethinking of the question. One could call it a revolution in the relations between masters and slaves. This belongs to the presuppositions of New Testament Christology and anthropology. Whenever it is rightly heard, it is bound to produce a fermenting unrest in human history, until its goal is reached. We shall have to enquire of the Old Testament what the motives, forms and aims of this change of attitude were.

This also brings us to the anthropological problem of man's liberty among men. The late book of Ecclesiastes formulates it precisely (8.9): 'All this I observed while applying my mind to all that is done under the sun, when man lords it over man (*šalaṭ hā'ādām be'ādām*) to his hurt.' When we were considering the Priestly document's doctrine of man, we saw that such a lordship of man over man was for God's image out of the question.[2] The two diametrically opposite institutions of monarchy and slavery will serve as examples to show us how this lordship none the less came into existence and how it was overcome.

1. Critique of the monarchy

(a) The empires of the ancient East traced their beginnings back to a monarchy which descended from heaven and which was begotten in the divine pantheon. For Israel, on the other hand, the monarchy as a primal mythical and cosmic phenomenon was completely alien. Those of Israel's neighbours which were related to her sociologically and ethnically – the Edomites, the Moabites, the Ammonites and the Aramaeans – introduced the monarchy long before Israel itself. The ancient Canaanite city states and the Philistines, who had immigrated from beyond the Mediterranean, had had a dynastic constitution from time immemorial. Early Israel, however, in its first centuries knew the monarchy at most as a temptation.

This is shown in exemplary fashion by the fable of Jotham in Judg. 9.8–15. This is a very old anti-monarchical document, which in its present literary context belongs to the first attempt at establishing the monarchy in Israel, which was made by Abimelech in Shechem.[3] This political satire is unique of its kind:

> The trees once went forth to anoint a king over them; and they said to the olive tree, 'Reign over us'. But the olive tree said to them, 'Shall I leave my fatness, by which gods and men are honoured, and go to sway over the trees?' And the trees said to the fig tree, 'Come you, and reign over us.' But the fig tree said to them, 'Shall I leave my sweetness and my good fruit, and go to sway over the trees?' And the trees said to the vine, 'Come you, and reign over us.' But the vine said to them, 'Shall I leave my wine which cheers gods and men, and go to sway over the trees?' Then all the trees said to the bramble, 'Come you, and reign over us.' And the bramble said to the trees, 'If in good faith you are anointing me king over you, then come and take refuge in my shade; but if not, let fire come out of the bramble and devour the cedars of Lebanon.'

This fable exposes the monarchy to resounding laughter. What irony, for the bramble to praise its shade and at the same time to threaten the cedars, which give the finest shade of all! Since it has little to offer itself, the bramble wants to destroy those who have so much to give. According to this, anyone who wants to be king is 'only a scoundrel, only someone who really has nothing to contribute to the welfare of the whole'.[4] The theme of the criticism is the monarchy's lust for power, which destroys the best in life; the form the criticism takes is the satire; and its aim is to prevent the establishment of the monarchy, so that the forces which are of benefit to life can develop freely.

Here the specific starting point of early Israelite history has its quite concrete effect. Israel derives its history, not from any mythically celebrated and politically tested monarchy, but from a group of slaves who had been liberated from Egypt. They are indebted for this deliverance to Yahweh; but it is significant that even for him the title of king is not typical in the early period.[5] Pre-eminently and as a general rule Yahweh is understood as being the liberator from the Egyptian captivity. The most frequent and most important confessional statement is that he has led Israel out of Egypt.[6] If only because Yahweh as liberator belongs from the outset to the enslaved, he cannot really be compared with an ancient oriental potentate. It is therefore a fact well worth noting that the polemic against the monarchy in Israel is older than the institution of the monarchy itself and that this specific difference from her neighbours is indissolubly bound up with her faith in Yahweh.[7]

(*b*) The monarchy only found an entry into Israel under Saul and David, and its original purpose was to ward off the ever-increasing danger from the Philistines. But Saul's reign already came up against criticism (I Sam. 10.27; 13.7–15), as did David's in a different way (II Sam. 12.1ff.; 15.1ff.; 24.1ff.),[8] and finally (and to an extreme degree) Solomon's. As early as the second generation, David's dynasty ran into a crisis which led to the break up of the greater kingdom.

The revolt was triggered off by the severe forced labour which Solomon imposed on the men belonging to the house of Joseph (I Kings 11.26ff.). The revolt was at first suppressed by threatening its leader, Jeroboam, and through Jeroboam's subsequent flight into Egypt. But after Solomon's death, Rehoboam did not follow the advice of the old men, who advised him to lighten the forced labour; in the words of the account in I Kings 12.7 they even recommended him to 'be an *'ebed* (servant) to this people and serve them, and agree to their demands' (cf. Mark 10.43f.). But Rehoboam preferred to listen to his crude contemporaries, declaring 'My little one is thicker than my father's loins . . . I will add to your yoke. My father chastised you with whips, but I will chastise you with scorpions' (I Kings 12.10f.).[9] To this the people in Shechem answered rebelliously (v. 16):

> What portion have we in David?
> To your tents, O Israel!

Then Jeroboam, who had returned from Egypt, was raised to be anti-king over the ten tribes, as the representative of those doing forced labour. Rehoboam only retained Judah. Thus the dominion of the Davidic kings was decimated simply because of the enslaving of Israel's free men. David's empire broke up because the king did not respect the freedom of Israel's people.

(*c*) But the monarchy of the Northern Kingdom was not spared criticism either, and the criticism grew the more that the monarchy assimilated itself to the kingly laws of its neighbours. Through his marriage with the

Phoenician princess Jezebel, King Ahab was in a position of special temptation. His claims cut across the ancient Israelite laws governing land tenure.[10] According to I Kings 21, Naboth's vineyard borders on the palace grounds belonging to the king's winter residence at Jezreel. The king wants to acquire the vineyard for a vegetable garden, in return for suitable compensation. But Naboth replies (v. 3): 'Yahweh forbid that I should give you the inheritance of my fathers.' The statement is a splendid piece of evidence for an Israelite's farmer's independence of the king. This freedom is based on the fact that Yahweh had given the land to the patriarchs. The king, well aware of Israel's essential character, gives way in impotent rage. But his wife, who has been brought up as a Phoenician princess, applies absolutist Canaanite standards and meets Ahab ironically (v. 7) with: 'Do you now govern Israel?' She understands how to push Naboth aside as a blasphemer against God and the king. But she is immediately challenged by the prophet Elijah's word of judgment. He proclaims the end of the dynasty. The monarchy will be measured against the measure of freedom which it allows those who have been liberated by Yahweh. From this time on the monarchy is constantly accompanied by the censure of Yahweh's prophets, the most acute criticism of the Northern Kingdom coming from Amos. But in his vigorous attacks on the oppressor, and his threats of Yahweh's judgment (e.g., 2.6–8; 4.1; 5.11f.), neither Amos nor any other of the prophets calls the oppressed to rebellion. The guilty are always attacked directly (cf. I Cor. 7.20–24).

(*d*) From the history of the Davidic dynasty we need only mention one example: the prophetic saying which Jeremiah directs against King Jehoiakim (22.13–19):

> Woe to him who builds his house by unrighteousness; who makes his neighbour serve him for nothing . . . Your father upheld the cause of the poor and needy; Is not this to know me? But you have eyes and heart only for your dishonest gain.

For a king to strive for his own gain and, out of a self-assured lust for pleasure, to keep wages back from the worker instead of helping the oppressed and needy to find freedom: this is a misunderstanding of what is in Yahweh's eyes the only legitimate kingly office in Israel. It contradicts Yahweh's justice, which protects the freedom of all and wants to lead men out of every form of slavery. That is why Jeremiah reminds King Jehoiakim of the example set by his father Josiah. In the form of an indictment, and with the threat of a dishonourable burial for the exploiter (vv. 18f.), Jeremiah proclaims the law of God anew. Anyone who robs his fellow man of his freedom, anyone who cheats him of his just dues and torments him, even if he be the king himself, has robbed himself of his own future and his own honour.[11]

(*e*) From the prophetic criticism of the monarchy, there arises among the theologians of the Deuteronomic reform a picture which finds its literary form in the 'law of the king' in Deut. 17.14–20. First of all the king is warned to keep his chariot forces small and not to 'cause the people to return to Egypt' (v. 16); there was apparently fear that Yahweh's deliverance from Egypt might be revoked through political dependence on Egypt (Isa. 30.1ff.), or even that Israelite soldiers might be sent to Egypt in exchange for teams of chariot horses (cf. I Kings 10.26–29).[12] In the second place the king is forbidden to keep a large harem (v. 17a); Solomon is a prime example of the way in which the sovereign can be led away from Yahweh through numerous women (I Kings 11.1–13). Finally, the king is not to increase the royal treasure (v. 17b). The notion behind this is undoubtedly the heavy 'social burdens which an exaggerated display of splendour at the king's court means for the people'.[13] According to this, the very things on which the power and prestige of an oriental potentate are founded are not to interest the Israelite king at all.

Instead he is to turn his attention to the study of the Torah, reading in it 'all the days of his life' (v. 19a). Here two things are particularly deserving of notice. First, the king is to have a second copy of the Torah made for this daily study; the original document is, and remains, in the hand of the Levitical priests, who are in this respect above him (v. 18). Secondly, the purpose of the study of the Torah is the king's own way of life (v. 19b) and not, as might perhaps be expected, the royal administration of justice in Israel.

The meaning of these instructions only becomes completely understandable when we remember how the monarchy is viewed in the context of the laws about the administrative powers.[14] Deut. 16.18–18.22 can be interpreted as 'the coherent draft of a constitution', and in that connection it is interesting that the different offices are not developed from the starting point of the kingly functions; on the contrary, typical royal tasks (cf. I Sam. 8.20) are taken away from the king: the administration of the law is given over to the 'judge' belonging to the group of the Levitical priests (17.8–13; 16.18–20), and the conduct of war is assigned to the militia, together with the priests (20.1ff.). The prophets, as Moses' successors, are responsible for the living interpretation of the Torah (18.15ff.).

But what, then, is left over for the king? He is simply to be the model

Israelite (17.19b), the 'representative' of the people. He is chosen 'from among his brethren' (v. 15) and his heart 'may not be lifted up above his brethren' (v. 20). The real ruler in Israel is Yahweh, through his Torah; the priests protect it, the prophets interpret it, and the judges apply it. But the king, as brother among brothers, is to be the pattern Israelite, who lives according to Yahweh's will. The rule of the Torah as it has been written down is secured by the division of powers indicated above. The monarchy is given completely different functions through a diminution of the normal powers assigned to the ruler and through the indirect elevation of his fellow-countrymen to be his brothers. A truly revolutionary view of the monarchy!

(*f*) The transformation of the image of kingship in Israel is shown from yet another side. In the intercession for the king in Ps. 72 (on the day of his accession?) high expectations are expressed. These certainly include hopes for world-wide fullness of blessing under his rule, but what is especially characteristic is the way in which the general demand for righteousness is brought to a quite definite point. The king's pre-eminent task appears to be care for all the oppressed (vv. 2–4).

> May he defend the cause of the poor of the people,
>   give deliverance to the children of the needy,
>   and crush the oppressor (v. 4).

> May he deliver the needy when he calls,
>   the poor and him who has no helper.
> May he take upon himself the cause of the weak and needy
>   and save the lives of the needy.
> From oppression and violence may he redeem their life;
>   may their blood be precious in his sight (vv. 12–14).

The king, who is to administer Yahweh's law in Israel (v. 1), is judged precisely by whether he intervenes on behalf of those who are most in need of help. Either the king is the king of the weakest, or he is no true king in Israel.

(*g*) A final group of texts testifies to the disturbance which the Old Testament documents bring into established conditions of rule. These are the Servant Songs in Deutero-Isaiah. In these the true ruler shows himself as the one who offers his back to the smiters and his cheeks to those who pull out the beard (50.6), one who is despised, rejected by men, a man of sorrows, acquainted with grief (53.3), seized upon by oppression and judgment, with no one to care about his case (53.8), one who is given a grave among criminals (v. 9). He bears these sorrows for others (53.4f.):

> For our salvation he was chastised.
> His wounds make us whole.

This man, therefore, is not only a brother among brothers, like the king of Deut. 17, nor, like the king of Ps. 72, is he simply on the side of all the oppressed; he exchanges roles; he takes the other's place. He bears the punishment and misery, and they go free. But in this very way he too, the one who is utterly humiliated, whom nobody counted (v. 3), becomes the one before whom at the end the kings of the earth shall shut their mouths (52.15). The last song of the suffering Servant begins:

> Behold, my servant shall prosper (52.13).

Why? It is not an empty paradox that is being taught here: the deeply reviled servant is the true lord. The paradox is actually fulfilled. He is the one whose ear Yahweh has opened, who did not turn away rebelliously from the consequences of his will (50.5), who did not break the bruised reed and did not quench the dimly burning wick. In this way he faithfully exercised Yahweh's law of mercy (42.3), and was therefore exposed to shame and spitting (50.6). The one who as servant did not seek his own rights, God has made lord; and it is lord that he will prove him to be. Who could avoid turning from these Servant Songs to Phil. 2.5–11? Here the explicit and implicit criticism of the monarchy in the Old Testament reached its unsurpassable peak.

Perhaps one should add how the lonely, almost despairing Preacher of remotely comparable wisdom transfers it into everyday life (Eccles. 10.4):

> If the anger of the ruler rises against you,
>   do not leave your place,
>   for deference will make amends
>   for great offences.

The quiet victory over the rage of the powerful springs from knowledge of the abysmal perverseness of the way in which power is held (Eccles. 10.5–7):

> This is an error which I have seen under the sun,
>   as it were an error proceeding from the ruler.
> Folly is set in many high places,
>   and the rich sit in a low place.
> I have seen slaves on horses,
>   and princes walking on foot like slaves.

In the criticism of the monarchy, faith in the God of Israel provokes an enormously wide range of reflection.

2. *Critique of the law of slavery*

As a control, we must now examine, on the basis of some important examples, the way in which the Old Testament comes to terms with the institution of slavery. Slavery too was part of the social structure of the Near East in ancient times. It had two roots, basically speaking: great numbers of slaves were brought in as prisoners of war; and in addition there was a smaller number who, in their own country, got into debt and were therefore forced to sell their bodies, lives and working capacity into a debtor's slavery. Lev. 25.6 lists four types of dependent workers: the male slave (*'ebed*), the female slave (*'āmā*), the hired labourer (*śākīr*) and the foreign worker or stranger (*tōšāb*) (EVV sojourner). In addition we must mention a second type of female slave, the *šipḥā* or virgin bondmaid, who was primarily assigned to the service of mistress of the house,[15] whereas the *'āmā* belonged to her master.

(*a*) The slave law in Ex. 21.2–6 has in mind the slave who has been forced to sell himself out of economic necessity. After six years his debt is to count as having been paid off. He is then to be freed (v. 2). The Code of Hammurabi §117 provides for the slave's release after only three years.[16] If the slave came as a married man, his wife is released with him (v. 3). If his master gave him a wife from the group of slaves born in the house, and if the two have children, the woman remains in the house, with her children (v. 4; the children stay with the mother). The difference between the slave and a piece of the master's property only becomes clear in the case discussed in vv. 5f., where a slave declares:

> I love my master, my wife, and my children;
> I will not go out free.

On the strength of this his master can bore through his ear at the doorpost of the house, thus, by means of this archaic legal act, sealing an agreement that the slave is to remain permanently in the house. The concept of what to be free means and the idea of love envisaged in v. 5 herald the break-through of the human factor into the idea of the 'possession of property'.

(*b*) This becomes still clearer in the regulations about injuries to slaves. Ex. 21.20f. says:

> When a man strikes his slave, male or female, with a rod and the slave dies under his hand, he shall be punished (*nāqōm yinnāqēm*; Sam. *mōt yūmat*). But if the slave survives a day or two, he is not to be punished; for the slave is his own property (*ki kaspō hū'*).

Both cases are dealing with blows inflicted with a stick. The stick pre-supposes that the master's intention in the first place was to discipline the slave, not to kill him. It is only when death takes place at once that it is certain that the master went too far; then either murder or manslaughter is presumed. The death of the person responsible for the slave's death is then demanded. Probably the juridical assembly had to carry out the punishment. According to this, the slave's life is fundamentally speaking no less valuable than the life of his master. If the slave only dies later, the intention to kill is no longer assumed; the master bears the damage, since he has contributed to the loss of his own capital (*kaspō*). Here the old idea of the law of property is force.

In Ex. 21.26f. it is different: 'When a man strikes the eye of his slave, male or female, and destroys it, he shall let the slave go free for the eye's sake.' The same is true even if he only knocks out a tooth. Here the law of property has receded entirely behind the law governing personal rights. The master's incapacity for dealing humanely with a slave may have motivated the regulation that the man was to be freed. Here the Book of the Covenant goes decisively further in the slave's interests than the Code of Hammurabi. There, according to § 199, a master has to pay his slave half of his value when he breaks a bone or puts out an eye. There is no talk of setting free, let alone that the slave should be freed in return even for a knocked-out tooth. In Israel the master's rights of possession over a slave find their clear limits where the slave is physically injured.

(*c*) Humanity is considered even more strongly in the law about the female slave in Ex. 21.7–11. Release after six years, as in the case of the male slave, is not fundamentally envisaged (v. 7). Does she count more as permanent property, or is the personal bond and obligation considered to be stronger in her case? The second explanation is the more probable. For v. 8 goes on to take the case where a master has grown tired of a woman slave. Here the first possibility is that her kindred or clan should be allowed to buy her freedom; she may not be sold to foreigners; here the slave as person is apparently paramount. An alternative, which appears in v. 9, is to give her to his son; in this case the former slave must be treated according to the law that applies to daughters. Verse 10 further presupposes that the slave was at first the only one in the household. For the case is considered in which the master takes another slave in addition. In this event he must curtail neither his first slave's food, nor her clothing, nor her marital rights. If he cannot afford what is necessary for two slaves, the first one is to be allowed to go free without paying any compensation. All in all, therefore, it is by no means a loveless relationship that is presupposed; it is a positively intimate one, full of solicitous concern. It is evidently for this reason that the woman slave is not in principle to be freed after six years. The man and wife relationship is thought of primarily as a lasting one, even with the slave. If the relationship comes to an end, then it always ends in freedom. The regulations which govern the exceptions all have the interests of the slave in mind, not those of her master.

(*d*) Deuteronomy brings quite new ideas into play for slavery, just as it does for the monarchy. Deut. 15.12–18 speaks of 'your brother'[17] and decrees that after six years

> you shall not let him go empty handed; you shall furnish him liberally out of your flock, out of your threshing floor, and out of your wine press; as Yahweh your God has blessed you, you shall give to him (vv. 13f.).

According to this passage the relationship to the slave is not to be governed by the compulsions of a law, but in the light of the gifts that the slave's master has received from God. In addition two facts are impressed on the owner, so that the freeing of the slave who works for him does not appear as injustly harsh (v. 18a): first, he should remember that he himself was a slave in the land of Egypt and that Yahweh gave him freedom (v. 15b); thus solidarity with his fathers also constitutes full solidarity with the slave. Secondly, a clear reckoning is presented: six years' service as slave are the equivalent of the wages of a hired labourer (v. 18a).[18] Deuteronomy adds once more (v. 18b):

> So Yahweh your God will bless you in all that you do.

In this way the preacher strives not only for rigid obedience but for a definite decision of conscience and an inward assent springing from gratitude and a sense of the bond existing between master and slave before Yahweh.

We may remind ourselves here of the Deuteronomic version of the sabbath commandment.[19] It stresses repeatedly that above all slaves of both sexes must have rest. The reason is once again the remembrance of Israel's slavery in Egypt (5.14f.). The actual wording stresses that

> your manservant and your maidservant may rest as well as you (*lᵉmaʿan yānūaḥ ʿabdᵉkā waʾᵃmātᵉka kāmōkā*).

This is one of the first expressions of a thrust towards the idea of equal rights as a means of overcoming social differences.

Much too little attention has been paid up to now to the Deuteronomic regulation about runaway slaves in Deut. 23.15f.:

You shall not give up to his master a slave who has escaped from his master to you; he shall dwell with you, in your midst, in the place which he shall choose within one of your towns, where it pleases him best; you shall not oppress him.

As far as we can see, this law is unique in the ancient East.[20] Everywhere else the handing over of a runaway slave counts as a self-evident rule; cf. also I Sam. 30.15. The free Israelite, however, who remembers the acts of his God in salvation history, should sympathize with the escaped slave rather than with his master. Here we can not only see the trend towards the observance of humane treatment of the slave – a trend which we could already observe in the Book of the Covenant;[21] there is also an obviously growing tendency to put slaves on the same level as freemen. This is therefore a step in the direction of their emancipation.

Thus in Deuteronomy the constant remembrance that Yahweh liberated Israel from Egyptian bondage leads to clear conclusions: the slave is to be released with liberal gifts, so that he can partake of the freeman's 'blessing'; he is to rest 'as well as you'; and a runaway slave is to be subjected to no pressure of any kind.

Another reason for the equality of master and slave, above all before the court of justice,[22] is later to be found in Job's 'oath of innocence' (Job 31.13, 15):

> If I have disregarded the rights of my manservant (*mišpaṭ*
> *ʿabdī*) or my maidservant,
> when they brought a complaint against me (*berībām*[23]
> *ʿimmādī*).
> . . .
> Did not he who made me in the womb make him?
> and did not one fashion us in the womb?

Here belief in creation inspires the notion of equality.

(*e*) The Law of Holiness goes beyond Deuteronomy in one particular respect. For it draws a further conclusion from the acknowledgment of the deliverance from the Egyptian bondage (Lev. 25.39f.):

> If your brother becomes poor beside you, and sells himself to you, you shall not make him serve as a slave (*lōʾ taʿabōd bō ʿabōdat ʿebed*): he shall be with you as a hired servant (*śākīr*), as a sojourner (*tōšāb*; i.e. a foreign worker).

The reason is given in v. 42:

> For they are *my* servants, whom I brought forth out of the land of Egypt; they shall not be sold as slaves.

And v. 43 draws the psychological conclusion:

You shall not rule over him with harshness, but shall fear your God.

The necessary supply of slaves may be met by buying from neighbouring peoples, as well as by using the children of foreign workers (*tōšābīm*) and their descendants who have been born in the country.[24]

(*f*) The wage-earner too (*śākīr*) finds his own protection. His daily earnings are to be paid out to him regularly and punctually. Jeremiah reproaches King Jehoiakim with keeping back the labourers' wages (Jer. 22.13).[25] Deut. 24.14f. orders that a poor and needy worker who is paid by the day must have his earnings paid out to him on the same day, before sundown, whether he belongs to the people of Israel or comes from a foreign country.

For he is poor, and sets his heart upon it; lest he cry against you to Yahweh, and it be sin in you.

Again the Deuteronomic preacher puts himself in the psychological situation of the man who is in need. Lev. 19.13b warns categorically against keeping back the labourer's wage until the following morning. In the context of the text, such behaviour is on the same level as sharp practice and robbery (v. 13a). The point by which the employer has to pay may seem unimportant to him – but the law-giver thinks of the labourer's needs.

(*g*) The message of freedom takes yet another remarkable form in the Law of Holiness in Lev. 25.8ff., where a great year of emancipation (*dᵉrōr*) is proclaimed. It is the fiftieth year, in which after seven times seven years everyone is to return as a free man to his kindred or clan, and everyone is also to get back possession of the land he owns. It is the great Year of Liberation, known as the Year of Jubilee or Jobel Year, because it is to be opened by the blowing of the ram's horn (*yōbēl*). As a pledge of freedom it is – particularly because it is a Utopian regulation – a token that Israel can view and can endure all lack of liberty only as something provisional.

The hope of freedom pushes forward in ever new forms, even in periods of the greatest general distress, such as the Babylonian exile and the years that succeeded it. Isa. 61.1ff. announces the messenger of peace, who proclaims liberty to the captive and in Yahweh's name publishes the year of peace, to comfort all the sad. In Joel 2.28f. the eschatological outpouring of the Spirit, which mediates direct, free knowledge of God, lays hold not only of young and old, women and men, but also of slaves, as well as freemen. Finally, in the psalms of lament the concept of the poor and the oppressed (*'ānī*) to an increasing degree 'practically contains a legal claim upon Yahweh',[26] because it is to them above all that he has given the solemn assurance of his support (cf. Pss. 22.24; 12.6; and frequently). Is not everything here pressing towards the goal where in Christ Jesus the antithesis between slaves and freemen is abolished altogether (Gal. 3.28)?

3. On the road to freedom

In two series of observations running in opposite directions, we have shown critical impulses in the attitude to the monarchy and the attitude to slavery in the Old Testament proclamation. Summing up, the Old Testament view of man as a dependent is guided by certain basic principles:

(*a*) The equal status of masters and slaves is founded on the recognition of the God of Israel as the one who liberated the slaves from Egypt; and, in passing, also on the recognition of the one Creator of all men (Deut.; Job 31).

(*b*) As a rule the idea of a political and economic revolution as a mere reversal of the existing conditions of sovereignty is completely alien. The secession of the Northern Kingdom from the Davidic dynasty under Rehoboam/Jeroboam (I Kings 12) is an exception, It shows that the same problems arise in the kingdom of the rebels as arose under the rule that they have shaken off (I Kings 21; Amos). The man who asserts himself cannot truly liberate himself.

(*c*) What is fundamental for the true revolution is the perception that everyone is in origin himself a slave who has been liberated by God's act. The double revolution from above is based on understanding of the slave's mind; and this revolution takes the form first of a changed attitude to the slave's psychological situation, and secondly of an alteration in his external conditions (Deut.; the Law of Holiness).

(*d*) The true Lord of lords is the exemplary brother (Deut. 17), the ruler who liberates the oppressed (Ps. 72), the servant who takes the burden of others on himself (Deutero-Isaiah).

(*e*) The parallelism of concrete measures and Utopian schemes is characteristic of the Old Testament (cf. for example the slave laws and the 'mirror for magistrates' in the Book of the Covenant, with the law of the king in Deuteronomy and the enactment of the Year of Jubilee in the Law of Holiness). Provisional improvements in detail and the expectation of complete freedom are not mutually exclusive; they belong together.[27]

(*f*) As a whole the different kinds of Old Testament schemes seek for alterations in existing conditions which should be in line with God's liberating rule, which is perfected in his servanthood. The proclamation of God's fundamental acts in the past and those that are to come introduces a ferment into existing conditions.

(*g*) The goal is a community of the masters and slaves who have been freed through the outpouring of the divine Spirit. For masters and slaves alike need liberation through the direct knowledge of God (Joel 2.28f.; Mal. 4.5f.; Gal. 3.28; Col. 3.22–4.1).

Thus the Old Testament sees men in the midst of social tensions as being on the road to freedom, between the declaration of Yahweh's early acts in salvation history and those future acts which prophecy has proclaimed.

XXIII

The Wise and the Foolish (Teachers and Pupils)[1]

Man is on the road to freedom as long as he is a learner. All his life, he has to gain wisdom in dealing with the world and his fellow men. Thus upbringing is not just a matter between parents and children.[2] Let us look at the question of where wisdom was communicated in Israel, and how it related to the individual's conduct of life, to public power and to the fear of God.

1. *School*

In so far as the wise man is the person who is learned and knowledgeable, his wisdom presupposes schooling; but the Old Testament only allows us to surmise what educational conditions were like in Israel. In many cases a man is called wise if he is versed in a particular skill – in the technique of fashioning metals (I Kings 7.14), in goldsmith's work and wood-carving (Ex. 31.3), in spinning (Ex. 35.25) – or if he is a skilled seafarer (Ezek. 27.8; Ps. 107.27), or a statesman and soldier (Isa. 10.13). For most of these crafts and professions the 'father's house' will have been the 'school'.[3]

But Israel also uses the term 'wise' (*ḥākām*) for the teacher. Thus Jer. 18.18 mentions the teacher next to the professional groups of priests and prophets. As the transmitter of knowledge, we find the teacher mentioned at the head of collections of maxims (Prov. 22.17; 24.23). It emerges from Prov. 25.1 that 'wise men' of this kind had their school at the king's court, for the reference tells us that a collection of the proverbs of Solomon are to be ascribed to 'the men of Hezekiah, king of Judah'. These wise men are therefore in the first place 'scribes' (Prov. 22.20; Eccles. 12.10), and then 'scholars', who study the traditions of the fathers (Job 8.8), but who also investigate the complexities of things themselves (Eccles. 8.1, 5, 17; 12.9); thus they become 'teachers' (Prov. 8.10; Job 15.18; Eccles. 12.9) and 'counsellors' (Jer. 18.18; II Sam. 16.20, 23; 17.1–14). The people who listen to them are therefore not only 'pupils' (*limmūd*), who 'hear' and learn the right answers morning by morning (Isa. 50.4); they are also kings (II Sam. 14.2ff.), the sons of kings (II

Sam. 16.15ff.), royal officials (II Sam. 20.16) and all kinds of people needing advice (II Sam. 20.22).

Egyptian and Babylonian parallels, as well as sufficient indications within the Old Testament itself, allow us to settle the question about schools to some extent: a school for princes, officials and the sons of the higher classes was connected with the court at Jerusalem, and it may have continued to exist as a temple school in the post-exilic period.[4] We can see from the collections of maxims in the book of Proverbs, however, that the work of the teachers was not confined to court and priestly circles,[5] but that fundamentally speaking they had something to say to everyone.[6] It is therefore the question whether in many country towns in Israel the elders who carried out justice at the city gates did not also manifest themselves as 'wise men' in the general education of the young and in advising the people.[7] Wherever it be: only by turning in at the house of wisdom will the inexperienced, easily misled, simple person (*peti*) become learned (Prov. 9.4, 16). Prov. 13.20 teaches:

> He who walks with wise men becomes wise,
>> but the companion of fools will suffer harm.

Thus much more has to be learnt from teachers than knowledge of a profession.

2. The conduct of life

Wisdom covers the whole conduct of life. Wisdom and way (*derek*= conduct, behaviour) belong together.[8] Thus both the wise and the foolish are to be found in all stations of life. Prov. 14.8 says:

> The wisdom of a prudent man is to discern his way,
>> but the folly of fools is deceiving.

Wisdom about life of this kind does not only feed on its own insight (Prov. 28.26):

> He who trusts in his own understanding is a fool;
>> but he who walks in wisdom will be delivered.

The wise man does not dispense with guidance of the experienced (Prov. 10.21):

> The lips of the righteous feed many,
>> but fools die for lack of sense.

Here the wise are called the righteous. This corresponds to a basic feature of the ancient collection in Prov. 10–15, where the righteous man is generally equated with the wise one.[9] For (10.8)

> the wise of heart will heed commandments,
>> but a prating fool will come to ruin.

And (Prov. 14.16):

> A wise man is cautious and turns away from evil,
> but a fool throws off restraint and is sure of himself.

To be familiar with this wisdom about life 'has to do with character rather than with intellect'.[10] It affects the whole of life. All ill-considered, over-hasty and reckless action is suspect here (Prov. 19.2b):

> He who makes haste with his feet misses his way.

Thus property that has been too quickly acquired is also mistrusted (Prov. 13.11):

> Wealth hastily gotten[11] will dwindle,
> but he who gathers little by little will increase it.

Cf. also 21.5; 28.20, 22. Speech is most adversely affected by hastiness (Prov. 29.20); the wise man is sparing of words (10.19):

> When words are many, transgression is not lacking,
> but he who restrains his lips is prudent.

Wisdom always shows itself most accurately in the right word. A clear mind can express itself concisely (Prov. 17.27):

> He who restrains his words has knowledge,
> but he who has a cool spirit is a man of understanding.

On the other hand the fool prepares his own downfall by needless chatter (Prov. 18.7):

> A fool's mouth is his ruin,
> and his lips are a snare to his own life.

Kindness of speech as well as circumspection is a mark and a blessing of the wise (Prov. 16.24):

> Pleasant words are like a honeycomb,
> sweetness to the soul and health to the body.

Thus even the very words of the wise or the fool decide the salvation or disaster – indeed the life or death – of the whole person.[12] Anyone who wants to be and to remain true man should in quiet reflection pay attention to the path he is taking and the words he speaks, and above all to the words of wisdom, which are practical guidance in the art of living. In their trueness to life, the maxims often give direct pleasure through their very form of expression, or amuse us with their sometimes witty comparisons, for example:

> Like a dog that returns to his vomit
> is a fool that repeats his folly (Prov. 26.11).

> A dripping roof on a rainy day
> and a contentious woman are alike (Prov. 27.15).[13]

3. *Wisdom and power*

Wisdom has significance for public life as well. It is the truly supreme power in society, showing itself superior to both power and riches. Cf. Prov. 24.1–6:

> Be not envious of evil men,
> nor desire to be with them;
> 2 for their minds devise violence,
> and their lips talk of mischief.
> 3 By wisdom a house is built,
> and by understanding it is established;
> 4 by knowledge the rooms are filled
> with all precious and pleasant riches.
> 5 A wise man is mightier than a strong man,
> and a man of knowledge than he who has strength;[14]
> 6 for by wise guidance you can wage your war,
> and in abundance of counsellors there is victory.

It is in accordance with such insight that Israelite wisdom should know no education for the real soldierly 'virtues' and achievements, and no training in warlike behaviour.[15] Instead it aims to promote insight into the despicableness and senselessness of all acts of violence (Prov. 16.32):

> He who is slow to anger is better than a hero in war,
> and he who has self-command than he who takes a city.

But the slighting criticism of everything warlike is not a withdrawal into a life of privately shuttered 'inwardness'. On the contrary, the criticism is inspired by the certainty that this is a better way of achieving the aims of public life (Prov. 21.22):

> A wise man scales the city of heroes
> and brings down the stronghold in which they trust.

True victories are always only to be reached through 'wise' political solutions – never through military intervention. The same applies to economic affairs (Prov. 16.16):

> To get wisdom is better than gold;
> to get understanding is to be chosen rather than silver.

A house owes its strength, not to the size of the stones it is built with, or the strength put into it by its builders, but to the calculations of the architect and the knowledgeable care of the bricklayers (Prov. 24.3); and in the same way all economic management requires as its first premise knowledge of what can usefully be stored without its deteriorating in value (24.4), and the ability to dispense with a thing for a time (Prov. 21.20):

> Precious treasure (and oil) is in the wise man's dwelling,
>   but a foolish man fritters it away.

Joseph's clever management proved to be a blessing for Egypt and for the whole world (Gen. 41.39ff.). The wise man knows the constructive power of the good and the destructive power of evil. 'Good is that which does good.'[16] Consequently the prudent man's decision in favour of whatever is better has considerable social importance.

Those who rule must therefore above all acquire the insight of the wise.[17] Justice and righteousness are the foundations of their throne (Isa. 9.6). Just as the sensible farmer divides the wheat from the chaff in the threshing process, so (Prov. 20.26)

> a wise king winnows the wicked,
>   and drives the wheel[18] over them.

It is part of wisdom's paradox that it is not the strong and the rich who secure a king's throne but the helpless and the poor – that is, when the king intervenes on their behalf (Prov. 29.14):

> If a king judges the poor with equity
>   his throne will be established for ever.

In saying this, are not the teachers of the court school introducing a positively messianic component into the art of government?[19] They know that wisdom is always a definite political factor. Certainly, the real territory of Yahweh's wisdom is the 'heart', as the understanding and will[20] of the individual; but that is precisely the way in which it affects the greater movements of history. The author of the Court History of David well knows how to depict this phenomenon.[21] The voices of wise women intervene in events (II Sam. 14.2ff.; 20.16ff.). The failure and downfall of David and his sons is perceived in terms of the categories of wisdom: David's secret adultery sets up far-reaching consequences that penetrate far into major politics as well (II Sam. 11f.), just as does his weakness in the upbringing of his sons Amnon and Adonijah (II Sam. 13.21; I Kings 1.6)[22] and the arrogance of Absalom and Adonijah (II Sam. 15.1; I Kings 1.5). Absalom allows himself to be advised by two wise men in his struggle against his father – by Ahithophel and Hushai (II Sam. 16.20–17.12). Wisdom no doubt comes into being in the most private sphere, but for that very reason it is the heart of the domination of the world which is laid upon man.

If a man wants to manifest himself as God's image and therefore as a good steward of creation and a good administrator of history, he has to reject the crimes of stupidity and foolishness; he needs enlightenment through the wisdom that permeates all the decisions of life. But in the midst of this perception, we are faced with an inscrutable obscurity. According to II Sam. 17.14, Absalom and the men of Israel decide in favour of Hushai's counsel, for Yahweh thwarts Ahithophel's better advice, in order to bring about Absalom's downfall. In the same way Yahweh can also completely confuse the excellent wisdom of Pharaoh's advisers (Isa. 19.11–14). The discovery that 'Yahweh loved him' (II Sam. 12.24) has a more decisive influence on Solomon's future than all the wisdom of his rivals put together. But it is just such inexplicable obscurities that are not outside the range of Israel's wisdom.

4. *Discernment and the fear of God*

For according to frequently emphasized experience, the crowning characteristic of discernment is the fear of God (Prov. 1.7; 9.10; 15.33; Job 28.28; Ps. 111.10). This is true of professional skill, the discreet conduct of life, and social and political decisions. Anyone who wants to judge man's potentialities correctly must weigh the importance of the fear of God for his insights.

How can this be done? The starting point for Israel's teachers was the certainty that the subjects of knowledge, i.e., the whole world of man, are the creation of God. But this creation is governed by an order which manifests its laws to the understanding man (Ps. 104.24): 'In wisdom hast thou made all thy works.' Cf. Ps. 145.10–12:

> All thy works give thanks to thee, O Yahweh,
> and all thy saints bless thee!
> They speak of the glory of thy kingdom,
> and tell of thy power,
> to make known to the sons of men thy[23] mighty deeds,
> and the glory and splendour of thy[23] kingdom.

The fear of God as the beginning of perception therefore first of all evokes the confidence to open one's mind to the teaching and the call of the world of phenomena (Prov. 8; Job 28; 12.7–9).[24] The truth that knowledge of the world can be wisdom for men is founded objectively on the world as creation.

But subjectively too the fear of God is the beginning of understanding (Prov. 2.6):

> For Yahweh gives wisdom;
>> from his mouth come perception and understanding.

Where else than from his word should man gain the realization that the world is his creation? Where else could he gain the courage to trust himself to the principles which he here perceives? Who should grant him the openness for the reality that he encounters and the independence of all inwardly distorted foolishness? Capacity for perception is just as much a creation of Yahweh's as all the subjects of perception themselves.

But in this way the fear of God also brings man insight into the limitations of his knowledge (Job 38f.; Prov. 25.2):

> It is the glory of God to conceal things.

Anyone who is not aware of the dark borders of reality and the impenetrable veil covering the total pattern of things has exchanged the actual world for a self-made illusion. In this Job remains the master teacher of all the wise. He acknowledges (Job 26.12–14):

> By his power he whips up the sea;
>> by his understanding he smites Rahab.
> By his wind the heavens are made fair;
>> his hand pierces the fleeing serpent.
> Lo, these are but the outskirts of his ways;
>> and how small a whisper do we hear of him!
>> For the thunder of his power who can understand?

The fear of God is the crown of wisdom, because wisdom is first and last God's wisdom, in which man participates on the basis of the few whispered words he perceives. Next to Job, Ecclesiastes is most aware of the limits set for the wise: the future is closed to him (8.7), he cannot discover the total coherence of all events from their beginnings to their end (3.11), and he is not capable of finding out what the work of God is in everything that is under the sun (8.16f.). Thus the truly wise man is burdened by the divine incognito, yet is at the same time a 'hymnist of the divine mysteries'[25] (Prov. 30.1–4):

> I laboured with God,
>> I laboured with God,
>>> so that I might understand it.
> For surely I am stupider than anyone,
>> and have not the understanding of a man.

> I have not learned wisdom
>> that I might have knowledge of the Holy One.
> Who has ascended to heaven and come down?
>> Who has gathered the wind in his fists?
> Who has wrapped up the waters in a garment?
>> Who has established all the ends of the earth?
> What is his name, and what is his son's name?
>> Surely you know!

Humility is wisdom's indispensable accompaniment (Prov. 18.12):

> Before destruction a man's heart is haughty,
>> but humility goes before honour.

Thus the narrator of the story in the Court History of David paints David on the flight before Absalom as a humble man (II Sam. 15.25f., 30; 16.10–12),[26] who as such remains victor. On the other hand Absalom and Adonijah[27] prove the truth that

> Pride goes before destruction,
>> and a haughty spirit before a fall (Prov. 16.18).

Pride is the twin of foolishness. For arrogance which abandons the fear of God also robs man of his future. Only the humble remains truly man, for wisdom sets him on the true path of the fear of Yahweh.[28]

XXIV

The Individual and the Community[1]

The life of the individual in ancient Israel is always firmly integrated in the bonds of his family and thus of his people. Wherever he is set apart or isolated, something unusual, if not something threatening, is happening, although it is also ultimately something essential if man is truly to become man.

1. *The individual in Israel's social order*

In a miniature sociology of early Israel, let us first ask what the groups in the community were by which the individual was surrounded. In the story of Achan's theft, we are given a vivid account of the way in which, by drawing lots among the whole people, Joshua arrives at the guilty person by means of a gradual process of elimination. First of all he collects the whole people (Josh. 7.16–18)

> tribe by tribe, and the lot fell on the tribe of Judah; and he brought near the 'clans'[2] of Judah, and the lot fell on[2] the the clan of the Zerahites; and he brought near the clan of the Zerahites 'family by family',[2] and the lot fell on the family[2] of Zabdi; and he brought near his family man by man, and the lot fell on Achan the son of Carmi, son of Zabdi, son of Zerah, of the tribe of Judah.

The text makes the divisions clear.

(*a*) The individual is a member of his family, which is called '*house*' (*bayit*) or 'father's house' (*bēt 'āb*) (Gen. 24.38, 40). Josh. 7.17f. shows that this means the larger, patriarchal family group; for the house takes its name not from Achan's father, Carmi, but from his grandfather, Zabdi. He is the 'head' (*rō'š*) of the family group (cf. I Chron. 24.31; Num. 25.15). Since we must assume that Achan is an adult, he can have children himself, so that four generations live together in the patriarchal family group; in addition to the men, there were the married women and the unmarried daughters, as well as slaves of both sexes, persons without full citizenship and 'sojourners', or resident foreign workers.[3] If we remember that families had numerous children, and that an Israelite might easily be a father at twenty, a grandfather at forty, and a great-grandfather at sixty,[4] and that the younger brothers of the head of the family, with their descendants, could also belong to the patriarchal family, it is easy to see how a family group of this kind could provide the militia with a 'fifty' (I Sam. 8.12).[5]

(*b*) The family groups were members of their kindred or 'clan' (*mišpāḥā*), just as in Josh. 7.17 the 'house' of Zabdi belongs to the 'clan' of Zerah. Since the clan provided a 'thousand' for the militia (Micah 5.2; I Sam. 8.12; cf. Amos 5.3; I Sam. 10.19; the Hebrew word means 'thousand' in each case) it will probably have consisted of about twenty family groups. The clan settled as a whole; for example, the clan of Ephrathah, of which David (who belonged to the family group of Jesse) was a member, lived as a whole in Bethlehem (Micah 5.2). The clan was led by the elders, who also exercised justice (I Kings 21.8ff.).

(*c*) The clans were united in the tribe (*šēbeṭ*, later *maṭṭe*[6]). Thus the clan of Zerah (Josh. 7.16f.), as well as the clan of Ephrathah (Micah 5.2) belonged to the tribe of Judah; whereas Saul's clan, the Matrites, belonged to the tribe of Benjamin (I Sam. 10.21); cf. Num. 26.6f., 57f. In the semi-nomadic period, the tribes formed a travelling community, as the wanderings of the tribe of Dan show, when they moved from the foothills between the mountains and the coastal plain west of Jerusalem to the region round the sources of the Jordan.[7] The tribes then lived with their clans in a particular area; this region sometimes gave the tribe its name; Judah was probably named after the southern part of the West Jordan mountains, and Ephraim after their central section.[8] At the head of every tribe stood the tribe's leader (*nāśī*) (Num. 7.2; 31.13; 32.2; Ex. 22.28). His name may perhaps be a reminder of his function to act as spokesman in the tribal confederation; he was the one who 'raised his voice' (*nś' qōl*).[9]

(*d*) The community of all the tribes was called '*Israel*' or '*the house of Israel*'. As *Yahweh's people* it formed a unity (Josh. 24.9f., 31; Judg. 5.11; II Sam. 1.12).[10] In the early period the conduct of war seems to have been more a matter for the individual tribes and smaller groups of tribes, whereas 'Israel' was largely bound together as God's people through its common acknowledgment of Yahweh's saving acts (Judg. 5.11) and through the proclamation of the divine law. In the period before Israel became a nation, the 'judge of Israel' (Micah 5.1) was probably at the head of the tribal confederation; according to the list of the so-called 'minor judges' in Judg. 10.1–5; 12.7–15, he was probably chosen from the tribes in turn by the amphictyonic council of the tribal spokesmen.[11] The 'judges of Israel' probably had to decide difficult cases that had not yet been settled by the law passed down by tradition, and had also to provide for the periodic proclamation of the divine law in Israel (cf. Deut. 31.9–13; I Sam. 7.15–17). But these conditions cannot be precisely clarified, historically.

(*e*) In the period after Israel became a *nation*, the king seems to have become the supreme court of appeal to an increasing degree (II Sam. 15.2ff.; Jer. 26.10ff., 20ff.). But the tradition that has been passed down to us shows that in the period of the kings above all a series of prophets, as accusers, made the law of God the theme of discussion, particularly with regard to the kings themselves (Hos. 7.3ff.; 8.4ff.; Isa. 1.21ff.; 3.13ff.; Jer. 22).

(*f*) In the post-exilic period Israel was constituted as a '*congregation*' ('*ēdā*),[12] a religious community. Beside the governor appointed by the foreign empire as occupying power, the congregation was headed by the high priest (Hag. 1.1) and a council of elders (Joel 1.2).

In the different epochs of Israel's history – in the great revolutionary changes from the days before she became a nation to the period of the kings, and then to the Babylonian exile and to the post-exilic period – the fate of the individual in Israel was largely the fate of his people. The acknowledgment made by the farmer (according to Deut. 26.5–10) when he delivered up his first fruits in the sanctuary is indicative: here the change-over from 'I' to 'we' and back again to 'I' is typical of the fact that the history of the individual coincides completely with the history of God's people, in the changes experienced, in the troubles endured, and in the benefits enjoyed:

A wandering Aramean was *my* ancestor; and he went down into Egypt . . . The Egyptians treated *us* harshly and afflicted *us* . . . Then *we* cried to Yahweh the God of *our* fathers . . . and Yahweh brought *us* out of Egypt . . . He brought *us* into this place and gave *us* this land . . . And behold, now *I* bring the first of the fruit of the ground, which thou, O Yahweh, hast given *me*.

It was always an unusual proceeding when from the whole of the nation, the tribe, the clan, the family, a single individual was sought out and particularly chosen. It could mean a special disaster, as when the criminal Achan was sought for (Josh. 7.10–18); but it could also mean Yahweh's particular election, as in the casting of lots that made Saul king (I Sam. 10.17–24). Let us consider the two possibilities of separating out an individual *from* the whole or *for* the whole.

2. *The individual as one expelled from society*

We first meet the individual as someone who has been expelled from society in the case where, like Achan, he has offended against the principles of God's law, thereby committing an 'infamous deed in Israel' of which it it must be said 'such a thing is not done in Israel'.[13] Just as characteristic is the phrase, which recurs again and again in Deuteronomy, charging Israel to 'purge th: evil' from her midst, e.g. 17.12:

> The man who acts presumptuously, by not obeying the priest who stands to minister there before Yahweh your God, or the judge, that man shall die; so you shall purge the evil from Israel.

Here, at the place which Yahweh has chosen (17.8ff.), the point at issue is the supreme decisions of the central court, which could not be made by the local judges (16.18ff.). Cf. further Deut. 13.5; 17.7; 19.19; 22.22; and frequently elsewhere. In order to defend the fellowship of the community as a whole, the one who threatens it with injury must as an individual be discovered and expelled. The law of God in its oldest forms (as in the dodecalogue of curses in Deut. 27.15–26) has already appealed to the individual.

But there is also loneliness that is due to false accusation. The man who is praying in Ps. 25 sees himself encompassed by his enemies (vv. 2, 19), who deny his innocence in a particular instance and set traps for him (vv. 15, 21). He appeals to Yahweh (vv. 15f.):

> My eyes are ever toward Yahweh,
>> for he will pluck my feet out of the net.
> Turn thou to me, and be gracious to me,
>> for I am lonely and afflicted.

The word 'lonely' (*yāḥīd*) means here the misery of segregation and isolation,[14] which imply wretchedness and affliction – and indeed loneliness as a longed-for benefit that gives active pleasure is alien to the Old Testament in general. To be alone and to have no one beside one involves dangers which the fugitive in particular is aware of. When David, pursued by Saul, turns aside to visit Ahimelech, the priest at Nob, Ahimelech asks him (I Sam. 21.1): 'Why are you alone, and no one with you?' 'Alone' (*lebad*) here means much the same as separated, cut off, for *bad* is the part which has been split off from the whole.[15] The segregated person is easily overpowered. That is why Ahithophel's advice to Absalom aims at making a surprise attack on David at night with 12,000 men, so that David's companions will panic and take flight (II Sam. 17.2b) and 'I will strike down the king alone (*lebaddō*).' The psalms of lament often speak of the misery of loneliness, Most movingly of all, in Ps. 102 a man who is near death (v. 23) and mocked by his enemies (v. 8) prays (vv. 6–7):

> I am like a vulture[16] of the wilderness,
>> like an owl in ruined places;

> I lie awake and I 'complain'[17]
> like a lonely (*bōdēd*) bird on the housetop.

The wilderness, the ruins, the lonely bird are a graphic description of an existence of complete abandonment. This is the legally regulated fate of the leper (Lev. 13.46): 'He shall remain unclean as long as he has the disease; since he is unclean, he shall dwell alone in a habitation outside the camp.'

Although loneliness is never exalted, and is not sought after, even for meditation or out of asceticism, the man who trusts in Yahweh can find a word of affirmation even for this affliction. Lam. 3.28 introduces the lonely man with the same words that are used of the leper in Lev. 13.46 (*yēšēb bādād*). But now we are told of the lonely (Lam. 3.25–33):

> Yahweh is good to those who wait for him,
> to the soul that seeks him.
> It is good 'to hope silently'[18]
> for the salvation of Yahweh.
> It is good for a man that he bear
> the yoke in his youth.
> Let him sit alone (*yēšēb bādād*) in silence
> because he has laid it on him;
> let him put his mouth in the dust –
> there may yet be hope.
> . . .
> For the Lord will not cast off for ever,
> but though he cause grief, he will have compassion
> according to the abundance of his saving acts;
> for he does not 'of his own accord'[19] afflict
> and grieve the sons of men.

In Pss. 42/43 the speaker is one who has been carried away into a foreign land (42.6). In his forsakenness he misses particularly the services of the congregation (42.4). When in his loneliness he 'thirsts' for God (42.1f.), this means in concrete terms that he longs to take part once more in the pilgrimages to the sanctuary, in order there to find the assurance of the God who is his joy (43.3f.). In the expectation that one day he will again praise his God there, he can encourage himself to hope even in the torment of isolation (42.5, 11; 43.5). In the prayer of the accused man which we find in Ps. 4, trust also breaks through at the end (v. 8):

> In peace I sleep directly I lie down,
> for, solitary though I be (*lᵉbēdād*),
> thou Yahweh makest me dwell in safety.[20]

Thus the Old Testament shows loneliness as segregation, as a result of just or false accusation, persecution, or sickness. It always means misery. But Yahweh is attainable even for those who are cut off, for the separated and the isolated. With him loneliness can be endured and overcome.

3. *The individual as one called and chosen*

Election can also lead to loneliness. Here Yahweh shows himself as the origin of a man's segregation. This theme takes on considerable importance in the Old Testament.

Right at the beginning of the story of the patriarchs – and thus at the beginning of the history of Israel's blessing as well – the Yahwist sets down Yahweh's command to Abraham: a thrice emphasized command of separation (Gen. 12.1):

> Go from your country,
>> and from your kindred,
>> and from your father's house
>> to the land that I will show you.

This setting apart of Abraham is by no means a curse; on the contrary, it is bound up with the manifold promise of blessing, and ultimately corresponds to the promise that in this Abraham 'all the families of the earth can find blessing' (vv. 2f.). The theme is repeated in notes of a different (Elohistic?) origin, which are sprinkled here and there in the account. In Gen. 15.2 Abraham complains that he goes alone and childless ('*arīrī*), only then to discover under the night sky that his descendants are to be as numerous as the innumerable stars (v. 5). When they are scattered in exile, the people are still, in their loneliness and abandonment, to remember the story of Abraham (Isa. 51.2b):

> When he was but one I called him,
>> and I blessed him and made him many.[21]

The story of Jacob too tells of a great loneliness in which, separated from his two wives, his maids and his eleven children, he 'was left alone (*lebaddō*)' (Gen. 32.24a) in the night at the ford of the Jabbok, in order to be both smitten (v. 25) and blessed (29b) by the great Unknown who fell upon him (v. 24b).

Thus every story of election is first the story of a setting apart, just as every call and revelation first of all takes its recipient into loneliness. In the framework of the revelation on Sinai, Ex. 24.2 emphasizes:

> Moses alone (*lebaddō*) shall come near to Yahweh;
>> but the others shall not come near,
>> and the people shall not come up with him.

The receiver of revelation is not only set far apart from the people; the present context tells us (v. 1) that he is separated even from those who at first went up to the mountain with him – from Aaron, Nadab, Abihu and seventy elders.

The passing on of a message of revelation to someone who has been marked out for a special task can also take place in strict privacy. Thus the prophet Ahijah the Shilonite approaches Jeroboam (I Kings 11.29) 'at that time, when Jeroboam went out of Jerusalem . . . and the two of them were alone (*lᵉbaddām*) in the open country.' In this lonely place Ahijah tears his coat into twelve pieces and gives Jeroboam ten of them, as a sign that he is to assume the lordship over the ten tribes of Israel whom Yahweh is going to tear away from the house of David (vv. 30ff.).

Jeremiah's complaint shows most clearly and most movingly how the call of the classic prophets not only took place in the remoteness of unusual events, but also led to intense isolation. Through his proclamation he has become a laughing stock and an object of mockery to his hearers (20.7f.). He is surrounded by suspicion and persecution (20.10; 15.10f., 15). And he sees himself as an outcast, excluded from every kind of fellowship (15.17):

> Never do I sit joyously in the company of the merrymakers. I sit alone (*bādād yāšabtī*), under the weight of thy hand. For thou hast filled me with indignation.

The wording (*bādād yāšabtī*) is reminiscent of the casting out of the leper.[22] But the distress of the man called to be prophet is even worse than the suffering of the one who is isolated though sickness; for he can still turn to Yahweh.[23] But Jeremiah cries to his God (15.18b):

> Thou art for me like a deceitful brook,
> like waters that do not keep their word.[24]

Ezekiel, too, from the very outset sees himself confronted through Yahweh's command with an unruly Israel, a 'rebellious house' (Ezek. 2.3–5); a man can only shrink back aghast from such a task, but that is what Ezekiel is not to do (vv. 6f.). Where the God of Israel subordinates men to the task of being his emissary, lonely individuals arise in the midst of a firmly established social order. This phenomenon even has its literary repercussions. The collecting of the prophetic sayings leads for the first time to a body of writings which is no longer anonymous but is passed down under the names of the individual prophets.

But the prophets do not only encounter the people as individuals; they also collect their hearers into a new community, which differs from the natural order of society. Thus, even in an early phase of his ministry,

Isaiah's proclamation of judgment collected disciples, to whom he was able
to entrust the word he preached (Isa. 8.16). An opposition group formed
round him which stood in clear antithesis to official Jerusalem circles. The
prophet had to arm this group against opinions which were widespread
among the people (Isa. 8.11–13):[25]

> For Yahweh spoke thus to me as his strong hand was laid upon me,
> 'hindering me' from walking the way of this people, saying:
>
>> Do not call conspiracy
>> all that this people calls conspiracy,
>> and do not fear what they fear,
>> nor be in dread.
>> Yahweh of hosts, him you shall 'call conspirator'!
>> Let him be your fear, and let him be your dread!

Thus the prophet establishes a group which assembles round the Immanuel
sign ('God is with us') (7.14; cf. 8.16–18). Out of the judgment a purified
(1.25ff.) 'remnant' congregation (Isa. 7.3; cf. 4.2ff.) will emerge.[26]

Before Yahweh's word not only the prophet himself but also the hearers
of the word become individuals. Such individualization is clearly shown
from the time of Jeremiah onwards, e.g., 4.4: 'Circumcise yourselves for
Yahweh and remove the foreskin of your hearts!' Ezekiel urges the responsibility of each individual in even more precise terms (Ezek. 18.30):
'Therefore I will judge you, every one according to his ways, says Yahweh.'
In the Deuteronomic admonition personal devotion becomes authorita-
tively enjoined (Deut. 6.4f.):

> Hear, O Israel: Yahweh is our God, Yahweh alone. You shall love
> Yahweh your God with all your devotion, with all your desire and with
> all your powers.[27]

In this way the Deuteronomic preachers with their address to the individual are aiming at a reformed congregation. But will the truly new
congregation of the covenant be realized in any way other than through the
power of the promise? Scepticism with regard to the reforming optimism
of the Deuteronomists may have entered into Jer. 31.33f., where it is
proclaimed as Yahweh's promise:

> I will put my law with them, and I will write it upon their hearts . . .
> And no longer shall each man have to teach his neighbour and each
> his brother, saying, 'Know Yahweh', for they shall all know me, from
> the least of them to the greatest, says Yahweh; for I forgive their
> iniquity and will utter the remembrance of their sin no more.

Thus the old, firmly established people of the covenant is led by way of complete individualization into a new community. Even within the Old Testament, this means something like 'the detachment of the individual from the suggestive power of the collective, of the *polis*, of the *gens*, through his confrontation with the will of God: with the love of God that is directed towards him, with the divine demand that is addressed to him, and with the invitation of faith that applies to him. He is given the courage to say: *si omnes, ego non* – though all, yet not I.'[28] We may well consider that it is not the least of the Bible's contributions to anthropology that man should understand himself for the first time when he is an individual, summoned through the call of the incomparable voice out of the bonds of his heritage and called to a new covenant.

Then, with the message of Jesus Christ, the promise is realized that men of all nations shall partake in this process – which means that they partake in man's becoming truly man (Gen. 12.3b; Isa. 45.14f.; 52.10; Zech. 8.23[29]).

XXV

The Destiny of Man[1]

Not a few Old Testament texts are impelled by the question: what is man's actual destiny? The decisive answers all point in the same direction. In view of the changes in language, the difference in the way of looking at things, and the multiplicity of literary genres in the thousand years of Old Testament history, the discovery of this consensus of opinion must be called an outstanding phenomenon in the history of thought.[2] Particularly since nothing is further from the Old Testament's intention than a systematic anthropology, it is both fascinating and illuminating to find analogous tendencies in its various strata.

The source of man's destiny is not questioned in the Bible, even though elsewhere it may be a point of controversy whether that destiny is decided by a struggle between the gods, by the decision of blind fate, or by the individual self. From the oldest hymns, laws and stories about man in the primeval era, through prophecy, the Deuteronomic centre and the great histories, down to the assailment of Job, the scepticism of Ecclesiastes and the eschatology of the apocalyptic writings – in all these, the varying modes of theological thinking leave us in no doubt that Yahweh, the God of Israel, is the Determining One. 'Yahweh our God, Yahweh is one alone' (Deut. 6.4). As Israel's Saviour and Judge, as man's Creator and Protector, he has through his human messengers left no doubt as to the goal of man's destiny.

1. *To live in the world*

He is destined to live and not to fall victim to death. Clearly though the Yahwist's primeval history sees the threatening doom of death, yet the story shows Yahweh, who has made man 'a living being' (Gen. 2.7), untiringly concerned to save him from premature death, through warning (2.17), protective mark (4.15) and merciful preservation (6.8); it is only with pain that he decides in favour of the great annihilating judgment of the Flood (6.6) and he suspends its repetition for all time, in spite of man's unaltered wickedness (8.21ff.). Man is destined for life.

In the Joseph story, completely different though it is in kind, the strained relationship between Joseph and his brothers is suddenly snatched out of all its sombreness and is set in the light of a clearly destined goal, in Joseph's words of address (Gen. 45.5): 'Now do not be distressed, or angry with yourselves, because you sold me here; for God sent me before you to preserve life.' At the end he explains still more clearly (50.20): 'As for you, you meant evil against me; but God meant it for good, to bring it about that many people should be kept alive, as they are today.' The final sentences are unambiguous: in spite of human waywardness, Israel is destined for life.

Deut. 30.15–20 sums up the trend of Yahweh's commandments. They set life and salvation, death and evil before Israel's eyes. But the intention is that she should 'choose life, that you and your descendants may live' (v. 19).

The wisdom of Proverbs – which is completely different in kind, both in its ruling interests and its methods of argument – ultimately points to the same goal, publishing its intention with complete finality (Prov. 13.14):

> The teaching of the wise is a fountain of life,
>   that one may avoid the snares of death.

Or 15.24:

> The wise man's path leads upward to life,
>   that he may avoid the world of the dead beneath.

In prophecy, even with the most sombre preacher of judgment, Amos, it is noticeable how in the very midst of his message about the end of Israel, the word of God beams out (5.4): 'Seek me and live!' Isaiah makes it clear that all judgment is Yahweh's 'alien work' (28.21). And Hosea has come to perceive that the overdue death penalty pronounced on his refractory son Israel (11.1–7) has been withdrawn by Yahweh (v. 8):

> How could I give you up, O Ephraim!
> How could I surrender you, O Israel!

Ezekiel by no means put life and death before his hearers as if they were of equal weight. Yahweh declares that he has no pleasure in death but wants life. 'So turn, and live!' (18.32). Even over the valley of dead bones the call goes out (37.14):

> I will put my vital power[3] within you
>   and you shall live.

In the psalms of lament, wherever we saw the psalmist in extremest danger, it was evident that Yahweh and death are far removed from one another.[4] Trust pioneers new ways (Ps. 16.10):

> Thou dost not give me up to the world of the dead,
> or permit thy faithful one to see the Pit.

Although the problem of death is far from solved in any fundamental sense in the Old Testament, yet the tendency is clear: man is destined to live. That this main trend strives towards the word of life of the New Testament is a fact that can hardly be missed. In a world in which survival is threatening to become increasingly improbable, the biblical insight into man's destiny is ground for a new expectation of life.

But what should man live *for*? Only answers which affect the 'worldliness' of this life can be expected from the Old Testament.

2. *To love his fellow-men*

He is destined to love and to overcome hate. The relationship of man to his fellows is orientated towards this goal. The rule of man over man is not in accordance with his destiny but is 'for his hurt', as Ecclesiastes recognizes (8.9). The Yahwist has pointed out man's right relationship to his fellows in the archetypal image of Adam's discovery of his wife: in the jubilation of his loving recognition, the being alone, which is not good for him, has found its end, and the help fitting for him has found its creaturely realization (Gen. 2.18–23). But we are soon shown how hard it is for man not to allow his destiny of helping and loving to be wrested from him through the powers of temptation (Gen. 3) or envy (Gen. 4).

So that man does not lose track of his destiny among his fellows, Israel is taught through ever-new precepts to deal rightly with men, until the crowning sentence in Lev. 19.17f.[5] is reached, with its command that a man should love his neighbour as his own self, not excluding the stranger (v. 34) or even the enemy (Ex. 23.4f.; Prov. 25.21f.).[6] Love (Ex. 21.5)[7] and a feeling of complete solidarity can enter even into the relations between masters and slaves (Deut. 15.12–18; 23.15f.).[8] The only true king in Israel is the one to whom the poor are precious (Ps. 72.2–4, 12–14).[9] Micah 6.8 can put it in the concisest of terms:

> He has showed you, O man, what is good, and what Yahweh requires of you: nought but to do justice, and to love kindness, and to walk heedfully with your God.[10]

This also exposes the basis of all prophetic indictments of the social order. They see man becoming inhuman wherever he denies his fellow men recognition, justice and kindness. The wisdom of Proverbs comes to the sober conclusion (Prov. 15.17):

> Better is a dinner of herbs where love is
> than a fatted ox and hatred with it.

But even in the Old Testament the ultimate goal of man's mutual dealings and relationships embraces the whole world of the nations. Guided by Yahweh's edicts from Zion, they are all to cease from learning the techniques of war (Isa.2.2–4).[11] Thus, varied though the different points of departure are, the direction of man's life among his fellow men is clearly determined. Its goal is love. But man has not only to do with man.

3. To rule over creation

His destiny in the world of extra-human creation is just as unequivocal; it is to rule. The Priestly document has reduced this most stringently to a definition by saying that the intention of man's creation in God's image was that he should rule over the earth, and in particular over his own first rivals, the animals (Gen.1.26, 28).[12] Even earlier, the Yahwist in his story-like way expressed his joy over man's capacity for controlling the world's potentialities: he can produce musical instruments and learn the arts of playing zither and flute (Gen.4.21), he can mine and fashion minerals and iron (v.22). As husbandman, he learnt to cultivate the vine and discovered its power to overthrow him (Gen.9.20f.). He invented materials which made it possible for him to put up giant buildings (11.3f.). But did not this ancient narrator already see the danger that man would himself be dominated by the potentialities of the creation which he was himself designed to dominate – as when wine deprives Noah of his will-power and puts him at the mercy of his son's shamelessness (9.21f.); or when the unguessed-at technique of building drew man on the one hand into the intoxication of self-praise (11.4a) and on the other into projects motivated by fear (v.4b)? Wherever man is overpowered by the things which he himself is meant to overpower, inhuman man is born.

In Israel's wisdom writings rule over nature becomes an archaic science. I Kings 4.33 reports Solomon's wisdom in the things of nature. According to this passage, botany and zoology particularly were studied at the court in Jerusalem:

> the trees, from the cedar that is in Lebanon to the hyssop that grows out of the wall; he spoke also of beasts, and of birds, and of reptiles, and of fish.

The encyclopaedic lists which belonged to the science of Egypt and Mesopotamia merely accumulated the names of natural phenomena; Israelite wisdom was distinguished from this by the fact that it did not merely enumerate animals and plants, but also brought out the connections between them in poetical descriptions.[13]

The triumph of human technology in mining is celebrated by Job 28. 1–10; men hollow out the innermost parts of the earth and illuminate them, hanging in the shafts on ropes, where not even the sharp eye of the hawk can penetrate, so that they may win the most costly precious metals and gems:

> Surely there is a mine for silver
>> and a place for gold where they may refine it.
> Iron is taken out of the earth
>> and copper is smelted from the ore.
> Men put an end to darkness,
>> and search out the rock, enveloped in night.[14]
> Men with lamps hollow out the shaft,
> they hang without support for their feet,
>> far from men, they swing to and fro.
> Out of the earth sprouts corn for bread;
>> but underneath men burst it asunder with fire.
> Its rocks are the place of sapphires,
>> and it has dust of gold.
> That path no bird of prey knows,
>> and the hawk's eye has not seen it.
> The proud beasts have not trodden it;
>> the lion has not passed over it.
> Man puts his hand to the flinty rock,
>> and overturns mountains by the roots.
> He cuts out channels in the rocks,
>> and his eye sees every precious thing.

But why is man's domination of the world described here with so much artistry? To make it all the clearer that for all his searchings and investigations man cannot discover wisdom itself, 'the meaning implanted in creation'.[15] 'Only God understands the way to it' (v. 23). Thus belief in creation secures the factual nature of man's wordly rule, which deviates sharply from a sacral interpretation of the world,[16] yet leads clearly to the fear of God (Job 28.28).

Psalm 8 celebrates man's destiny to rule over extra-human creation in a quite different way.[17] It leads to the final, decisive and all-embracing recognition by emphasizing that the crowning of man to be steward over the world is (in view of his minuteness in relation to the universe and his pitiable need of providing care) anything but a matter of course, and certainly does not have its ground in man himself (vv. 3f.).

4. *To praise God*

Man is destined to praise God. The man in Ps. 8, who discovers his superiority in the world, is unable to express this fact through praise of himself; he can only find words of praise addressed to God (vv. 5f.):

> Thou hast made him lack but little of the divine
> and hast crowned him with glory and honour.
> Thou hast given him dominion over the works of thy hands;
> thou hast put all things under his feet.

And the framework of the whole psalm is the antiphon (vv. 1, 9):

> O Yahweh, our Lord,
> how glorious is thy name
> in all the earth!

In Ps. 8, therefore, man's destiny to praise God and therefore to enter into a grateful dialogue with his Creator is not pushed aside by his fascination with his own capabilities; for he also keeps himself and his own neediness in view (v. 4):

> What is man that thou art mindful of him,
> and the son of man that thou dost care for him?

Remembering the acts of God proclaimed in Israel, he is bound to recognize this other aspect of his nature,

That very act of salvation at the Reed Sea (Ex. 14) which was the foundation of Israel's faith in Yahweh, led inevitably to the primitive hymn (Ex. 15.21):

> Sing to Yahweh, for he has triumphed gloriously;
> the horse and his rider he has thrown into the sea.

But Israel also grasped the prophetic proclamation of judgment in its final intention when she was able to answer with such doxologies as we find included in the book of Amos (4.13; 5.8; 9.5f.), or with hymns of thanksgiving such as are heralded in Isa. 12, at the end of the first collection of the sayings of Isaiah (chs. 1–11). Where the praise of God is absent, man has misunderstood the discord between his neediness and his capabilities. Here too inhuman man is not far away. The Psalter – passed down to us as 'the Book of Praises'[18] – has with its hymns grasped that man's final destiny is to praise God. Here we can only remind ourselves of the multiplicity of the calls to praise that meet man when, with his experiences drawn from history and from creation, he turns into the sanctuary, there to pay homage to the only Merciful One, even in the complaints that he unfolds before God. As examples, we may turn in conclusion to Pss. 145 and 148.

Psalm 145 sees the connection between the works of creation which man discovers and his destiny of praise (vv. 5f.):

> I will tell of thy wondrous works.
> They speak of the might of thy terrible acts.
> I will declare thy greatness.

The works of God which man explores speak a language which provokes him to a hymn of praise (vv. 10–12).[19] And in praise fragmentary perceptions turn into a unity and a whole, together with the still unexplored secrets which continue to threaten even the most thoroughly established knowledge.[20] Thus the hymn of praise not only manifests life's final destiny ('the living, the living he thanks thee!' Isa. 38.19), but also man's destiny to rule over the world.

Finally, however, Ps. 148 shows how man, from the kings of the earth down to the choir of children (vv. 11–13), together with all the works of creation, from the constellations down to the smallest things that creep on the earth (vv. 3–10), are bound together in the fellowship of praise. The destiny of men differs so deeply and is so deeply divided; but their common destiny, to join together in love, is fulfilled in their coming together in the praise of God:

> Kings of the earth and all peoples,
> princes and all rulers of the earth!
> Young men and maidens together,
> old men, at one with children!
> Let them praise the name of Yahweh,
> for his name alone is exalted.

In praise such as this the destiny of man – his destiny to live in the world, his destiny to love his fellow men, and his destiny to rule over all non-human creation – finds its truly human fulfilment. Otherwise man, becoming his own idol, turns into a tyrant; either that or, falling dumb, he loses his freedom.

NOTES

I. *Introduction*

1. See especially *Kirchliche Dogmatik* III/2.
2. Here and for the following passages see E. Jüngel, 'keine Menschenlosigkeit'.
3. E. Bloch, *Atheismus*, p. 378.
4. Gen. 3.9.
5. Ps. 8.4; Job 7.17.
6. Ex. 3.11; II Sam. 7.18; cf. Gen. 18.27.
7. III/2, p. vii; ET p. ix.
8. F. Delitzsch, *System der biblischen Psychologie*, ²1861; J. Koeberle, *Natur und Geist nach der Auffassung des AT*, 1901; J. Pedersen, *Israel – its Life and Culture* I–II, 1927.
9. K. Galling, *Das Bild vom Menschen in biblischer Sicht*, 1947; W. Eichrodt, *Das Menschenverständnis des AT*, 1947 (ET 1951); W. Zimmerli, *Das Menschenbild des AT*, 1949.
10. Cf. K. Galling, op. cit., pp. 6f.; W. Zimmerli, op. cit., pp. 3f.
11. A. R. Johnson, *The Vitality of the Individual in the Thought of Ancient Israel*, 1949.
12. G. Pidoux, *L'homme dans l'Ancien Testament*, 1953.
13. L. Köhler, *Der hebräische Mensch*, 1953 (ET 1956).
14. See the monographs and essays cited in the first note of each of the following chapters; also F. Maass, '*ādām*', cols. 81f.
15. W. Pannenberg, *Was ist der Mensch? Die Anthropologie der Gegenwart im Lichte der Theologie*, 1962; H. R. Müller-Schwefe, *Der Mensch – das Experiment Gottes*, 1966; H. Gollwitzer, *Krummes Holz – aufrechter Gang. Zur Frage nach dem Sinn des Lebens*, 1970; J. Moltmann, *Mensch. Christliche Anthropologie in den Konflikten der Gegenwart*, 1971, and the books cited there, pp. 171f. n. 14 (ET p. 120).
16. L. Köhler, *Mensch*, p. 2; ET p. 13.
17. G. v. Rad has already stressed that Israel's ideas of man 'can only be understood in the light of the distinctive nature of her faith' (*Theol. AT* II, p. 369; ET II, pp. 347f.). Cf. here J. Moltmann, *Mensch*, an outline of a Christian anthropology as 'theology in action'; he already notifies his readers in the introduction that 'a book about "Man" will inevitably slip into being a book about God' (p. 9; cf. p. 33; ET pp. 9, 19).

Preliminary Remarks to Part One

1. Cf. for example E. Jüngel's remarks on the separation between soul and body in death according to Plato's *Phaedo* (*Tod*, pp. 61ff., 68ff.).

2. Cf. provisionally J. Hessen, *Platonismus*, pp.98ff.; T. Boman, *Denken*, pp.11ff.; ET pp.17ff.; J. Barr, *Semantics*, pp.8ff.

3. B. Landsberger, *Eigenbegrifflichkeit*, p.17; G. v. Rad, *Weisheit*, pp.42f.; ET pp.26ff. See also 'soul' as a parallel to 'neck' (Prov.3.22), or 'hand' beside 'throat' (Ps.143.6).

4. G. v. Rad, op. cit., pp.75f.; ET p.53.

5. K. H. Fahlgren, '*ṣᵉdaqā*', p.126, termed as synthetic in the first place that view of life which sees religion, ethics and economics, not as completely independent phenomena but merely as different sides of the same thing.

6. Cf. J. Koeberle, *Natur und Geist*, pp.84ff., 178ff.; J. Pedersen, *Israel*, pp.106ff.; A. R. Johnson, *Vitality*, pp.1f.

7. H. Plessner, 'Anthropologie', col.412.

8. J. Moltmann, *Mensch*, p.23; ET pp.10f.

II. nepeš – *Needy Man*

1. *Literature*: L. Dürr, '*nepeš*'; J. Pedersen, *Israel*, pp.99–259; J. H. Becker, *Nefesj*; M. Seligson, *nps mt*; G. Widengren, *VT* 4; G. Pidoux, *L'Homme*, pp.10–19; A. Murtonen, *Soul*; D. Lys, *Nèphèsh*; W. Schmidt, 'Begriffe', pp.377–382; A. R. Johnson, *Vitality*, pp.2–22; F. Scharbert, *Fleisch*.

2. KBL p.626; according to D. Lys (p.119), 757 times.

3. See p.8 above.

4. D. Lys's attempt to order the *n.* texts historically and thus to discern a development in the meaning has produced no results worth mentioning; apart from small variants a 'polysémie' is evident from the earliest to the latest literary strata in the Old Testament (pp.194–196).

5. On Prov.23.7, the grudging man is like 'something horrible in the throat' and 'something bitter for the neck', cf. the Instruction of Amen-em-opet ch.XI (*ANET*, p.423a; *AOT*, p.42), G. Widengren, *VT* 4, pp.100f. and B. Gemser, *Sprüche*, pp.86f.

6. The Old Testament only talks 21 times in all about Yahweh's *n.* (A. R. Johnson, *Vitality*, p.8 n.1); when Yahweh according to Amos 6.8 swears by his *n.*, the phrase probably contains a reminiscence of an ancient oath ceremony, in which the man swearing the oath touched his throat; see here H. W. Wolff, BK XIV/2, p.326. In Amos 6.8 too mention of Yahweh's *n.* is associated with his abhorrence. See p.25 below.

7. Read *napšah* with BHS.

8. Cf. the related use of '*ap* for nose and 'snorting'; E. Johnson, "*ānap*", p.375.

9. Cf. W. v. Soden, *GAG* §73b, and W. Schmidt, *Begriffe*, p.378.

10. Cf. W. v. Soden, *AHw*, p.736, and D. Lys, *Nèphèsh*, p.119; see also p.20 below.

11. *AHw*, p.738.

12. Cf. J. Aistleitner, *WB*, p.211, with C. H. Gordon, *UT* p.446, and G. Widengren, *VT* 4, pp.98ff.

13. A. R. Johnson, *Vitality*, pp.7, 13.

14. Cf. earlier E. Dhorme, *L'Emploi* (1923), pp.18f.; later above all A. R. Johnson, *Vitality*, pp.4ff.

15. See p.13 above.

16. See BHS.

17. Still H. J. Kraus's view (*Psalmen*, p.716).
18. W. v. Soden, *ZAW* 53, 1935, pp.291f.
19. L. Dürr, '*nepeš*, p.268; *maḥmal n.* in Ezek.24.21, 25, could also be that 'which one wears on the neck', an ornament and jewel; cf. Prov.3.22.
20. L. Dürr, ibid., p.267; he reminds us on p.264 of *Enuma eliš* IV 31 (cf. *ANET*, p.66a), where Marduk is given the command, when he is invested with the sword: 'Go . . . cut Tiamat's throat!' (*a-lik-ma nap-ša-tu-aš pu-ru-ʿ-ma*). The Yahwist and Deuteronomy use *hikkā* with double acc.: to attack someone 'with respect to the neck' (Gen.37.21; Deut.19.6, 11), also Jer.40.14f.; here *n.* designates the precise vital spot at which the stroke meets the person. It is only the wording with simple accusative that understands *n.* as 'person' or 'life' (Lev.24.17f. and Num.35.11, 15, 30; see here p.9 below). Cf. J. Scharbert, *Fleisch*, pp.24, 43, 64.
21. Cf. L. Dürr, p.264, also Ps.22.20a.
22. See pp.12f. above.
23. But see p.24 below.
24. See BHK.
25. Cf. V. Wagner, *Rechtssätze*, p.4; J. Oelsner, on the other hand, thinks of 'throat' (*Körperteile*, pp.13ff.).
26. See p.111 below.
27. See pp.102ff. below.
28. Cf. J. Scharbert, *Fleisch*, p.23.
29. The parallels *n.* – *gargārōt* (neck) reminds us that by using the word *n.* to term the man addressed a person, there is still an echo of the 'throat' for the Israelites. G. Gerleman, '*ḥyh*', p.553, stresses that the term *ḥayyīm* 'contains a higher degree of objectivity', that is to say signifies 'a possession or, more correctly, a saving gift' whereas *n.* 'is viewed as an inherent principle of life bound up with the body'. See further pp.555f.
30. E.g., by M. Noth, *Leviticus*.
31. In Gen.2.19 *n. ḥayyā* in this sense seems to be a later addition to the Yahwist text.
32. Cf. A. R. Johnson, *Vitality*, p.15 n.3.
33. W. Schmidt, 'Begriffe', p.381; '*nephesh* is man as individual, in so far as he has an independent existence.'
34. F. J. Stendebach, *Mensch*, pp.130f.
35. See pp.7f. above.
36. For statistics see p.13 and n.6 above.

III. bāśār – *Man in his Infirmity*

1. *Literature*: G. Pidoux, *L'Homme*, pp.18f.; A. R. Hulst, '*kol-bāśār*'; Schweizer-Baumgärtel-Meyer, '*sarx*'; W. Schmidt, 'Begriffe', p.382; J. Scharbert, *Fleisch*; D. Lys, *bāśār*; G. Gerleman, '*bāśār*'; N. P. Bratsiotis, '*bāśār*'.
2. D. Lys, *bāśār*, p.18.
3. Ibid., p.131. Exceptionally, *bāśār* is once applied to the world of vegetation together with *nepeš*; according to Isa.10.18 forest and vineyard were destroyed *minnepeš weʿad bāśār*, which is probably intended to mean that not only has life been destroyed (in the sap) but dead material (the dead wood) as well.
4. 61 times according to Gerleman, '*bāśār*, p.377.

5. Cf. K. Elliger, *Leviticus*, pp. 191ff., contrary to J. Scharbert, *Fleisch*, p. 49; but cf. Lev. 15.19, where the female *b.* is mentioned. See ch. VII n. 5 below.

6. Cf. W. Zimmerli, BK XIII 547.

7. About 50 times according to G. Gerleman, '*bāśār*', p. 377.

8. See BHK (so also RSV).

9. O. H. Steck, *Paradieserzählung*, p. 95.

10. W. Reiser, 'Verwandtschaftsformel'.

11. On the other hand *dām* (blood) is not used in the Old Testament as it is in Accadian (W. v. Soden, *AHw* p. 158) as a term for ('blood') relationship.

12. Cf. E. Dhorme, *L'Emploi*, p. 9.

13. A. R. Hulst, '*kol-bāśār*', pp. 29, 64.

14. See p. 22 above.

15. See also below p. 54.

16. Cf. Ezek. 16.26; 23.20 and pp. 27f. above. In Paul too 'the flesh' is the term for human weakness: II Cor. 5.16f.; 11.18. On the ethical frailty of *b.* cf. N. P. Bratsiotis, '*bāśār*', col. 863.

IV. rūaḥ – *Man as he is Empowered*

1. *Literature*: J. Koeberle, *Natur und Geist*; G. Pidoux, *L'Homme*, pp. 19–22; W. Bieder, 'Geist'; J. H. Scheepers, *gees*; D. Lys, *Rūach*; A. R. Johnson, *Vitality*, pp. 23–37 and 83–87; W. Schmidt, 'Begriffe', pp. 382–383; J. Scharbert, *Fleisch*.

2. D. Lys, *Rūach*, p. 152; according to J. H. Scheepers, *gees*, in 144 instances.

3. D. Lys, ibid.

4. See ch. II n. 6 above.

5. See p. 26 above. *r.* is applied 10 times to animals (Gen. 6.17; 7.15, 22; Ezek. 1.12, 20f.; 10.17; Eccles. 3.19, 21; Isa. 31.3), and 3 times to idols (Jer. 10.14 = 51.17; Hab. 2.19; cf. Isa. 41.29).

6. Cf. D. Lys, *Rūach*, p. 336.

7. See pp. 13 and 20 above.

8. See BHK (so also RSV).

9. See BHS.

10. Gen. 6.17; 7.15, 22. Eccles. 3.19, 21 stresses that animals have the same breath as men.

11. On this point see pp. 44f. below.

12. Cf. Judg. 15.19; I Sam. 30.12 and p. 33 above.

13. Cf. p. 33 above.

14. Cf. W. Zimmerli, BK XIII 244. According to Luke 4.14 Jesus goes into Galilee 'in the power of the spirit'.

15. D. Lys, *Rūach*, p. 336 and passim. See below p. 38.

16. See pp. 30f. above and H. W. Wolff, BK XIV/2, p. 80; on the following passage ibid., p. 78.

17. Cf. L. Perlitt, 'Mose', pp. 601–603.

18. See pp. 33f. above.

19. J. Koeberle, *Natur und Geist*, p. 204.

20. See pp. 33f.

21. See pp. 34f.

22. See p.54 below.
23. See above p.37. on Deut.34.9.

V. lēb(āb) – *Reasonable Man*

1. *Literature*: F. Delitzsch, *Psychologie*, pp.248–265; J. Koeberle, *Natur und Geist*, pp.211–228; E. Dhorme, *L'Emploi*, pp.112–128; F. Baumgärtel, '*lēb*'; F. H. v. Meyenfeldt, *Hart*; G. Pidoux, *L'Homme*, pp.24–28; A. R. Johnson, *Vitality*, pp.75–87; W. Schmidt, '*Begriffe*', pp.383–386; F. Stolz, '*lēb*'.
2. KBL; cf. F. Stolz, '*lēb*', p.861, following F. H. v. Meyenfeldt, *Hart*.
3. See p.43 below.
4. On Ps.38.10 see below p.42; cf. J. Hempel, *Heilung*; for another view see F. Stolz, op. cit., p.861.
5. A New Assyrian prophetic saying talks about the 'beams of the heart', which is quite unusual in Accadian: 'I, the mistress (= Istar of Arba'il) speak with thee. I watch over the beams of thy heart.' According to this, the fear is that the beams of the heart might break down, therefore failing to 'support' the house of the heart. I have taken the text (BM, Department of Western Asiatic Antiquities, K.4310 = 4R 68 = 4R² 61 II 16–40) from K. Deller, who numbers it NASP 1d in his compilation of New Assyrian prophetic sayings. Incidentally the Accadian *libbu* has a range of meaning similar to the Hebrew *l.*; cf. W. v. Soden, *AHw*, pp.549f.
6. W. v. Soden, *AHw*, p.550.
7. See BHS.
8. Perhaps the statement even embraces: 'You expand my knowledge', just as I Kings4.29 praises Solomon's 'largeness of mind', in the sense of his wide knowledge and capabilities; see p.47 below. *reḥab lēb* is used in the sense of pride, arrogance (i.e., *lēb* in the sense of self-conceit) in Prov.21.4; Ps.101.5 (next to 'haughty looks'); cf. *reḥab nepeš* in Prov.28.25.
9. See p.34 above on Gen.45.27.
10. See p.37 above.
11. J. Hempel, *Heilung*, pp.253f. Cf. for example *nw'* in Isa.7.2 and 29.9.
12. See pp.34f. above.
13. G. Pidoux (p.25) counts 400 passages here; see pp.40f. above on I Sam. 25.37.
14. Cf. F. Stolz, '*lēb*', p.861.
15. Egyptian Wisdom is also aware of the great importance of hearing. Cf. H. Brunner, 'Herz'; and the same author's *Erziehung*, pp.110ff., 131ff.: 'The organ with which man receives wisdom was called the heart by the Egyptians' (p.110).
16. On the wider meaning of *špṭ* see M. Noth, BK IX 51.
17. Cf. G. v. Rad, *Weisheit*, pp.376f.; ET pp.296f.: 'What he, the paradigm of the wise man, wished for himself was not the authoritative reason which reigns supreme over dead natural matter, the reason of modern consciousness, but an 'understanding' reason, a feeling for the truth which emanates from the world and addresses man. . . . The Solomon of I Kings3 could – regarded objectively – have said that he would yield to Yahweh so that the world might not remain dumb for him but that it might be understood by him.'
18. See also II Kings5.26, for example.

19. Cf. K. Elliger, BK XI 184f.
20. But see below p.53 on II Sam.15.6.
21. In the case of the arrogant heart one ought also to think of 'self-conceit'; see p.46 above.
22. It is in this sense that the denominative verb *lbb* niphal in Job 11.12 is formed: to acquire understanding or insight, to come to one's senses. The origin of an appreciation of art as a human talent is the heart (Ex.35.25); in the sense of being a 'gift', artistic ability comes from the divine *rūaḥ* (Ex.31.3); see p.35 above.
23. See p.38 above.
24. Cf. J. Vollmer, *Rückblicke*, p.87.
25. According to LXX; cf. BHK.
26. Cf. W. Eisenbeis, *šlm*, pp.340f.; on the somewhat different linguistic usage in Chronicles, see pp.347f. In a private letter K. Deller has drawn my attention to the fact that in Accadian *libbašu gummur* (to devote the heart entirely) is used of the king's eunuchs, his closest advisers and his vassals. Thus we find in a letter to Esarhaddon (ABL VI, 620 r.6): 'A servant whose heart cleaves undividedly to his masters [i.e. Esarhaddon and the crown-prince Ashurbanipal] am I.'
27. See p.38 above.
28. See p.24 above.
29. Cf. Num.16.28 and p.53 above.
30. See BHS.
31. See p.53 above.
32. See p.53 above.
33. See pp.49f. above.
34. See pp.48f. above. Cf. W. Schottroff, *Gedenken*, pp.116f., 226ff.
35. M. Noth, BK IX 197.
36. All the 26 passages in the Old Testament dealing with the heart of God have been considered in this section.

VI. *The Life of the Body*

1. *Literature*: J. Koeberle, *Natur und Geist*, pp.187f.; E. Dhorme, *L'Emploi*, pp.8–11; L. Morris, 'blood'; G. Pidoux, *L'Homme*, pp.49–53; H. Graf Reventlow, 'Blut'; K. Koch, 'Blut'; A. R. Johnson, *Vitality*, pp.71–74; G. Gerleman, '*dām*'.
2. Above all from *ḥayyīm*; on *nepeš* see pp.11ff. above; on *rūaḥ* pp.32ff. above.
3. See BHK.
4. J. Koeberle's view; see *Natur und Geist*, pp.187f.
5. Together with B. Gemser, *Sprüche*; H. Ringgren, *Sprüche*, and BHK, as in Prov.24.12 and Job7.20.
6. Gen.2.7, see p.22 above.
7. Cf. G. Pidoux, *L'Homme*, p.51.
8. See p.19 above.
9. See pp.19f. above.
10. G. Gerleman, '*dām*', p.448.
11. Cf. K. Elliger, *Leviticus*, pp.226–228. It ought to be observed that the blood belongs to Yahweh by right, but not physically, as is undoubtedly the case

with the breath, especially in the book of Job (see pp. 34ff. above). The view (widespread in Mesopotamia) that mankind had been created out of the blood of a slaughtered god (for evidence see now F. Maass, "*ādām*", cols. 82f.) finds no acceptance in the Old Testament.

12. See p. 163 below.
13. K. Koch, *Blut*, p. 406=444.
14. In Nahum 3.1 subsequently applied to Nineveh; cf. J. Jeremias, *Kultprophetie*, pp. 29ff.
15. Cf. H. Graf Reventlow, 'Blut', and K. Koch, 'Blut', pp. 400f.=437f.
16. II Kings 3.22 mentions the redness of blood; Gen. 49.11 and Deut. 32.14 talk about the 'blood of the grape'.

VII. *The Inner Parts of the Body*

1. *Literature*: E. Dhorme, *L'Emploi*, pp. 109–137; G. Pidoux, *L'Homme*, pp. 29f.; A. R. Johnson, *Vitality*, pp. 73–75; L. Rost, 'Leberlappen'; C. Westermann, '*kbd*'; Freedman-Lundbom, '*beṭen*'.
2. See pp. 40f. above.
3. With LXX and B. Gemser, *Sprüche*, I have inserted *lō*' before the final word.
4. See pp. 41f. above.
5. Only once are the external male genitals called 'privy parts', or *mᵉbūšim* (Deut. 25.11); see also *bāśār*, p. 27 above; *raglayim*, ('legs') is found more frequently (Ezek. 4.25; Judg. 3.24; Isa. 6.2). On *yād* in Isa. 57.8, 10 as the male member, cf. A. S. van der Woude, '*yād*', pp. 669f. *yārēk* (loins, hip, thigh) is used for the generative organ, where a man's children are termed 'those who proceeded out of his *yārēk*' (Gen. 46.26; Ex. 1.5; Judg. 8.30), and in the ancient swearing ceremony 'to lay the hand under someone's *yārēk*' (Gen. 24.2; 47.29).
6. See pp. 59f. above.
7. E. Dhorme, *L'Emploi*, p. 109, points out that the inner parts of the body, as organs known precisely only to soothsayers and physicians, represent an interest of the first order for Semitic psychology.
8. J. Aistleitner, *WB* 144.
9. Cf. E. Dhorme, op. cit., p. 129.
10. That is to say *kābēd* in the Masoretic text.
11. Cf. L. Rost, 'Leberlappen'.
12. Cf. M. Jastrow, jr., *Religion*, pp. 245–406; W. Zimmerli, BK XIII 490.
13. So KBL and others.
14. E. Dhorme, *L'Emploi*, pp. 129f.
15. See p. 96 below.

VIII. *The Form of the Body*

1. *Literature*: E. Dhorme, *L'Emploi*, pp. 19–42, 91–109, 137–161; A. R. Johnson, *Vitality*, pp. 39f., 50–75; L. Delekat, 'Wörterbuch' ('*eṣṣem*, pp. 49–52); G. Gerleman, BK XVIII 63–75; H. U. v. Balthasar, *Herrlichkeit* III/2/1, 120–125; A. S. van der Woude, '*zᵉrōa*'' and '*yād*'.
2. L. Delekat observes that the plural of 'bones' is usually *ᵃṣāmōt*, whereas the masculine plural form generally means 'limbs'.
3. See pp. 28f. above. On the meaning 'genitals' for *raglayim* and also for *yārēk* (thigh, hip) see ch. VII n. 5 above.

4. A. S. van der Woude, '*yād*', p.667: rather more than 1600 instances.
5. This makes all textual considerations unnecessary; cf. H. Wildberger, BK X 33.
6. L. Köhler, *Mensch*, p.10; ET p.22.
7. G. Gerleman, BK XVIII 74f.
8. It is probably the colour of his hair that is meant, rather than the colour of his skin; cf. Gen.25.25.
9. The translation follows the rendering of O. Plöger in *Daniel*; even Abigail's quick understanding is praised as well as her beauty (I Sam.25.3).
10. Cf. G. Gerleman, BK XVIII 63–72.
11. Cf. G. Gerleman, op. cit., p.199: the writer is thinking of 'the threads that run between the front and back beams of the weaver's loom'.
12. Cf. T. Boman, *Denken*, pp.62ff.; ET pp.77ff.
13. The translation follows G. Gerleman, op. cit.
14. On the text cf. H. Wildberger, BK X 135f.

IX. The Nature of Man

1. *Literature*: A. R. Johnson, *Vitality*, pp.40–50; F. Maass, "*ādām*'; G. v. Rad, *Weisheit*; J. Moltmann, *Mensch*, pp.30–37, 152–156; ET pp.16ff., 105ff.; G. Liedke, "*ōzen*'.
2. Cf. A. R. Johnson, op. cit., pp.40f. *pānīm* occurs in its different combinations 2,100 times (KBL) – far more than three times as often as *rō'š*.
3. Following LXX.
4. Text following F. Horst, *Hiob*, and translation adapted from RSV accordingly.
5. See p.47 above.
6. G. v. Rad, *Weisheit*, p.399; ET p.314. Cf. also G. v. Rad, *Predigten* (ed. U. v. Rad, 1972), p.81.
7. Cf. J. Moltmann, *Mensch*, pp.30ff.; ET pp.16ff.
8. Cf. J. Moltmann, pp.153ff.; ET pp.106ff.
9. Cf. G. v. Rad, *Deut.* p.51; ET p.72.
10. Cf. C. Barth, 'Antwort'.
11. Cf. M. Bierwisch, 'Strukturalismus', *J.Ihwe* (ed.), *Literaturwissenschaft und Linguistik*, vol.1 (1971) p.71: 'There is clear evidence to support the supposition that the learning of language is conditioned by biological dispositions, which are by no means confined to the external organs, but which embrace deeply-lying neuro-physiological structures. In the first place, the capacity for learning a language is a characteristic confined to the species man. No other living thing is capable of learning even fragments of a natural language. The capacity for language is accordingly bound up with particular specific factors of the innate human disposition.'

X. The Old Testament Concept of Time

1. *Literature*: W. Vollborn, *Zeitverständnis*; C. H. Ratschow, 'Zeitproblem'; W. Eichrodt, 'Heilserfahrung'; J. Muilenburg, 'Time'; J. Barr, *Time*; M. Sekine, 'Zeitauffassung', pp.66–82; T. Boman, *Denken*, pp.104–133, 140–142 (ET pp.123–154, 161–163) and 209–212 (no ET); J. R. Wilch, *Time*; G. v. Rad,

Weisheit, pp. 182–188 and 295–306 (ET pp. 138–143 and 228–237); G. Delling, '*chronos*'.

2. Cf. 2.7 and p. 115 below.

3. See p. 51 above

4. See p. 83 above.

5. H. W. Wolff, 'Jahwist'.

6. M. Sekine, 'Zeitauffassung', pp. 67f., calls time as a framework, external time.

7. J. R. Wilch, *Time*, p. 164: 'The word '*ēth* was used in the OT in order to indicate the relationship or juncture of circumstances, primarily in an objective sense and only secondarily in a temporal sense, and to direct attention to a specifically definite occasion or situation.' Cf. Isa. 49.8 and II Cor. 6.1f.

8. Secondary, according to M. Noth, *Leviticus*, p. 31; ET p. 31.

9. G. v. Rad, 'Tag', p. 946; ET pp. 943f.

10. Cf. C. Westermann, BK I 235 and pp. 137ff. below.

11. See BHK.

12. Cf. E. Janssen, *Juda*, pp. 74f.

13. Cf. E. Jenni, "*hr*', p. 115 ('*ahªrit*=what comes afterwards); cf. also the discussion between T. Boman, *Denken*, pp. 128f. (ET pp. 149f.) and 210f., and J. Barr, *Semantics*, pp. 76f. Deserving attention in a wider context is the 'biblisch-theologische Meditation über die Erinnerung', by R. Bohren, *Predigtlehre* (1971), pp. 160ff: 'Remembrance teaches the language of hope. Memory is enthusiasm for the old pointing in the direction of the future; it is saga moving towards prophecy; it is a step backwards in a forward direction!' (p. 163).

14. Cf. K. Elliger, BK XI 184f., 238f.

15. Cf. E. Jenni, "*ōlām*'.

16. See p. 75 above.

17. Cf. J. Moltmann, *Freigelassene*, pp. 42f.; ET pp. 56f.

18. Cf. K. Galling, 'Zeit'.

19. J. R. Wilch, *Time*, pp. 117ff.

20. G. v. Rad, *Weisheit*, p. 183; ET p. 139. On the personally engaged 'critical individuality' of Ecclesiastes, which is that of an 'acute observer and independent thinker' see M. Hengel, *Judentum*, pp. 210–240 (cit. from p. 214); ET pp. 115–130 (116). G. v. Rad, on the other hand, has drawn attention (p. 305; ET p. 236) to the loss of confidence in Ecclesiastes, through which happenings do not only 'appear' differently but actually become different. Consequently the limits of knowledge also become clearer.

21. Cf. W. Zimmerli, *Weltlichkeit*, pp. 54f. The common formula 'in its season' means the 'right' time, such as is envisaged for the harvest, for example, or for a meal (Hos. 2.11; Pss. 1.3; 145.15 and frequently elsewhere).

22. See p. 48 above.

23. W. Zimmerli, *Prediger*, p. 172.

XI. *Creation and Birth*

1. *Literature*: L. Löw, *Lebensalter*, pp. 42–45; E. Würthwein, 'Psalm 139'; O. H. Steck, *Paradieserzählung*; F. Maass, "*ādām*'; J. G. Plöger, "*ªdāmā*'; W. Zimmerli, *Weltlichkeit*, pp. 20–44; C. Westermann, "*ādām*'.

2. As G. v. Rad holds, *Genesis*, p. 59; ET p. 82. In Gen. 2–3 it is only the later

addition 3.20 which calls the mother of mankind Eve, 'the mother of all living'.
3. See p.29 above and C. Westermann, BK I 318.
4. See p.22 and p.60 above.
5. See *AOT* pp.134, 135; cf. further evidence in F. Maass, "*ādām*', pp.82f.,
and W. Zimmerli, *Weltlichkeit*, pp.25f.
6. S. Morenz, *Religion*, p.192; F. Maass, op. cit., p.84; now above all E. Otto,
'Mensch', pp.338f. The statement seems to derive, not from a mythological
story, but from a play on the words *rmṭw*=man and *rmyt*=tear.
7. C. Westermann, BK I 311.
8. On the relationship formula in the bridegroom's paean of praise in 2.23 see
p.29 above.
9. See p.93 above.
10. Cf. KBL³, J. G. Plöger, "*ᵃdāmā*', p.95 and C. Westermann, "*ādām*',
pp.41f.
11. On the connection between vv.23 and 25 cf. W. H. Schmidt, *Schöpfungsgeschichte*, pp.124ff. That the terrestrial animals do not receive a blessing like the
fish and the birds is probably connected with the fact that the blessing in 1.22
and 1.28 brings such an increase with it that water and land are 'filled'. But as far
as the land is concerned, this is reserved for man (W. H. Schmidt, p.147).
12. But see Ps.139.15 and p.97 below.
13. Cf. W. H. Schmidt, op. cit., pp.164ff.
14. On man as the 'image of God' (vv.26f.) see p.163 below.
15. Cf. E. Würthwein, 'Psalm 139', pp.185–189.
16. Cf. Ps.16.7, Jer.12.2 and pp.65f. above.
17. This (Ps.139.16) is the only instance of *gōlem* in the Old Testament; the
word means the 'unfinished' being (cf. KBL³). In Ex.21.22 the fruit of the
pregnant woman's womb is designated by the usual word for child, in the plural
(*yᵉlādīm*). Job 3.10 speaks of the 'doors of the mother's womb' (*daltē beṭen*). That
the length of a woman's pregnancy is familiar as a theme can be deduced indirectly from the verses in Job 39.1f.:

> Do you know when the mountain goats bring forth?
> Do you observe the calving of the hinds?
> Can you number the months that they go great with young?
> Do you know the time when they bring forth?

18. An Assyrian account gives this as the primal origin of wise men and
heroes: *AOT* pp.135f.
19. Cf. F. Horst, *Hiob*, p.19.
20. See BHK (so also RSV) and F. Horst, op. cit., on this passage.
21. Cf. also Ezek.37.5f. and p.27 above.
22. F. Maass, "*ādām*', col.92.

XII. *Life and Death*

1. *Literature*: C. Barth, *Errettung*; G. v. Rad, *Theol. AT* I, pp.285–293 and
414–420; II, pp.371f.; ET I, pp.272–279, 387–391; II, pp.349f.; V. Maag,
'Tod'; L. Wächter, *Tod*; E. Jüngel, *Tod*; W. Zimmerli, *Weltlichkeit*, pp.111–124;
G. Gerleman, '*ḥyh*'.
2. *derek kol hā'āreṣ*, 'what is usual all over the earth', is also the way in which
conjugal intercourse is described in Gen.19.31; cf. Gen.31.35.

3. G. v. Rad, *Deut.*, p. 146; ET p. 205.

4. Cf. H. W. Wolff, 'Geschichtswerk'.

5. G. v. Rad, *Gen.* (^{1}1952), p. 214; ET p. 245.

6. Manasseh too, according to II Chron. 33.20, was buried 'in his house', i.e., under the floor or in a wall. On the various types of normal cave burials outside the dwelling place, see K. Galling, *BRL*, cols. 237–252.

7. G. v. Rad, *Deut.*, p. 150; ET p. 210.

8. Places for libations were found in the necropolis of Ras Shamra, witnessing to the ancient Ugaritic custom of making gifts of drink (L. Wächter, *Tod*, p. 184).

9. Cf. C. Westermann, *Jes.*, p. 318; ET p. 401.

10. Gilgamesh epic, plate 12 (*AOT*, pp. 183–186). Cf. C. Barth, *Errettung*, pp. 76–91.

11. *AOT*, pp. 206–210. On the Old Testament way of dealing with the myth, cf. A. Ohler, *Elemente*, p. 218: 'As mere poetic decoration the myths are no longer taken really seriously . . . The myths are detached from their real context and robbed of their original meaning by becoming metaphors for God's actions in history.'

12. Further evidence in L. Wächter, *Tod*, pp. 78f.; on the pyramid texts, coffin texts, and on the Book of the Dead, see H. Kees, 'Pyramidentexte'.

13. On Dan. 12.3 see p. 110 below.

14. Cf. L. Wächter, op. cit., pp. 51ff. for the synonymous use of *šeʾōl* on the one hand and *qeber* (grave), *bōr* (Pit), and *šaḥat* (Pit) on the other. As a rule the mention of *šeʾōl* means a heightened expression of distress.

15. G. v. Rad, *Theol. AT* I, p. 290; ET I, p. 277.

16. Cf. W. Zimmerli, BK XIII 219f. On the Egyptian cult of Osiris, cf. S. Morenz, *Religion*, p. 58 and passim; on the reflection of the Phoenician cult of Adonis in Hos. 6.1f., cf. H. W. Wolff, BK XIV/1, 150.

17. Cf. H. J. Kraus, *Gott*.

18. Cf. G. Gerleman, *hyh*, pp. 554f.

19. G. v. Rad, *Theol. AT* I, p. 289; ET I, p. 276.

20. Cf. M. Noth, *Lev.*, p. 123; ET p. 143; and K. Elliger, *Leviticus*, p. 261.

21. On the meaning of 'hand' see pp. 67f. above.

22. Cf. G. v. Rad, *Theol. AT* II, pp. 371f.; ET II, pp. 349f.; C. Barth, *Errettung*, p. 151: 'One should note, however, that the praise of Yahweh also has the function of being a token of vitality'.

23. E. Jüngel, *Tod*, pp. 99, 138; cf. also p. 145, and H. Gollwitzer, *Holz*, pp. 285f.: 'Communion with God is life.'

24. E. Jüngel, op. cit., pp. 138f.: 'By identifying himself with the dead Jesus, God actually exposes himself to the aggressive divine alienation of death; he exposes his own godhead to the power of negation . . . in order that he can in this very way be present for all men.'

25. W. Zimmerli, *Weltlichkeit*, p. 116.

26. Pss. 15; 24.3–6; Ezek. 18.5–9. See here W. Zimmerli, op. cit., pp. 122f. It is true that in the laments for the dead that have come down to us from Israel the name of Yahweh does not occur (H. Jahnow, *Leichenlied*, p. 56); but it is hardly conceivable that in Israel these too were not 'meant for Yahweh's ears'; cf. E. Gerstenberger, 'Mensch', pp. 65ff. (67).

27. Cf. C. Barth, *Errettung*, pp. 165f.; G. v. Rad, *Theol. AT* I, 419f.; ET I, p. 390.

28. G. v. Rad, 'Gerechtigkeit', pp. 432ff. = 242ff., has discovered the

connections in the history of the tradition. Cf. also G. v. Rad, *Weisheit*, pp. 263ff.; ET pp. 203ff.

29. V. Maag, 'Tod', pp. 30f.

30. See pp. 41f. above.

31. E. Jüngel, *Tod*, pp. 30ff.

32. See p. 106 above.

33. So the German version of the Jerusalem Bible. On the text see H. J. Kraus, *Psalmen*.

34. So v. Maag, *Tod*, p. 25; cf. C. Barth, *Errettung*, p. 38 and passim; W. Baumgartner, 'Auferstehungsglaube', p. 125.

35. C. Barth, op. cit., p. 118: 'Anyone who is in the power of Sheol to even the smallest degree finds himself in actual fact absolutely within its power.'

36. See pp. 108ff.

37. E. Jüngel, *Tod*, p. 94; cf. L. Wächter, *Tod*, p. 65.

38. Goethe, *Faust* Pt. II, Act V.

39. Cf. L. Wächter, *Tod*, pp. 89–97.

40. Semaḥot 3.8, according to G. Quell, *Tod*, p. 37.

41. G. Quell, ibid.

42. E. Jüngel, *Tod*, p. 101.

43. H. Schulz, *Todesrecht*. Cf. Ex. 21.12ff.; Deut. 27.15ff.

44. Cf. E. Jüngel, *Tod*, p. 99: 'Sin . . . destroys relationship. Death is the summing up of this urge towards lack of relationship. In so far death is anthropologically not only, and not for the first time, to be found at the end of life; in the striving towards lack of relationship it can be present as an active possibility at any time.' Cf. also Eph. 2.1; John 5.24; Luke 15.24.

45. See p. 47 above.

46. See p. 94 above.

47. Paul takes up this view of created man as being mortal man in I Cor. 15.42 ('sown in mortality') and 47 ('the first man was from the earth, a man of dust'). Cf. E. Schweizer, *choikos*, pp. 466f.; ET pp. 477f. On the other hand in Rom 5.12 Paul challenges Gen. 3 and the view upheld in Ps. 90.8ff. ('As sin came into the world through one man and death through sin . . .'). To distinguish between the created being's frontier of life and death as an enemy was Karl Barth's concern in *Kirchliche Dogmatik* III/2, pp. 776ff. (ET pp. 637ff.). See H. Gollwitzer, *Holz*, p. 286: 'Our desire for immortality is a revolt against our creatureliness.'

48. See p. 91 above. On the problem of human sacrifice cf. Ex. 22.29 with Deut. 12.31, Gen. 22, and G. Quell, op. cit., pp. 9–11.

49. On the following section see H. Gese, 'Psalm 22'.

50. See p. 106 on Ps. 88.10–12 and Isa. 38.18.

51. See p. 110 above.

52. See p. 109 above.

XIII. *To be Young and to Grow Old*

1. *Literature*: L. Löw, *Lebensalter*, pp. 12–20; 119–138; 227–239; 279–351; L. Köhler, *Mensch*, pp. 27–33, 48–100; ET pp. 41–46, 61–113; J. Conrad, *Generation*.

2. The figures given here are calculated according to Alfred Jepsen in his *Chronologie* and his appendix to W. Rudolph, *Hosea*, pp. 271ff., in comparison

with the information given in the books of Kings. Only Jehoahaz, Jehoiachin and Zedekiah are missing from the following list of the Davidic kings after Solomon, since we do not know how long they lived after they were deposed and taken prisoner.

3. L. Köhler, *Mensch*, p.30 (ET p.44), starting from different premises, arrived at an average age of 47 to 48 years old.

4. According to the *Brockhaus Encyclopaedia*[17] XI (1970) p.232, in the decade from 1951–1960 the average expectation of life in India was 42 years for men, 41 for women. In Togoland it was 32 for men and 39 for women. The comparative figures given by the *Encyclopaedia Britannica* (1973) for the United States (1959–61) were 67 for men and 73 for women; and for England and Wales (1961–63) 68 for men and 74 for women.

5. Cf. C. Westermann, BK I, pp.478f. There is a moving scene in Gen.47.8f., in which the aged Jacob stands in the foreign land before Pharaoh and, in answer to Pharaoh's question about his age, declares not without bitterness that with his 130 years he looks back to a shorter and harder pilgrimage than his fathers. Abraham was 175 years old, according to Gen.25.7, Isaac 180 according to Gen.35.28. Cf. G. v. Rad, *Gen.*, pp.334f.; ET pp.402f.

6. Cf. the beginning of Jesus' ministry at 'about 30 years of age', according to Luke 3.23. See also I Chron.23.3.

7. Cf. M. Noth, *Num.*, p.63; ET pp.69f.

8. David became king when he was 30 years old, according to II Sam.5.4.

9. On Hos.1.8 cf. H. W. Wolff, BK XIV/1, 23. The Egyptian Instruction of Ani gives as reason for the admonition to care for the ageing mother, etc.: 'Her breast was in thy mouth for three years' (*ANET*, p.420; *AOT*, p.38). The day when the child was weaned could be celebrated as a feast (Gen.21.8).

10. Cf. J. Conrad, *Generation*, pp.9f. The circumcision was 'probably originally an apotropaic act at the beginning of puberty' (K. Elliger, *Leviticus*, p.157). Later it took place on the eighth day (Gen.17.12; 21.4; Lev.12.3; Luke 2.21).

11. Cf. L. Köhler, *Mensch*, p.32; ET p.46; K. Elliger, *Leviticus*, pp.380ff.: 'Not only the actual priestly business but also the numerous subordinate services (cf. Josh.9.21ff.) have long been firmly in the hands of particular professional clerical groups, who are not inclined to accept any stranger among them' (p.386). A shekel generally corresponds to about 11.5 grams of silver – rather less than half an ounce (cf. K. Galling, *BRL*, col.187, and A. Strobel, 'Masse', cols.1167f.).

12. See pp.71ff. above.

13. I Sam.16.12; II Sam.14.25f.; see pp.69f. above.

14. See p.120 above and J. Conrad, *Generation*, p.11.

15. See recently G. v. Rad, *Weisheit*, p.67; ET p.45.

16. As in the Palestinian winter; cf. W. Zimmerli, *Prediger*, p.240.

17. The arms.

18. The legs (so W. Zimmerli, ibid.). K. Galling, 'Prediger', p.122, thinks of bent backs.

19. The teeth.

20. The eyes.

21. The ears become deaf.

22. The voice.

23. Cf. K. Galling, op. cit., on this passage.
24. The singing falls silent.
25. The hair becomes grey.
26. Walking becomes difficult, there is no more running and jumping.
27. No stimulus and no aphrodisiac helps the old man any more.
28. Cf. K. Galling, op. cit., on this passage.
29. Cf. K. Galling, ibid., on this passage.
30. See BHK (so also RSV).
31. H. J. Hermisson, 'Weisheit', p. 145, points to models from wisdom literature which are evident in the speech of the aged Barzillai.
32. Cf. J. Conrad, *Generation*, pp. 9, 57 and passim.
33. *lēaḥ*, root *lḥḥ*, moist, fresh, full of sap.

XIV. *Waking and Working*

1. *Literature*: W. H. Schmidt, *Schöpfungsgeschichte*, pp. 194f., 205–207, 219–221; C. Westermann, BK I, pp. 271–273, 299–302, 367f.; G. v. Rad, *Weisheit*, pp. 92–101, 165–181; ET pp. 65–73, 124–137.
2. Cf. C. Westermann, BK I, p. 272.
3. Cf. W. H. Schmidt, *Schöpfungsgeschichte*, pp. 142, 147. On the view taken by the Priestly document, see further p. 160 below.
4. C. Westermann, op. cit., pp. 300f.: 'Work is therefore seen here as being part of the essence of man's nature. A life without work would not be an existence worthy of man' (p. 300). Cf. further O. H. Steck, *Paradieserzählung*, pp. 85f.
5. The stories of the creation and the Garden of Eden were probably linked together at a later stage; this is also suggested by the 3rd fem. suffix in 2.15b *β*, which is quite in accordance with *'ᵃdāmā* in 2.5; 3.23 but is now related to *gan*; see W. H. Schmidt, *Schöpfungsgeschichte*, pp. 206f. See also O. H. Steck, op. cit., p. 48.
6. Cf. G. v. Rad, *Weisheit*, pp. 166ff; ET pp. 125ff. *ḥārūṣ* (industrious) occurs solely in Proverbs (5 times), *'āṣēl* (lazy) 14 times in Proverbs and once in Ecclesiastes, *'aṣlā* and *'aṣlūt* (laziness) once each in Proverbs. We therefore have to do here with a theme that is quite particular to the wisdom of the proverbial sayings.
7. See BHK.
8. See BHK (so also RSV).
9. G. v. Rad, *Weisheit*, pp. 167f.; ET pp. 125f.
10. On the 'fear of God' interpreted as obedience and trust, cf. G. v. Rad, op. cit., p. 92, ET pp. 65f., and the literature mentioned there. Prophecy and its attitude to poverty might also be considered here; cf. H. W. Wolff, BK XIV/2, 126, 200ff. H. U. v. Balthasar, *Herrlichkeit* III/2/1, p. 119, says: 'Through prophecy and the warnings of the nation's downfall through God's judgment, which the prophets proclaimed and which later came to pass, Israel was drawn into an all-pervading attitude to existence: poverty which, having been utterly robbed and deprived by God's judgment, can only hope to receive all justice and every good thing at God's hand.'

XV. *Sleep and Rest*

1. *Literature*: G. v. Rad, 'Ruhe'; A. Alt, *Recht*; A. J. Heschel, *Sabbath*, E. Jenni, *Sabbatgebot*; E. Lohse, '*sabbaton*'; A. R. Hulst, 'Sabbatgebot'; V. Fritz,

Israel, pp.42–48; N. E. Andreasen, *Sabbath*; W. H. Schmidt, 'Dekalog'; M. Tsevat, 'Sabbath'.

2. Prov.10.22; see pp.131f. above.

3. See p.132 above.

4. See BHK (so also RSV).

5. See p.132 above.

6. J. Moltmann, *Freigelassene*, p.39; ET p.54: '"It's all *for nothing* any way", says the nihilist and falls into despair. "It's really all *for nothing*", says the believer, rejoicing in the grace which he can have *for nothing*, and hoping for a new world in which all is available and may be had *for nothing*. "Ho, everyone who thirsts, come to the waters, and he who has no money, come, buy, and eat. Come, buy wine and milk without money and without price", so the prophets of the Old and New Testaments promise (Isa.55.1; Rev.22.17).'

7. C. A. Keller, 'Das quietistische Element', p.89, points out that 'according to Isaiah one aspect of sin is a frenetic activity, a bustle of business that passes God by'. Cf. H. W. Wolff, *Frieden*, pp.18ff.

8. Cf. G. v. Rad, 'Ruhe'.

9. E. Jenni, '*yōm*', p.710.

10. Cf. *šbt* in other connections, Gen.8.22; Josh.5.12; Isa.14.4; and V. Fritz, *Israel*, p.44.

11. *leqaddešō* could in Deut.5.12 be taken at second hand from Ex.20.8; cf. A. R. Hulst, 'Sabbatgebot', pp.153f.

12. A. Alt, *Recht*: BAL, pp.71f.=*Kl. Schr.* I, p.331=*Grundfragen*, p.256; ET p.132 n.125.

13. Cf. W. Zimmerli, *Weltlichkeit*, p.80, also on what follows; see also M. Tsevat, *Sabbath*, pp.451ff.

14. Cf. K. Barth, III/4, 51–79, ET pp.47–72. The Jewish interpreter A. J. Heschel writes (*Sabbath*, p.10): The meaning of the Sabbath is to celebrate time rather than space . . . It is a day on which we are called upon to share in what is eternal in time, to turn from the results of creation to the mystery of creation; from the world of creation to the creation of the world.' Isa.66.23 proclaims the sabbath (as well as the day of the new moon) as the day of worship before the face of Yahweh.

15. See p.95 above.

16. *weyinnāpeš* is applied here to the slave child in need of refreshment and to the foreign worker just as it is applied to the Creator in Ex.31.17; cf. p.138 above.

17. '*ōneg*=a pleasure, a delight.

18. See pp.135f. above.

19. Cf. E. Lohse, '*sabbaton*', pp.3f., ET pp.3f. and W. H. Schmidt, 'Dekalog', pp.208f.

20. V. Fritz, *Israel*, pp.47f., on 4.a, bα; 5.29f.

21. W. Vischer, 'Nehemia', p.609.

22. On the use of *leᶜōlām* in legal language see p.89 above.

23. Cf. E. Kutsch, 'Sehen', p.170, and *Verheissung*, p.76.

24. Perhaps the Priestly document also thought of the seventh day as being the great day of revelation. For it describes the fundamental Sinai event in Ex.24.15–18 as follows: Yahweh's glory remains veiled in a cloud for six days; but on the seventh day Yahweh calls to Moses out of the cloud, and the glory of

Yahweh is revealed to the Israelites as a consuming fire on the top of the mountain. Thus for the Priestly document the seventh day as the day of completed creation is also the day of completed revelation. Cf. C. Westermann, BK I, 236f.

25. Cf. G. v. Rad, 'Ruhe', pp.109f.=107f.; ET pp.101f. 'The seventh day is the sign of the resurrection and the rest of the age to come' (*Vita Adae et Evae* 51.2 [*AP* II, p.153]; cf. A. J. Heschel, *Sabbath*, p.114, also pp.73ff.: 'The Sabbath is an example of the world to come.').

XVI. Sickness and Healing

1. *Literature:* L. Köhler, *Mensch*, pp.33–47; ET pp.46–60; J. Scharbert, *Schmerz*; G. v. Rad, *Theol. AT* I, pp.285–293; ET pp.272–279; J. Hempel, 'Arzt' and *Heilung*; P. Humbert, 'Maladie'; T. Struys, *Ziekte*; K. Seybold, 'Krankheit' and *Gebet*; C. Westermann, 'Heilung'; F. Stolz, 'ḥlh'; E. Neufeld, 'Hygiene'; T. Collins, 'Tears'; V. Hamp, 'bākāh'.

2. According to F. Stolz, 'ḥlh', p.568, 110 times in the Old Testament in all principal parts of the verb and in several substantive formations, of which the most common ḥºlī occurs 24 times. Cf. J. Scharbert, *Schmerz*, pp.36ff.

3. The exception is the expression ḥillā pānīm=to soothe (15 times).

4. On the unsolved problem of the precise diagnosis, see F. Horst, *Hiob*, pp.26f.; J. Hempel, *Heilung*, pp.250f.

5. See BHS.

6. timhōn lēbāb; on the meaning of lēbāb see p.48 above.

7. See p.41 above; cf. Ps.38.10.

8. See pp.40f. above.

9. See p.106 above.

10. Cf. T. Collins, 'Tears'; also V. Hamp, 'bākāh'.

11. Cf. KBL and J. Hempel, 'Arzt', col.810.

12. On the cleansing, healing and strengthening effect of oil, as the ancient East knew it, cf. E. Kutsch, *Salbung*, pp.1–6; F. Hesse, 'mšh', p.485; ET pp.496f.

13. It is probable that ointments were also compounded to ward off insects; cf. Gen.37.25; Ex.30.23f.; I Kings 10.10; and E. Neufeld, 'Hygiene', pp.59–62.

14. On Elisha's instructions (II Kings 5.10ff.) G. v. Rad remarks ('Naaman', p.299): 'We only grasp the full affront of this scene when we remember that the Jordan and its water did not enjoy even the faintest degree of sacral value for ancient Israel.' Cf. the healing and enlivening power of water from the sanctuary in Ezek.47.1ff. (8f.), also John 5.7.

15. Cf. W. F. Kümmel, 'Melancholie'.

16. Cf. G. Gerleman, BK XVIII, 119, with pointers to Egyptian parallels. Especially powerful symptoms accompanying the experience of love also count as being a sign of 'sickness', like the symptoms accompanying menstruation, though we should term both entirely 'healthy' indispositions. The phenomena as such have the final word.

17. Cf. W. Rudolph, KAT XVII/2, 131.

18. It was different in Babylon and Egypt. In Mesopotamia surgeons (who are assigned to the craftsmen) are to be distinguished from physicians, who study lists of herbs and tablets of prescriptions, and belong among the priests; cf. E. Ebeling, 'Arzt'. In Egypt the 'house of life' which belonged to the larger sanctuaries is probably to be interpreted as a medical school; cf. H. Bonnet, RÄRG,

pp.417f. with H. de Meulenaere, 'Ärzteschule'. There were probably two reasons why internal medicine was not developed in Israel: first, a shrinking from dissection because of pollution through the corpse (see p.105 above); and secondly, conclusions drawn from the analogy between animals and man did not appear cogent because of man's special position in creation (Gen.2.18–23; 1.26f.). Cf. J. Hempel, *Heilung*, pp.244f.; also P. Humbert, 'Maladie', pp.1ff., 23ff.

19. Cf. G. v. Rad, *Weisheit*, p.178; ET p.134.
20. Cf. C. Westermann, 'Heilung' III. Even Saul's outbreaks of rage were caused by 'an evil spirit from Yahweh' (I Sam.16.14; 18.10; 19.9). On the psalms of sickness and healing cf. K. Seybold, 'Krankheit'. On II Kings 5.6f. cf. G. v. Rad, 'Naaman', pp.298f.
21. Cf. J. Hempel, *Heilung*, p.282f.
22. J. Hempel, 'Arzt', col.820.
23. Cf. C. Westermann, op. cit. III.
24. G. v. Rad, *Theol. AT* I, p.287; ET I, p.274.
25. Ecclus.38.1, 12ff., but see also v.15 and p.146 above.
26. See pp.106f. above.

XVII. *The Hope of Man*

1. *Literature*: C. Westermann, 'Hoffen'; T. C. Vriezen, 'Hoffnung'; J. van der Ploeg, 'L'Espérance'; W. Zimmerli, 'Hoffnung' (1966) and *Hoffnung* (1968); H. D. Preuss, *Zukunftserwartung*; C. Westermann, '*yhl*'.
2. On Gen.1.26, 28 and 2.5, 15; 3.23 see pp.128ff. above.
3. See pp.90f. above.
4. Cf. W. Zimmerli, *Hoffnung*, pp.12ff., ET pp.6ff.; C. Westermann, '*yhl*', p.727f.
5. Cf. Prov.10.27, 'The years of the wicked will be short.'
6. But cf. Prov.6.8.
7. Cf. BHK and W. Zimmerli, *Prediger*, p.216.
8. According to C. Westermann, 'Hoffen' (1952/53) p.21=ThB 24 (1964) p.221.
9. H. D. Preuß in *Zukunftserwartung* has described fully how Israel's expectation of the future was based on faith in Yahweh himself, and not on some impulse towards perfection or on a flight into the future motivated by historical disappointment.
10. G. v. Rad, *Theol. AT* I, p.355; ET I, p.343.
11. Cf. H. W. Wolff, 'Jahweglaube', pp.59–71, and 'Jahwe' (1969), pp.399f.= ThB 22 (²1973), pp.420f.; W. v. Soden, *Jahwe*; E. Jenni, *yhwh*.
12. On the following passage cf. C. Westermann, 'Hoffen', pp.39f.=237ff., also his article '*yhl*', pp.727ff.
13. On the meaning of *nepeš* see pp.15ff. above.
14. See pp.126f. above.
15. Cf. for example Ps.22.4f., 8f. (37.3, 5), with Ps.39.7.
16. Cf. W. Zimmerli, *Hoffnung*, p.17; ET p.9.
17. See pp.74ff. above.
18. For more detailed treatment see H. W. Wolff, 'Jahwist', pp.88–95=361–370.

19. Cf. Ps.76.6 and R. Bach, 'Bogen', p.26: 'Out of one of the centres of the Yahweh religion, the Old Testament already saw in Yahweh "the God of peace" (Rom. 15.33; 16.20). Human longing for peace is certainly to be taken seriously; but it must be clearly recognized that, according to the testimony of the Old Testament, Yahweh's will to peace (which springs from his jealous holiness) precedes all human longing for it.'

20. See W. Zimmerli's discussion with Ernst Bloch (*Hoffnung*, pp.163–178; ET pp.151–165).

21. Cf. J. Moltmann, *Mensch*, p.58; ET pp.30f.

XVIII. *God's Image – the Steward of the World*

1. *Literature*: J. J. Stamm, 'Imago'; O. Loretz, 'Mensch'; H. Wildberger, 'Abbild'; W. H. Schmidt, *Schöpfungsgeschichte*; O. Loretz, *Gottebenbildlichkeit*; C. Westermann, BK I, 197–222; F. Maass, "*ādām*'; W. Zimmerli, *Weltlichkeit*, pp.45–57.

2. Cf. chs.11 and 14 above.

3. See pp.128f. above.

4. On the structure of the final clause cf.1.14f. and W. H. Schmidt, *Schöpfungsgeschichte*, p.142 with n.4.

5. See BHS.

6. On the meaning of *yād*=hand=power see pp.68f. above.

7. Thus O. Loretz, *Gottebenbildlichkeit*, pp.62ff. Ps.8.5 expresses both the nearness and the distinction between God and man with the sentence: 'Thou hast made him little less than a divine being.'

8. E. Otto, 'Mensch', p.345. See also the details (pp.342ff.) about the significance of the Instruction for King Meri-ka-Re, according to which men as such are uniquely called 'images' of God. This phrase seems in Egypt to have meant either the role of gods played by priests in the cult, or inner, moral possession by a godhead; it never meant ruling functions, which are reserved for the king as the image of God.

9. *'enōs* (in Ps.8.4a) may perhaps mean man as the weakly, mortal being (Ps.103.15) corresponding to Accadian *enēšu* (to be weak, fragile). But see F. Maass, "*'enōs*', cols.373f.

10. K. Barth, III/1, 219; ET p.195.

11. W. H. Schmidt, *Gebot*, p.29.

12. G. v. Rad, 'Christliche Weisheit?', p.151.

13. N. H. Ridderbos, *Psalmen*, p.139. It is only in the messianic End-time that the relationship of the animals to one another, as well as the relation between man and beast, will be no longer marked by domination and conflict, but by peaceful play (Isa.11.6–8).

14. See pp.192ff. below. The 'image of God' is thus only appointed to rule over the whole extra-human creation and not for rule over men. Cf. F. Herzog, 'Menschenbild', p.516. On the other hand, man as the 'image of the creative God' is *ipso facto* 'not to be an image of nature and her powers' (J. Moltmann, 'Zukunft', p.315, cf. p.319).

15. *Mensch*, pp.112f.; ET pp.126f.

16. Cf. E. Jüngel, 'Grenzen'.

17. M. Hengel, 'Mensch', pp.125ff. Taking Jer.31.31ff. as his starting point,

M. Hengel shows how 'the Old Testament points beyond itself', 'that the demand on man was too great when he was called into partnership with God', and that 'the fact of being the image of God' is 'a commission . . . in which man in his concrete situation fails again and again'. But Jer. 31.31–34 'gives hope'. Cf. also Isa. 61.1–3.

XIX. *Man and Woman*

1. *Literature*: F. Horst, 'Ehe'; R. de Vaux, *Israel*, pp. 24–38; J. van Seters, 'Childlessness'; R. Goeden, *Sexualität*; U. Nembach, 'Ehescheidung'; W. Zimmerli, *Weltlichkeit*, pp. 35–44; N. P. Bratsiotis, "*iš*"; J. Kühlewein, "*iššā*"; G. J. Wenham, '*betūlāh*'.

2. See pp. 161f. above. This is already a demand for the basic recognition that a biblical anthropology without an intensive treatment of the social components would be of no avail; cf. chs. 20–25.

3. Cf. K. Elliger, *Leviticus*, p. 239, on Lev. 18.6–17; also H. Ringgren, "*āb*", pp. 8f.; Hoffner, '*bayit*', cols. 636f. and pp. 214f. below.

4. But see C. Westermann, BK I 317f.

5. See p. 21 above and Hos. 3.2, with the comments by H. W. Wolff, BK XIV/1, 76f.

6. II Sam. 3.14; Hos. 2.21f.; cf. BK XIV/1, 64. *betūlā* does not necessarily mean 'virgin' in the narrower sense; it is rather a girl of marriageable age, as G. J. Wenham has shown in '*betūlāh*'; cf. especially pp. 331f. on Deut. 22.13–21.

7. On Hos. 2.18, where the relationship to Yahweh is meant, cf. N. P. Bratsiotis, '*iš*, col. 248; on Gen. 2.23 see p. 172 below.

8. Cf. E. Kutsch, *Verheissung*, pp. 134ff.

9. Cf. H. W. Wolff, BK XIV/2, 34f.

10. M. Noth, BK IX/1, 241, 247f.

11. See further pp. 200f. below.

12. See here K. Elliger, *ZAW* 1955, and the same author's *Leviticus*, pp. 229ff.

13. L. Köhler, *Mensch*, pp. 78f.; ET p. 92.

14. N. P. Bratsiotis, "*iš*', col. 243.

15. See p. 93 above.

16. N. P. Bratsiotis, op. cit.

17. On v. 23a see p. 29 above.

18. Cf. the factual derivation of '*ādām* from the '*adāmā* in 2.7; see p. 94 above.

19. Just like the 'lordship' of the man over the woman, cf. 3.16b.

20. See p. 71 above. The old way of thinking in terms of the laws of possession (see pp. 166f. above) has here been completely overcome.

21. See pp. 102ff. above.

22. Cf. H. W. Wolff, BK XIV/1, 106ff.

23. Highly significant for the Israelite consciousness of such distinctions is the phrase, found in a number of different connections, 'an infamous deed in Israel' or 'such a thing is not done in Israel'. Cf. Gen. 34.7; Deut. 22.21; Judg. 20.6, 10; II Sam. 13.12; Jer. 29.23.

24. According to LXX and Vulgate.

25. Cf. K. Barth, III/4, p. 154; ET p. 139.

26. M. Noth, *Exod.*, pp. 185f.; ET p. 227. Cf. In Isa. 6.2 the seraphim in Yahweh's train; of their six pairs of wings, two cover the 'feet', which probably also indicates above all the region of the genitals (see ch. VII n. 5).

27. L. Köhler, *Mensch*, p.78; ET p.91. The story of David's adultery with Bathsheba (II Sam. 11) shows with exemplary sharpness how the purely physical longing (vv. 2f.) together with the adultery (vv. 4f.) draws a chain of crimes after it (vv. 6ff.). Cf. also Ezek. 23.14–17a with v. 17b.
28. K. Barth, III/4, p. 148; ET p. 133.

XX. *Parents and Children*

1. *Literature*: L. Löw, *Lebensalter*, pp. 130–134; L. Dürr, *Erziehungswesen*; J. Conrad, *Generation*; H. Ringgren, "*āb*"; J. Kühlewein, "*ēm*" and "*bēn*".
2. See p. 169 above.
3. On Gen. 1.28 see p. 162 above.
4. Cf. Lev. 27.1ff. and p. 121 above.
5. See p. 121 above.
6. Cf. J. Kühlewein, "*em*", p. 176, and the literature referred to there.
7. See pp. 174f. above.
8. On the possibility of tracing the admonitory discourses of the wisdom writings (e.g. in Prov. 22.17–24.21 and 31.3–9) back to instruction given by parents (especially the mother), cf. G. Liedke, *Rechtssätze*, p. 199. Paul compares his relationship as apostle to the church in Corinth with that of a father to his children (I Cor. 4.14ff.; II Cor. 6.13; 11.2).
9. Cf. G. v. Rad, *Weisheit*, pp. 165–181; ET pp. 124–137.
10. Cf. E. Jenni, "*āb*", p. 13.
11. Hos. 5.2; 7.12, 15; 10.10; and Prov. 3.11f.; Job 5.17; 33.12ff.; Ps. 118.18; cf. H. J. Kraus, *Erziehung*, pp. 268f. and H. W. Wolff, BK XIV/1, 125.
12. W. Zimmerli, BK XIII, 402.
13. In I Kings 19.4 Elijah – more 'tired of God' than tired of life – (G. v. Rad, *GPM* 20, 1966, p. 290) justifies his plea that he might be allowed to die with the words, 'I am no better than my fathers.' The zealot has become afraid (v. 3) and is hence no longer able to compare himself favourably with his fathers, especially if this is meant as a reference to his predecessors in the prophetic office. On the title 'father' for the prophet, see p. 180 above. Of the earlier prophets, only Moses is shown by the Yahwist in a state of similar despondency and readiness to die (Num. 11.15). On the difficulties of interpreting I Kings 19.4 cf. O. H. Steck, *Elia-Erzählungen*, p. 27.
14. The ancient Egyptians talked about 'the staff of the old', thinking of the son's duty to help his ageing father; cf. W. Helck, 'Altersversorgung', p. 158.

XXI. *Brothers, Friends and Enemies*

1. *Literature*: C. H. Gordon, 'Fratriarchy'; J. Fichtner, 'Nächsten'; F. Maass, 'Selbstliebe'; R. de Vaux, *Israel*, pp. 19, 37f., 53–55; T. C. Vriezen, 'Liebesgebot'; W. Zimmerli, *Weltlichkeit*, pp. 98–110; H. Ringgren, "*āḥ*"; E. Jenni, "*āḥ*".
2. On the meaning of this word see J. Fichtner, 'Nächsten', pp. 24ff. = 89ff.
3. Cf. M. Noth, *Lev.*, p. 134; ET p. 155.
4. C. H. Gordon, 'Fratriarchy'; cf. R. de Vaux, *Israel*, p. 19.
5. See pp. 168f. above.
6. R. de Vaux, op. cit., p. 54.
7. See p. 185 above on Deut. 13.6ff.

8. Further evidence in H. W. Wolff, BK XIV/2, 193f.

9. Half-brothers also count as brothers; in II Sam. 13.4 Amnon talks about his 'brother' Absalom, although according to II Sam. 3.2f. they had two different mothers. Thus the children of Leah, Rachel, Zilpah and Bilhah are bound together as brothers by their common father, Jacob. On the amphictyonic theory held by M. Noth and its confutation, see R. Smend, 'Amphiktyonie'.

10. Cf. G. v. Rad, *Gottesvolk*, pp. 12f., and compare Ex. 21.2 with Deut. 15.12, Ex. 21.16 with Deut. 24.7 and Ex. 22.24 with Deut. 23.20f.

11. Deuteronomy generally underlines the bond between the members of God's people by the addition of a suffix to *'āḥ*, generally in the form of address, 'thy brother'.

12. Cf. Lev. 25.36f.; Ex. 18.8, 13, 17; 22.12; Ps. 15.5 and W. Zimmerli, *Weltlichkeit*, p. 102.

13. Cf. Ex. 21.2–6 and p. 201 below.

14. See p. 197 below.

15. Cf. G. v. Rad, *Gottesvolk*, p. 50.

16. Cf. C. Westermann, *Erträge*, pp. 49f., 53f.; by the same author, BK I 381ff.

17. Following M. Noth's translation of v. 17b β, *Lev.*, p. 118 (ET p. 137 follows RSV).

18. J. Fichtner, 'Nächsten', WuD 40=*Gottes Weisheit*, p. 103.

19. The duty of hospitality applied to the stranger who was passing through (Gen. 18.1ff.; 19.1ff.; Judg. 19.11ff.).

20. L. Baeck, *Judentum*, p. 211; cf. M. Buber, *Glaubensweisen*, p. 69=701: '. . . as if it applied to you yourself'.

21. Cf. J. Fichtner, F. Maass, T. C. Vriezen.

22. J. Fichtner, 'Nächsten', p. 41=104.

23. Cf. Matt. 7.12 and K. Barth, I/2, pp. 426f.; ET pp. 387f.

24. F. Maass, 'Selbstliebe', p. 113.

25. See BHK.

26. S. Morenz, 'Kohlen'.

27. Cf. K. Koch, 'Vergeltungsdogma', pp. 4f, 7=134f., 137f.

XXII. *Masters and Slaves*

1. *Literature*: J. Hempel, *Ethos*, pp. 124–135; A. Alt, 'Anteil'; A. Jepsen, '*Amaᵇ*'; K. H. Bernhardt, *Königsideologie*, pp. 114–177; N. Lohfink, 'Sicherung'; W. H. Schmidt, 'Königtum'; J. P. M. van der Ploeg, 'Slavery'.

2. See p. 164 above.

3. Cf. H. J. Bocker, *Beurteilung*, p. 27, cf. p. 98.

4. G. v. Rad, *Weisheit*, pp. 63f.; ET p. 43.

5. It is only later that it acquires a restricted meaning for a polemical theology directed against the surrounding world; cf. above all the Enthronement Psalms 47, 93, 96–99 and the tradition recognizable in Isa. 6.5.

6. Cf. K. Galling, *Erwählungstradition*, pp. 5ff.; M. Noth, *ÜP*, pp. 50ff.; ET pp. 47ff.

7. Cf. K. H. Bernhardt, *Königsideologie*, pp. 116ff.

8. Cf. also L. Delekat, 'Tendenz'.

9. The whole narrative context 11.26–28, 40; 12.1ff. apparently goes back to

groups (of elders?) in Jerusalem 'who although basically affirming the Davidic kingdom, yet saw with disquiet the actual course of events under David and his successors and gave expression to their doubts' (M. Noth, BK IX, 271). On the text itself, see the explanation on p.125.

10. A. Alt, 'Anteil', pp.356ff.=375ff.
11. Cf. W. H. Schmidt, *Königtum.*
12. Cf. G. v. Rad, *Deut.*, pp.85f.; ET pp.119f.
13. H. J. Boecker, *Beurteilung*, p.30.
14. For the following passage I am indebted to N. Lohfink, 'Sicherung'.
15. Cf. Gen.16.1, 6; Ps.123.2; Prov.30.23; Isa.24.2; see also A. Jepsen, *Ama^h.*
16. *AOT*, p.392; *ANET*, pp.170f.
17. See p.187 above.
18. *mišne* does not mean the double but the equivalent; see G. v. Rad, *Deut.*, p.77; ET p.108.
19. See pp.136f. above.
20. J. P. M. van der Ploeg, 'Slavery', p.83.
21. In the Code of Hammurabi as well; see p.199 above.
22. See the warnings already found in the 'mirror for magistrates' in the Book of the Covenant against straining the law either to please the masses (Ex.23.2f.) or to please the rich (vv.6–8).
23. Perhaps the reading should be *b^eribāh*; see BHK.
24. Cf. the similar regulation about the levying of interest on loans in Lev. 25.35ff.; Deut.23.19f.; see p.187 above.
25. See p.195 above.
26. G. v. Rad, *Theol. AT* I, p.413; ET I, p.400.
27. See pp.199ff. above. Cf. in the New Testament the epistle to Philemon, I Cor.7.21–24; Col.3.22–4.1; Eph.6.5–9; I Tim.6.1f.; Titus2.9f.; I Peter2.18ff. See also E. Schweizer, 'Sklavenproblem'; G. Eichholz, *Paulus*, pp.278–283.

XXIII. *The Wise and the Foolish (Teachers and Pupils)*

1. *Literature*: M. Noth, 'Bewährung'; U. Skladny, *Spruchsammlungen*; H. H. Schmid, *Weisheit*; G. Fohrer, 'Weisheit'; H. J. Hermisson, *Spruchweisheit*; G. v. Rad, *Weisheit*; M. Saeb, '*ḥkm*'; N. C. Habel, 'Wisdom'.
2. See pp.178ff. above.
3. See pp.179f. above.
4. This is the conclusion of H. J. Hermisson's investigations; cf. his *Spruch-weisheit*, pp.113–136.
5. U. Skladny, *Spruchsammlungen*, p.66, sees in Prov.28f. a 'mirror for sovereigns'.
6. Cf. G. v. Rad, *Weisheit*, p.112; ET pp.81f.
7. H. J. Hermisson, *Spruchweisheit*, pp.88ff.; G. v. Rad, *Weisheit*, pp.31ff.; ET pp.17ff.
8. Cf. N. C. Habel, 'Wisdom', pp.135ff.
9. U. Skladny, op. cit., pp.7–13; cf. O. Plöger, 'Sentenzensammlungen', pp.404f.
10. G. v. Rad, *Weisheit*, p.89; ET p.64.
11. See BHK (so also RSV).

12. Cf. pp. 114f. above.
13. Cf. G. v. Rad, *Theol. AT* I, pp. 436f.; ET I, pp. 423f.
14. On the text see BHK. (So RSV.)
15. G. v. Rad, *Weisheit*, p. 115; ET p. 84.
16. G. v. Rad, ibid., p. 106; ET p. 77.
17. On Solomon's skill as ruler, see I Kings 3 and p. 47 above. To set riddles was not merely a royal game. The Queen of Sheba used riddles (*ḥîdōt*) to test whether Solomon's wisdom matched its reputation.
18. Cf. Isa. 28.27 and G. Dalman, *AuS* III, pp. 88f.
19. See p. 197 on Ps. 72; cf. Isa. 11.3f.
20. See pp. 46ff. above.
21. For the following passage cf. H. J. Hermisson, 'Weisheit', pp. 137–148.
22. See p. 179 above.
23. With LXX and others. (So RSV.)
24. G. v. Rad in the central thesis of his book *Weisheit in Israel* teaches afresh that the world releases a truth from itself and that the wisdom of the wise man consists in allowing himself to be set right by the order ruling in things, since in that he can trust to the secret of creation; cf. pp. 189–228, ET pp. 144–176: 'The Self-Revelation of Creation', as well as pp. 376f., 382ff., 404f. (ET pp. 296f., 301ff., 318f.). Here only an indication of the argument can be given, and the book itself is emphatically recommended.
25. G. v. Rad, ibid., pp. 372f., ET pp. 293f.; cf. also p. 146, ET pp. 108f.: 'The fear of God not only enabled a man to acquire knowledge, but also had a predominantly critical function in that it kept alive in the person acquiring the knowledge the awareness that his intellect was directed towards a world in which mystery predominated.'
26. H. J. Hermisson, 'Weisheit', pp. 140f.
27. See p. 210 above.
28. Cf. K. Barth, IV/4, p. 31, ET p. 28: 'There is no more intimate friend of sound human understanding than the Holy Spirit. There is no more basic normalising of man than in the doing of his work.' See also H. Gollwitzer, *Holz*, p. 361: 'The hearing of the Word of God preserves the freedom of reason from the constantly threatening dogmatization of science and scholarship and the excessive claims made on them, caused by the unfulfilled needs of faith; and it prevents man from expecting more from both science and scholarship than they can give.'

XXIV. *The Individual and the Community*

1. *Literature*: L. Rost, *Vorstufen*; E. Wächter, *Gemeinschaft*; R. de Vaux, *Israel*, pp. 3–61; H. Seidel, *Einsamkeit*; H. J. Zobel, '*bādād*'; Hoffner, '*bayit*'; E. Jenni, '*bayit*'.
2. See BHK.
3. Cf. Hoffner, '*bayit*', col. 636, and E. Jenni, '*bayit*', p. 7.
4. Cf. L. Köhler, *Mensch*, pp. 48ff.; ET pp. 61ff.
5. Cf. M. Noth, *GI*, p. 103; ET p. 108.
6. From the Priestly document onwards; cf. L. Rost, *Vorstufen*, pp. 41ff.
7. Cf. Judg. 1.34f.; 18.2, 27ff. and M. Noth, *GI*, pp. 66f., 150f.; ET pp. 67f., 149.

8. Cf. M. Noth, *GI*, pp. 56f., 60f.; ET pp. 56, 60.

9. Following M. Noth, ibid., p. 95; ET p. 98; see also his *System*, pp. 151ff., and L. Rost, *Vorstufen*, pp. 69ff.

10. On the problem of the number of the tribes, which varies between 10 (Judg. 5) and 12, and above all on the problem of the function of the tribal federation, cf. R. Smend, *Yahwekrieg*.

11. Cf. M. Noth, 'Richter'. On the following passage cf. G. C. Macholz, 'Gerichtsverfassung', pp. 180f.

12. Cf. L. Rost, *Vorstufen*, pp. 32ff.

13. See ch. XIX n. 23 above.

14. Cf. H. Seidel, *Einsamkeit*, p. 32.

15. Cf. KBL³; H. J. Zobel, '*bādād*, cols. 511f.

16. The Hebrew word is unexplained; it seems to mean an 'unclean desert bird'; cf. H. J. Kraus, *Psalmen*, p. 694.

17. See BHK.

18. Cf. H. J. Kraus, *Threni*, pp. 51, 53.

19. On *millibbō* see p. 56 above.

20. Cf. H. Seidel, *Einsamkeit*, pp. 29ff.

21. On Isa. 54.1 see p. 178 above.

22. On Lev. 13.46 see p. 218 above; cf. Lam. 3.28.

23. On the statements of confidence in the psalms of lament see pp. 152f. above.

24. For the image see Job 6.15–20.

25. On the text and on the 'group of intimates' which must be assumed here, as the people addressed, cf. H. Wildberger, BK X 335ff.

26. On the difference between the congregation of the people and the congregation of faith in the Old Covenant, see H. W. Wolff, 'Volksgemeinde und Glaubensgemeinde im Alten Bund'.

27. On the meaning of 'heart' and 'soul' see p. 53 above.

28. H. Gollwitzer, *Holz*, p. 300.

29. E. E. Hölscher, *Vom römischen zum christlichen Naturrecht* (1939), p. 87: 'This fact – whatever attitude one may take to the teaching of Christ and his church – means the only *really* revolutionary alteration in the structure of mankind because it has brought into the world the doctrine of the dignity of the individual.' Hölscher means the detachment of the individual, which he holds to be 'the greatest of all turning-points in human history – one we can perhaps see as being the only real turning-point at all' (H. Gollwitzer, loc. cit.).

XXV. *The Destiny of Man*

1. *Literature*: A. Alt, 'Weisheit'; H. J. Stoebe, 'demütig'; G. v. Rad, *Weisheit*; F. Maass, '*ādām*'.

2. F. Maass, '*ādām*', p. 91.

3. On *rūaḥ* see pp. 32ff. above.

4. See pp. 106f.

5. See pp. 188f. above.

6. See pp. 190f. above.

7. Cf. also Ex. 21.7–11 and p. 199 above.

8. See pp. 199ff. above.

9. See p. 197f. above.
10. Cf. H. J. Stoebe, 'demütig'. The prophetic sayings in Hos.4.1f.; 6.6; 12.7; Isa.1.17; Zech.7.7–10 sum up behaviour to one's fellow-men in a similar way.
11. See further p. 154 above.
12. See p. 163 above.
13. Cf. I Kings 4.32 and A. Alt, 'Weisheit'.
14. The text here and in the following lines is uncertain.
15. G. v. Rad, *Weisheit*, p. 193; ET p. 148.
16. G. v. Rad, ibid., p. 402; ET pp. 316f.
17. See p. 163 above.
18. This is M. Buber's rendering of the canonical heading. This heading also covers the songs of lament. They represent the 'muted accompaniment' to the hymns. In them the man who cannot himself remedy his situation of need, clings to the God of the testimonies. The laments document resistance to the temptation to renounce God (Job 2.9) no less than the songs of praise; cf. E. Gerstenberger, *Mensch*, pp. 64, 72.
19. See p. 211 above.
20. G. v. Rad, *Weisheit*, p. 256; ET pp. 198f. According to Phil.2.10f., the exaltation of the One who was crucified destines created beings for the confession of praise, 'Jesus Christ is Lord', a confession in which the heavenly, the earthly, and what is under the earth are united.

BIBLIOGRAPHY

Aistleitner, J., *WB*
    Wörterbuch der ugaritischen Sprache, ed. O. Eissfeldt, ³1967
Alt, A., 'Anteil'
    'Der Anteil des Königtums an der sozialen Entwicklung in den Reichen Israel
    und Juda' (1955), *KlSchr* III, pp. 348–72=*Grundfragen*, pp. 367–91
Alt, A., *Grundfragen*
    Grundfragen der Geschichte des Volkes Israel, ed. S. Herrmann, 1970
Alt, A., *KlSchr*
    Kleine Schriften zur Geschichte des Volkes Israel I–II, ²1959; III, 1959
Alt, A., 'Recht'
    'Die Ursprünge des israelitischen Rechts', BAL Phil.-hist. Klasse 86/1, 1934=
    KlSchr I, pp. 278–332=*Grundfragen*, pp. 203–57; ET, 'The Origins of
    Israelite Law', *Essays in Old Testament History and Religion*, 1966, pp. 79–132
Alt, A., 'Weisheit'
    'Die Weisheit Salomos', *ThLZ* 76, 1951, cols. 139–44=*KISchr* II, pp. 90–99
Andreasen, N. E., *Sabbath*
    The Old Testament Sabbath. A Traditio-Historical Investigation, Diss. Vander-
    bilt, 1971; *Dissertation Abstracts International* 32, 1971/72, 2781 A

Bach, R., 'Bogen'
    '"... der Bogen zerbricht, Spiesse zerschlägt und Wagen mit Feuer ver-
    brennt"', *PbTh*, pp. 13–26
Baeck, L., *Judentum*
    Das Wesen des Judentums, ⁴1926
Balthasar, H. U. von, *Herrlichkeit* III/2/1
    Herrlichkeit. Eine theologische Ästhetik. III/2, Theologie. 1, Alter Bund, 1967
Barr, J., *Semantics*
    The Semantics of Biblical Language, 1961
Barr, J., *Time*
    Biblical Words for Time, SBT 33, 1962
Barth, C., 'Antwort'
    'Die Antwort Israels', *PbTh*, pp. 44–56
Barth, C., *Errettung*
    *Die Errettung vom Tode in den individuellen Klage- und Dankliedern des Alten
    Testaments*, 1947
Barth, K., I/2
    Die kirchliche Dogmatik I: *Die Lehre vom Wort Gottes*, 2, 1938; ET, *Church
    Dogmatics* I: *The Doctrine of the Word of God*, 2, 1956
Barth, K., III/1, III/2, III/4
    Ibid., III, *Die Lehre von der Schöpfung*, 1, 1945; 2, 1948; 4, 1951; ET, ibid.,
    III, *The Doctrine of Creation*, 1, 1959; 2, 1960; 4, 1961

Barth, K., IV/4
Ibid., IV: *Die Lehre von der Versöhnung*, 4, 1967; ET, ibid., IV: *The Doctrine of Reconciliation*, 4, 1969
Baumgärtel, F., 'Geist'
'Geist im Alten Testament', *ThWNT* VI, 1959, pp. 357–66; ET, 'Spirit in the Old Testament', *TDNT* VI, pp. 360–67
Baumgärtel, F., '*lēb*'
'*lēb*, *lēbāb* im Alten Testament', *ThWNT* III, 1938, pp. 609–11; ET, *TDNT* III, pp. 606f.
Baumgartner, W., 'Auferstehungsglaube'
'Der Auferstehungsglaube im Alten Orient', *Zum Alten Testament und seine Umwelt*, 1959, pp. 124–46
Becker, J. H., *Nefesj*
Het Begrip Nefesj in het Oude Testament, 1942
Bernhardt, K. H., *Königsideologie*
Das Problem der altorientalischen Königsideologie im Alten Testament, VT Suppl. 8, 1961
Bloch, E., *Atheismus*
Atheismus im Christentum, 1968
Boecker, H. J., *Beurteilung*
Die Beurteilung der Anfänge des Königtums in den deuteronomistischen Abschnitten des 1. Samuelbuches, WMANT 31, 1969
Boman, T., *Denken*
Das hebräische Denken im Vergleich mit dem griechischen, [5]1968; ET of [2]1954, *Hebrew Thought Compared with Greek*, 1960
Bonnet, H., *RÄRG*
Reallexikon der ägyptischen Religionsgeschichte, 1952
Bratsiotis, N. P., '*'īš*'
'*'īš*', *ThWAT* I/2, 1971, cols. 238–52
Bratsiotis, N. P., '*bāśār*'
'*bāśār*', *ThWAT* I/6–7, 1972, cols. 850–67
Brunner, H., *Erziehung*
Altägyptische Erziehung, 1957
Brunner, H., 'Herz'
'Das hörende Herz', *ThLZ* 79, 1954, cols. 697–700
Buber, M., *Glaubensweisen*
Zwei Glaubensweisen, 1950= *Werke* I, 1962, pp. 651–782

Collins, T., 'Tears'
'The Physiology of Tears in the Old Testament', *CBQ* 33, 1971, pp. 18–38 and 185–97
Conrad, J., *Generation*
Die junge Generation im Alten Testament, AzTh I/42, 1970

Dalmann, G., *AuS*
Arbeit und Sitte in Palästina I–VII, 1928–42
Delekat, L., 'Tendenz'
'Tendenz und Theologie der David-Salomo-Erzählung', *Das ferne und das nahe Wort. Festschrift L. Rost*, BZAW 105, 1967, pp. 26–36

Delekat, L., 'Wörterbuch'
'Zum hebräischen Wörterbuch' *VT* 14, 1964, pp.7–66
Delitzsch, F., *Psychologie*
System der biblischen Psychologie, ²1861
Delling, G., '*chronos*'
'*chronos*', *ThWNT* IX, 1972, pp.576ff.; ET, *TDNT* IX, 1974, pp.581ff.
Dhorme, E., *L'Emploi*
L'Emploi métaphorique des noms de parties du corps en hébreu et en akkadien,
1923; reissued 1963
Dürr, L., *Erziehungswesen*
Das Erziehungswesen im Alten Testament und im antiken Orient, MVAG 36/2,
1932
Dürr, L., '*nepeš*'
'Hebr. *nepeš*=akk. *napištu*=Gurgel, Kehle', *ZAW* 43, 1925, pp.262–69

Ebeling, E., 'Arzt'
'Arzt', *RLA* I, 1928, pp.164f.
Eichholz, G., *Paulus*
Die Theologie des Paulus im Umriss, 1972
Eichrodt, W., 'Heilserfahrung'
'Heilserfahrung und Zeitverständnis im Alten Testament', *ThZ* 12, 1956,
pp.103–25
Eichrodt, W., *Menschenverständnis*
Das Menschenverständnis des Alten Testaments, *AThANT* 4, 1947; ET, *Man in
the Old Testament*, SBT 4, 1951
Eisenbeis, W., *šlm*
Die Wurzel šlm im Alten Testament, BZAW 113, 1969
Elliger, K., BK XI
Jesaja II, BK XI, 1970ff.
Elliger, K., *Leviticus*
Leviticus, HAT I/4, 1966
Elliger, K., *ZAW* 1955
'Das Gesetz Leviticus 18', *ZAW* 67, 1955, pp.1–25=*Kleine Schriften zum
Alten Testament*, ThB 32, 1966, pp.232–59

Fahlgren, K. H. *ṣedaqā*
ṣedaqā, nahestehende und entgegengesetzte Begriffe im Alten Testament, Diss.
Uppsala, 1932, pp.1–32, 44–54; cited from Fahlgren, 'Die Gegensätze von
ṣedaqā im Alten Testament', K. Koch (ed.), *Vergeltung*, pp.87–129
Fichtner, J., 'Nächsten'
'Der Begriff des "Nächsten" im Alten Testament', *WuD* NF 4, 1955, pp.23–
52=*Gottes Weisheit*, 1965, pp.88–114
Fohrer, G., 'Weisheit'
'Die Weisheit im Alten Testament', BZAW 115, 1969, pp.242–74
Freedman, D. N., and Lundbom '*beṭen*'
'*beṭen*', *ThWAT* I/5, 1972, cols.616–20
Fritz, V., *Israel*
Israel in der Wüste, Marburger Theologische Studien 7, 1970

Galling, K., *Bild vom Menschen*
 Das Bild vom Menschen in biblischer Sicht, Mainzer Universitäts-Reden 3, 1947
Galling, K., *BRL*
 Biblisches Reallexikon, HAT I/1, 1937
Galling, K., *Erwählungstraditionen*
 Die Erwählungstraditionen Israels, BZAW 48, 1928
Galling, K., 'Prediger'
 'Der Prediger', HAT I/18 (*Die fünf Megilloth*), ²1969, pp. 73–125
Galling, K., 'Rätsel'
 'Das Rätsel der Zeit', *ZThK* 58, 1961, pp. 1–15
Gemser, B., *Sprüche*
 Sprüche Salomos, HAT I/16, ²1963
Gerleman, G., '*bāśār*'
 '*bāśār*, Fleisch', *ThHAT* I, 1971, pp. 376–79
Gerleman, G., BK XVIII
 Ruth, Das Hohelied, BK XVIII, 1965
Gerleman, G., '*dām*'
 '*dām*, Blut', *ThHAT* I, 1971, pp. 448–51
Gerleman, G., '*hyh*'
 '*hyh*, leben', *ThHAT* I, 1971, pp. 549–57
Gerstenberger, E., 'Mensch'
 'Der klagende Mensch', *PbTh*, pp. 64–72
Gese, H., 'Psalm 22'
 'Psalm 22 und das Neue Testament', *ZThK* 65, 1968, pp. 1–22
Goeden, R., *Sexualität*
 Zur Stellung von Man und Frau, Ehe und Sexualität im Hinblick auf Bibel und Alte Kirche, Diss. Göttingen, 1969
Gollwitzer, H., *Holz*
 Krummes Holz – aufrechter Gang. Zur Frage nach dem Sinn des Lebens, 1970, ⁵1972
Gordon, C. H., 'Fratriarchy'
 'Fratriarchy in the Old Testament', *JBL* 54, 1935, pp. 223–31
Gordon, C. H., *UT*
 Ugaritic Textbook, AnOr 38, 1965

Habel, N. C., 'Wisdom'
 'The Symbolism of Wisdom in Proverbs 1–9', *Interpretation* 26, 1972, pp. 131–57
Hamp, V., '*bākāh*'
 '*bākāh*', *ThWAT* I/5–6, 1972, cols. 638–43
Helck, W., 'Altersversorgung'
 'Altersversorgung', *LÄ* I, 1972, pp. 158f.
Hempel, J., 'Arzt'
 'Ich bin der Herr, dein Arzt', *ThLZ* 82, 1957, cols. 809–26
Hempel, J., *Ethos*
 Das Ethos des Alten Testaments, BZAW 67, 1938
Hempel, J., *Heilung*
 Heilung als Symbol und Wirklichkeit im biblischen Schrifttum, ²1965
Hengel, M., *Judentum*
 Judentum und Hellenismus, 1969; ET, *Judaism and Hellenism*, 1974

Hengel, M., 'Mensch'
  '"Was ist der Mensch?"', *PbTh*, pp. 116–35
Hermisson, H. J., *Spruchweisheit*
  Studien zur israelitischen Spruchweisheit, WMANT 28, 1968
Hermisson, H. J., 'Weisheit'
  'Weisheit und Geschichte', *PbTh*, pp. 136–54
Herzog, F., 'Menschenbild'
  'Befreiung zu einem neuen Menschenbild? Anthropologische Überlegungen
  zum Problem der Lebensqualität', *EvKomm* 5, 1972, pp. 516–20
Heschel, A. J., *Sabbath*
  The Sabbath, its Meaning for Modern Man, 1951/52
Hesse, F., *'mšḥ'*
  'mšḥ und *māšîaḥ* im Alten Testament', *ThWNT* IX, 1972, pp. 485–500; ET,
  TDNT IX, 1974, pp. 496–509.
Hessen, J., *Platonismus*
  Platonismus und Prophetismus, ²1955
Hoffner, H. A., *'bayit'*
  'bayit', *ThWAT* I/5, 1972, cols. 629–38
Horst, F., 'Ehe'
  'Ehe im AT', *RGG*³ II, 1958, cols. 316–18
Horst, F., *Hiob*
  Hiob, BK XVI/1, 1968
Hulst, A. R., *'kol-bāśār'*
  'kol-bāśār in der priesterlichen Fluterzählung', *OTS* 12, 1958, pp. 26–68
Hulst, A. R., 'Sabbatgebot'
  'Bemerkungen zum Sabbatgebot', *Studia Biblica et Semitica. Festschrift Th. C.
  Vriezen*, 1966, pp. 152–64
Humbert, P., 'Maladie'
  'Maladie et médicine dans l'Ancien Testament', *RHPhR* 44, 1964, pp. 1–29

Jahnow, H., *'Leichenlied'*
  Das hebräische Leichenlied, BZAW 36, 1923
Janssen, E., *Juda*
  Juda in der Exilzeit, FRLANT 69, 1956
Jastrow, M., jr., *Religion*
  The Religion of Babylonia and Assyria, Handbooks on the History of Religions
  2, 1898
Jenni, E., *"āb'*
  "āb, Vater', *ThHAT* I, 1971, pp. 1–17
Jenni, E., *"āḥ'*
  "āḥ, Bruder', *ThHAT* I, 1971, pp. 98–104
Jenni, E., *"ḥr'*
  "ḥr, danach', *ThHAT* I, 1971, pp. 110–18
Jenni, E., *'bayit'*
  'bayit, Haus', *ThHAT* I, 1971, pp. 308–13
Jenni, E., *'yhwh'*
  'yhwh, Jahwe', *ThHAT* I, 1971, pp. 701–07
Jenni, E., *'yōm'*
  'yōm, Tag', *ThHAT* I, 1971, pp. 707–26

Jenni, E., "ʿōlām'
'Das Wort ʿōlām im Alten Testament', *ZAW* 64, 1952, pp. 197–248; ibid., 65, 1953, pp. 1–35
Jenni, E., *Sabbatgebot*
Die theologische Bedeutung des Sabbatgebotes, ThSt Zürich 46, 1956
Jepsen, A., 'Amaʰ'
'Amaʰ und Schiphchaʰ, *VT* 8, 1958, pp. 293–97
Jepsen, A., and Hanhart, R., *Chronologie*
Untersuchungen zur israelitisch-jüdischen Chronologie, BZAW 88, 1964
Jeremias, Jörg, *Kultprophetie*
Kultprophetie und Gerichtsverkündigung in der späten Königzeit Israels, WMANT 35, 1970
Johnson, A. R., *Vitality*
The Vitality of the Individual in the Thought of Ancient Israel, 1949, ²1964
Johnson, E., "ānap'
"anap', *ThWAT* I/3–4, 1971, cols. 378–89
Jüngel, E., 'Grenzen'
'Grenzen des Menschseins', *PbTh*, pp. 199–205
Jüngel, E., 'keine Menschenlosigkeit'
'. . . keine Menschenlosigkeit Gottes . . . Zur Theologie Karl Barths zwischen Theismus und Atheismus', *EvTh* 31, 1971, pp. 376–90
Jüngel, E., *Tod*
Tod, Themen der Theologie 8, 1971

Kees, H., 'Pyramidentexte'
'Pyramidentexte, Sargtexte und Totenbuch', *HdO* I.I.2, Ägyptologie: Literatur, ²1970, pp. 52–68
Keller, C. A., 'Das quietistische Element'
'Das quietistische Element in der Botschaft des Jesaja', *ThZ* 11, 1955, pp. 81–97
Koch, K., 'Blut'
'Der Spruch "Sein Blut bleibe auf seinem Haupt" und die israelitische Auffassung vom vergossenen Blut', *VT* 12, 1962, pp. 396–416=K. Koch (ed.), *Vergeltung*, pp. 432–56
Koch, K. (ed.), *Vergeltung*
Um das Prinzip der Vergeltung in Religion und Recht des Alten Testaments, WF 125, 1972
Koch, K., 'Vergeltungsdogma'
'Gibt es ein Vergeltungsdogma im Alten Testament?', *ZThK* 52, 1955, pp. 1–42=*Vergeltung*, pp. 130–80
Koeberle, J., *Natur und Geist*
Natur und Geist nach der Auffassung des Alten Testaments, 1901
Köhler, L., *Mensch*
Der hebräische Mensch, 1953; ET, *Hebrew Man*, 1956 (reissued 1973)
Kraus, H. J., 'Erziehung'
'Geschichte als Erziehung', *PbTh*, pp. 258–74=*Biblisch-theologische Aufsätze*, 1972, pp. 66–83
Kraus, H. J., 'Gott'
'Der lebendige Gott', *EvTh* 27, 1967, pp. 169–200=*Biblisch-theologische Aufsätze*, 1972, pp. 1–36

262   *Bibliography*

Kraus, H. J., *Psalmen*
    Psalmen, BK XV, ³1966
Kraus, H. J., *Threni*
    Threni, BK XX, ³1968
Kühlewein, J., "*ēm*'
    "*ēm*, Mutter', *ThHAT* I, 1971, pp. 173–77
Kühlewein, J., "*iššā*'
    "*iššā*, Frau', *ThHAT* I, 1971, pp. 247–51
Kühlewein, J., '*bēn*'
    '*bēn*, Sohn', *ThHAT* I, 1971, pp. 316–25
Kümmel, W. F., 'Melancholie'
    'Melancholie und der Macht der Musik. Die Krankheit König Sauls in der
    historischen Diskussion', *Medizinhistorisches Journal* (Hildesheim) 4, 1969,
    pp. 189–209
Kutsch, E., *Salbung*
    Salbung als Rechtsakt, BZAW 87, 1963
Kutsch, E., 'Sehen'
    'Sehen und Bestimmen. Die Etymologie von *bᵉrīt*', *Archäologie und Altes
    Testament. Festschrift K. Galling*, 1970, pp. 165–78
Kutsch, E., *Verheissung*
    Verheissung und Gesetz, BZAW 131, 1973

Landsberger, B., *Eigenbegrifflichkeit*
    Die Eigenbegrifflichkeit der babylonischen Welt, 1965
Liedke, G., "*zōen*'
    "*zōen*, Ohr', *ThHAT* I, 1971, pp. 95–98
Liedke, G., *Rechtssätze*
    Gestalt und Bezeichnung alttestamentlicher Rechtssätze, WMANT 39, 1971
Löw, L., *Lebensalter*
    Die Lebensalter in der jüdischen Literatur, Beiträge zur jüdischen Altertums-
    kunde 2, 1875.
Lohfink, N., 'Sicherung'
    'Die Sicherung der Wirksamkeit des Gotteswortes durch das Prinzip der
    Schriftlichkeit der Tora und durch das Prinzip der Gewaltenteilung nach den
    Ämtergesetzen des Buches Deuteronomium', *Testimonium Veritati. Festschrift
    W. Kempf*, Frankfurter Theologische Studien 7, 1971, pp. 143–55
Lohse, E., '*sabbaton*'
    '*sabbaton*', *ThWNT* VII, 1964, pp. 1–35; ET, *TDNT* VII, 1971, pp. 1–35
Loretz, O., *Gottebenbildlichkeit*
    Die Gottebenbildlichkeit des Menschen, 1967
Loretz, O., 'Mensch'
    'Der Mensch als Ebenbild Gottes', *Anima* 19, 1964, pp. 109–20=L. Scheffczyk
    (ed.), *Mensch*, pp. 114–30
Lys, D., *bāśār*
    La chair dans l'Ancien Testament. 'bāśār', 1967
Lys, D., *Nèphèsh*
    *Nèphèsh. Histoire de l'âme dans la révélation d'Israel au sein des religions proche-
    orientales*, EHPhR 50, 1959

Lys, D., *Rūach*
Rūach. Le souffle dans l'Ancien Testament, EHPhR 56, 1962

Maag, V., 'Tod'
'Tod und Jenseits nach dem Alten Testament', *SThU* 1964, pp. 17–37
Maass, F., *"ādām"*
"ādām", *ThWAT* I/1, 1970, cols. 81–94
Maass, F., *"ᵉnōs"*
"ᵉnōs", *ThWAT* I/3, 1971, cols. 373–75
Maass, F., 'Selbstliebe'
'Die Selbstliebe nach Leviticus 19,18', *Erlanger Forschungen* A 10, *Festschrift F. Baumgärtel*, 1959, pp. 109–13
Macholz, G. C., 'Gerichtsverfassung'
'Die Stellung des Königs in der israelitischen Gerichtsverfassung', *ZAW* 84, 1972, pp. 157–82
Meulenaere, H. de, 'Ärzteschule'
'Ärzteschule', *LÄ* I, 1972, pp. 79f.
Meyenfeldt, F. H. von, *Hart*
Het Hart (leb, lebab) in het Oude Testament, 1950
Moltmann, J., *Freigelassene*
Die ersten Freigelassenen der Schöpfung, Kaiser Traktate 2, 1971; ET, *Theology of Joy*, 1973
Moltmann, J., *Mensch*
Mensch. Christliche Anthropologie in der Konflikten der Gegenwart, Themen der Theologie 11, 1971; ET, *Man. Christian Anthropology in the Conflict of the Present*, 1974
Moltmann, J., 'Zukunft'
'Hoffnung und die biomedizinische Zukunft des Menschen', *EvTh* 32, 1972, pp. 309–26
Morenz, S., 'Kohlen'
'Feurige Kohlen auf dem Haupt', *ThLZ* 78, 1953, cols. 187–92
Morenz, S., *Religion*
Ägyptische Religion. Die Religionen der Menschheit 8, 1960
Morris, L., 'Blood'
'The Biblical Use of the Term "Blood"', *JTS* NS 3, 1952, pp. 216–27; ibid., 6, 1955, pp. 77–82
Müller-Schwefe, H. R., *Mensch*
Der Mensch das Experiment Gottes, 1966
Muilenburg, J., 'Time'
'The Biblical View of Time', *HTR* 54, 1961, pp. 225–71
Murtonen, A., *Soul*
The Living Soul. A Study of the Meaning of the Word naefaeš in the Old Testament Hebrew Language, StudOr XXIII/1, 1958

Nembach, U., 'Ehescheidung'
'Ehescheidung nach alttestamentlichem und jüdischem Recht', *ThZ* 26, 1970, pp. 161–71
Neufeld, E., 'Hygiene'
'Hygiene Conditions in Ancient Israel', *BA* 34, 1971, pp. 42–66

Noth, M., *Exod.*
    Das zweite Buch Mose. Exodus, ATD 5, ⁴1968; ET of ¹1959, *Exodus* OTL, 1962
Noth, M., *Lev.*
    Das dritte Buch Mose. Leviticus, ATD 6, ²1966; ET of ¹1962, *Leviticus*, OTL, 1965
Noth, M., *Num.*
    Das vierte Buch Mose. Numeri, ATD 7, 1966; ET, *Numbers*, OTL, 1968
Noth, M., 'Bewährung'
    'Die Bewährung von Salomos "göttlicher Weisheit"', *VT* Suppl. 3, 1955, pp.225-37=*GesStud* II, ThB 39, 1969, pp.99-112
Noth, M., BK IX/1
    Könige, BK IX/1, 1968
Noth, M., *GI*
    Geschichte Israels, ⁷1969; ET of ²1954, *History of Israel*, ²1960
Noth, M., 'Richter'
    'Das Amt des "Richters Israels"', *Festschrift A. Bertholet*, 1950, pp.404-17= *GesStud* II, ThB 39, 1969, pp.71-85
Noth, M., *System*
    Das System der zwölf Stämme Israels, BWANT 52, 1930
Noth, M., *ÜP*
    Überlieferungsgeschichte des Pentaeuch, 1948; ET, *A History of Pentateuchal Traditions*, 1972

Oelsner, J., *Körperteile*
    Benennung und Funktion der Körperteile im hebräischen Alten Testament, Diss., 1960
Ohler, A., *Elemente*
    Mythologische Elemente im Alten Testament, 1969
Otto, E., 'Mensch'
    'Der Mensch als Geschöpf und Bild Gottes in Ägypten', *PbTh*, pp.335-48

Pannenberg, W., *Mensch*
    Was ist der Mensch? Die Anthropologie der Gegenwart im Lichte der Theologie, 1962
Pedersen, J., *Israel*
    Israel, its Life and Culture I-II, 1927
Perlitt, L., 'Mose'
    'Mose als Prophet', *EvTh* 31, 1971, pp.588-608
Pidoux, G., *L'Homme*
    L'Homme dans l'Ancien Testament, Cahiers Théologiques 32, 1953
Plessner, H., 'Anthropologie'
    'Anthropologie II. Philosophisch', *RGG³* I, 1957, cols.410-14
Ploeg, J. P. M. van der, 'L'espérance'
    'L'espérance dans l'Ancien Testament', *RB* 61, 1954, pp.481-507
Ploeg, J. P. M. van der, 'Slavery'
    'Slavery in the Old Testament', *VT* Suppl. 22, 1972, pp.72-87
Plöger, J. G., "ᵃdāmā'
    "ᵃdāmā', *ThWAT* I/1, 1970, cols.95-105
Plöger, O., *Daniel*
    Das Buch Daniel, KAT XVIII, 1965

Plöger, O., 'Sentenzensammlungen'
'Zur Auslegung der Sentenzensammlungen des Proverbienbuches', *PbTh*,
pp. 402–16
Preuss, H. D., *Zukunftserwartung*
Jahweglaube und Zukunftserwartung, BWANT 87, 1968

Quell, G., *Tod*
Die Auffassung des Todes in Israel, 1925; reissued 1967

Rad, G. von, *Gen.*
Das erste Buch Mose, Genesis, ATD 2–4 (1949–53), ⁹1972; ET of 1956 ed.,
Genesis, OTL, 1961
Rad, G. von, *Deut.*
Das fünfte Buch Mose. Deuteronomium, ATD 8, ²1968; ET of ¹1964, *Deu-
teronomy*, OTL, 1966
Rad, G. von, 'Christliche Weisheit?'
'Christliche Weisheit?', *EvTh* 31, 1971, pp. 150–54
Rad, G. von, 'Gerechtigkeit'
'"Gerechtigkeit" und "Leben" in der Kultsprache der Psalmen', *Festschrift
A. Bertholet*, 1950, pp. 418–37 = *GesStud*, ThB 8, ⁴1971, pp. 225–47
Rad, G. von, *Gottesvolk*
Das Gottesvolk im Deuteronomium, BWANT 47, 1929
Rad, G. von, 'Naaman'
'Naaman: eine kritische Nacherzählung', *Medicus Viator, Festschrift R. Siebeck*,
1959, pp. 297–305
Rad, G. von, 'Ruhe'
'Es ist noch eine Ruhe vorhanden dem Volke Gottes', *ZdZ* 11, 1933, pp. 104–
11 = *GesStud*, ThB 8, ⁴1971, pp. 101–08; ET, 'There remains still a rest for the
people of God', *The Problem of the Hexateuch and Other Essays*, 1966, pp. 94–
102
Rad, G. von, 'Tag'
'"Der Tag" im AT', *ThWNT* II, 1935, pp. 945–49; ET, '"Day" in the OT',
TDNT II, 1964, pp. 943–47
Rad, G. von, *Theol AT*
Theologie des Alten Testaments I, ⁶1969, II, ⁵1958; ET of ¹1957–60, *Old
Testament Theology* I, 1962, II, 1965
Rad, G. von, *Weisheit*
Weisheit in Israel, 1970; ET, *Wisdom in Israel*, 1972
Ratschow, C. H., 'Zeitproblem'
'Anmerkungen zur theologischen Auffassung des Zeitproblems', *ZThK* 51,
1954, pp. 360–87
Reiser, W., 'Verwandtschaftsformel'
'Die Verwandtschaftsformel in Gen. 2, 23', *ThZ* 16, 1960, pp. 1–4
Reventlow, H. Graf, 'Blut'
'"Sein Blut komme über sein Haupt"', *VT* 10, 1960, pp. 311–27 = K. Koch
(ed.), *Vergeltung*, pp. 412–31
Ridderbos, N. H., *Psalmen*
Die Psalmen, BZAW 117, 1972

Ringgren, H., *'āb'*
"*āb'*, *ThWAT* I/1, 1970, cols.1–19
Ringgren, H., *'āḥ'*
"*āḥ'*, *ThWAT* I/2, 1971, cols.205–10
Ringgren, H., *Sprüche*
Sprüche/W. Zimmerli, *Prediger*. ATD 16/1, 1962, pp.1–122
Rost, L., 'Leberlappen'
'Der Leberlappen', *ZAW* 79, 1967, pp.35–41
Rost, L., *Vorstufen*
Die Vorstufen von Kirche und Synagoge im Alten Testament, BWANT 24, 1938,
reissued 1967
Rudolph, W., *Hosea*
Hosea, KAT XIII/1, 1966
Rudolph, W., KAT XVII/1–3
Das Buch Ruth, Das Hohelied, Die Klagelieder, KAT XIII/1–3, 1962

Saebø, M., *'ḥkm'*
'*ḥkm*, weise sein', *ThHAT* I, 1971, pp.557–67
Scharbert, J., *Fleisch*
Fleisch, Geist und Seele im Pentateuch, Stuttgarter Bibelstudien 19, ²1967
Scharbert, J., *Schmerz*
Der Schmerz im Alten Testament, BBB 8, 1955
Scheepers, J. H., *gees*
Die gees van god en die gees van die mens in die Oud Testament, 1960
Scheffczyk, L. (ed.), *Mensch*
Der Mensch als Bild Gottes, WF 124, 1969
Schmid, H. H., *Weisheit*
Wesen und Geschichte der Weisheit, BZAW 101, 1966
Schmidt, W., 'Begriffe'
'Anthropologische Begriffe im Alten Testament', *EvTh* 24, 1964, pp.374–88
Schmidt, W. H., 'Dekalog'
'Überlieferungsgeschichtliche Erwägungen zur Komposition des Dekalogs',
VT Suppl. 22, 1972, pp.201–20
Schmidt, W. H., *Gebot*
Das erste Gebot, TheolEx 165, 1969
Schmidt, W. H., 'Königtum'
'Kritik am Königtum', *PbTh*, pp.440–61
Schmidt, W. H., *Schöpfungsgeschichte*
Die Schöpfungsgeschichte, WMANT 17, ²1967
Schotroff, W.. *Gedenken*
'Gedenken' *im Alten Orient und im Alten Testament*, WMANT 15, ²1967
Schulz, H., *Todesrecht*
Das Todesrecht im Alten Testament, BZAW 114, 1969
Schweizer, E., Baumgärtel, F., and Meyer, R., *'sarx'*
'*sarx, sarkikos'*, *ThWNT* VII, 1964, pp.98–151; ET, *TDNT* VII, 1971, pp.98–151
Schweizer, E., *'choïkos'*
'choïkos', *ThWNT* IX, 1972, pp.460–68; ET, *TDNT* IX, 1974, pp.472ff.

Schweizer, E., 'Sklavenproblem'
'Zum Sklavenproblem im Neuen Testament', *EvTh* 32, 1972, pp. 502–6
Seidel, H., *Einsamkeit*
Das Erlebnis der Einsamkeit im Alten Testament, Theologische Arbeiten 29, 1969
Sekine, M., 'Zeitauffassung'
'Erwägungen zur hebräischen Zeitauffassung', *VT* Suppl. 9, 1963, pp. 66–82
Seligson, M., *nps mt*
The Meaning of nps mt in the Old Testament, StudOr XV/2, 1951
Seters, J. van, 'Childlessness'
'The Problem of Childlessness in Near Eastern Law and the Patriarchs of Israel', *JBL* 87, 1968, pp. 401–8
Seybold, K., *Gebet*
Das Gebet des Kranken im Alten Testament, BWANT 99, 1973
Seybold, K., 'Krankheit'
'Krankheit und Heilung. Soziale Aspekte in den Psalmen', *BiKi* 20, 1971, pp. 107–11
Skladny, U., *Spruchsammlungen*
Die ältesten Spruchsammlungen in Israel, 1962
Smend, R., 'Amphiktyonie'
'Zur Frage der altisraelitischen Amphiktyonie', *EvTh* 31, 1971, pp. 623–30
Smend, R., *Jahwekrieg*
Jahwekrieg und Stämmebund, FRLANT 84, 1963
Soden, W. von, *AHw*
Akkadisches Handwörterbuch, 1965ff.
Soden, W. von, *GAG*
Grundriss der akkadischen Grammatik, AnOR 33, 1952
Soden, W. von, 'Jahwe'
'Jahwe, "Er ist, Er erweist sich"', *WO* 3, 1966, pp. 176–87
Stamm, J., 'Imago'
'Die Imago Lehre von Karl Barth und die alttestamentliche Wissenschaft', Antwort, Festschrift K. Barth, 1956, pp. 8–98=L. Scheffczyk (ed.), Mensch, pp. 49–68
Steck, O. H., *Elia-Erzählungen*
Überlieferung und Zeitgeschichte in den Elia-Erzählungen, WMANT 26, ·1968
Steck, O. H., *Paradieserzählung*
Die Paradieserzählung. Eine Auslegung von Genesis 2,4b–3,24, BiblStud 60, 1970
Stendebach, F. J., *Mensch*
Der Mensch, wie ihn Israel vor 3000 Jahren sah, 1972
Stoebe, H. J., 'demütig'
'"Und demütig sein von deinem Gott" (Micha 6,8)', *WuD* 6, 1959, pp. 180–94
Stolz, F., 'ḥlh'
'ḥlh, krank sein', *ThHAT* I, 1971, pp. 567–70
Stolz, F., 'lēb'
'lēb, Herz', *ThHAT* I, 1971, pp. 861–67
Strobel, A., 'Masse'
'Masse und Gewichte', *BHHW* II, 1964, cols. 1159–69
Struys, Th., *Ziekte*
Ziekte en genezing in het Oude Testament, 1968

Tsevat, M., 'Sabbath'
'The Basic Meaning of the Biblical Sabbath', *ZAW* 84, 1972, pp. 447–59

Vaux, R. de, *Israel*
Ancient Israel. Its Life and Institutions (ET of *Les Institutions de l'Ancien Testament*, 1958–60), 1961
Vischer, W., 'Nehemia'
'Nehemia, der Sonderbeauftragte und Statthalter des Königs', *PbTh*, pp. 603–10
Vollborn, W., *Zeitverständnis*
Studien zum Zeitverständnis des Alten Testaments, 1951
Vollmer, J., *Rückblicke*
Geschichtliche Rückblicke und Motive in der Prophetie des Amos, Hosea und Jesaja, BZAW 119, 1971
Vriezen, Th. C., 'Hoffnung'
'Die Hoffnung im Alten Testament', *ThLZ* 78, 1953, cols. 577–87
Vriezen, Th. C., 'Liebesgebot'
'Bubers Auslegung des Liebesgebots Lev. 19,18b', *ThZ* 22, 1966, pp. 1–11

Wächter, L., *Tod*
Der Tod im Alten Testament, AzTh II/8, 1967
Wächter, L., *Gemeinschaft*
Gemeinschaft und Einzelner im Judentum, Aufsätze und Vorträge zur Theologie und Religionswissenschaft 16, 1959
Wagner, V., *Rechtssätze*
Rechtssätze in gebundener Sprache und Rechtssatzreihen im israelitischen Recht, BZAW 127, 1972
Wenham, G. J., 'b^etūlāh'
'b^etūlāh, "a girl of marriageable age"', *VT* 22, 1972, pp. 326–48
Wessetzky, V., 'Alter'
'Alter', *LÄ* I, 1972, pp. 154–56
Westermann, C., '*ādām*'
'*ādām*, Mensch', *ThHAT* I, 1971, pp. 41–57
Westermann, C., *Jesaja*
Das Buch Jesaja Kap. 40–66, ATD 19, 1966; ET, *Isaiah* 40–66, OTL, 1969
Westermann, C., BK I
Genesis, BK I, 1966ff.
Westermann, C., *Erträge*
Genesis 1–11, Erträge der Forschung 7, 1972
Westermann, C., 'Heilung'
'Heilung und Heil in der Gemeinde aus der Sicht des Alten Testaments', *Zehntes Seminar für christlichen ärztlichen Dienst* III/Feb. 1971 I–VI
Westermann, C., 'Hoffen'
'Das Hoffen im Alten Testament', *Theologia Viatorum* 4, 1952/53, pp. 19–70 = *Forschung am Alten Testament*, ThB 24, 1964, pp. 219–65
Westermann, C., '*yḥl*'
'*yḥl* piel/hiphil, warten', *ThHAT* I, 1971, pp. 727–30
Westermann, C., '*kbd*'
'*kbd*, schwer sein', *ThHAT* I, 1971, pp. 794–812

Widengren, G., *VT* 4
Review of M. Seligson, *The Meaning of nps mt in the Old Testament*, *VT* 4,
1954, pp. 97–102
Wilch, J. R., *Time*
Time and Event, 1969
Wildberger, H., 'Abbild'
'Das Abbild Gottes', *ThZ* 21, 1965, pp. 245–59, 481–501
Wildberger, H., BK X
Jesaja, BK X/1, 1972
Wolff, H. W., BK XIV/1
Hosea, BK XIV/1, ²1965
Wolff, H. W., BK XIV/2
Joel und Amos, BK XIV/2, 1969
Wolff, H. W., *Frieden*
Frieden ohne Ende, BiblStud 35, 1962
Wolff, H. W., 'Geschichtswerk'
'Das Kerygma des deuteronomistischen Geschichtswerks', *ZAW* 73, 1961,
pp. 171–86=*GesStud*, ThB 22, 1964=²1973, pp. 308–24
Wolff, H. W., 'Jahwe'
'Jahwe und die Götter in der alttestamentlichen Prophetie', *EvTh* 29, 1969,
pp. 397–416=*GesStud*, ThB 22, ²1973, pp. 418–41
Wolff, H. W., 'Jahweglaube'
'Jahweglaube und Selbstverständnis Altisraels', *Wegweisung. Vorträge zum
Bibelverständnis*, 1965, pp. 54–77
Wolff, H. W., 'Jahwist'
'Das Kerygma des Jahwisten', *EvTh* 24, 1964, pp. 73–98=*GesStud*, ThB 22,
1964=²1973, pp. 345–73
Wolff, H. W., 'Volksgemeinde'
'Volksgemeinde und Glaubensgemeinde im Alten Bund', *EvTh* 9, 1949/50,
pp. 65–82
Woude, A. S. van der, '*zᵉrōaʿ*'
'*zᵉrōaʿ*, Arm', *ThHAT* I, 1971, pp. 522–24
Woude, A. S. van der, '*yād*'
'*yād*, Hand', *ThHAT* I, 1971, pp. 667–74
Würthwein, E., 'Psalm 139'
'Erwägungen zu Psalm 139', *VT* 7, 1957, pp. 165–82=*Wort und Existenz.
Studien zum Alten Testament*', 1970, pp. 179–96

Zimmerli, W., BK XIII
Ezechiel, BK XIII, 1969
Zimmerli, W., 'Hoffnung'
'Der Mensch und seine Hoffnung nach den Aussagen des Alten Testaments',
Studia Biblica et Semitica, Festschrift Th.C. Vriezen, 1966, pp. 389–403
Zimmerli, *Hoffnung*
Der Mensch und seine Hoffnung im Alten Testament, VR 272, 1968; ET, *Man
and his Hope in the Old Testament*, SBT, Second Series 20, 1971
Zimmerli, W., *Menschenbild*
Das Menschenbild des Alten Testaments, TheolEx NF 14, 1949

Zimmerli, W., *Prediger*
   Prediger/H. Ringgren, *Sprüche*, ATD 16/1, 1962, pp. 123–53
Zimmerli, W., *Weltlichkeit*
   Die Weltlichkeit des Alten Testaments, VR 327, 1971
Zobel, H. J., *'bādād'*
   'bādād', *ThWAT* I/4–5, 1971/72, cols. 511–18

ABBREVIATIONS

ABL	R. F. Harper, *Assyrian and Babylonian Letters*, 1892–1914
ANET	*Ancient Near Eastern Texts Relating to the Old Testament*, ed. J. B. Pritchard, ³1969
AnOr	Analecta Orientalia (Rome)
AOT	H. Gressmann, *Altorientalische Texte zum Alten Testament*, ²1926
AP	R. H. Charles, *Apocrypha and Pseudepigrapha of the Old Testament*, 1913
ATD	Das Alte Testament Deutsch
AThANT	Abhandlungen zur Theologie des Alten und Neuen Testaments
AzTh	Arbeiten zur Theologie
BA	*The Biblical Archaeologist*
BAL	Berichte über die Verhandlungen der Sächsischen Akademie der Wissenschaften zu Leipzig
BBB	Bonner biblische Beiträge
BHHW	*Biblisch-Historisches Handwörterbuch*, ed. B. Reicke and L. Rost, 1966
BHK	Biblia Hebraica,³ ed. R. Kittel
BHS	Biblia Hebraica Stuttgartensia, ed. K. Elliger and W. Rudolph
BiblStud	Biblische Studien (Neukirchen)
BiKi	*Bibel und Kirche*
BK	Biblischer Kommentar (Neukirchen)
BWANT	Beiträge zur Wissenschaft vom Alten und Neuen Testament
BZAW	Beihefte zur *Zeitschrift für die alttestamentliche Wissenschaft*
CBQ	*Catholic Biblical Quarterly*
EHPhR	Etudes d'Histoire et de Philosophie Religieuse
ET	English translation
EvKomm	Evangelische Kommentar
EvTh	*Evangelische Theologie*
EVV	English versions
FRLANT	Forschungen zur Religion und Literatur des Alten und Neuen Testaments
GesStud	*Gesammelte Studien zum Alten Testament*
GPM	*Göttinger Predigtmeditationen*
HAT	Handbuch zum Alten Testament, ed. O. Eissfeldt
HdO	Handbuch der Orientalistik, ed. B. Spuler
HTR	*Harvard Theological Review*
JBL	*Journal of Biblical Literature*
JTS	*Journal of Theological Studies*
KAT	Kommentar zum Alten Testament (Gütersloh)
KBL	L. Koehler and W. Baumgartner, *Lexicon in Veteris Testamenti Libros*, 1953; ³1967ff.

LÄ	*Lexikon der Ägyptologie*, ed. W. Helck and E. Otto, 1972ff.
LXX	Septuagint
MVAG	Mitteilungen der Vorderasiatischen Gesellschaft
NF	Neue Folge
NS	New Series
OTL	Old Testament Library
OTS	*Oudtestamentische Studiën*
PbTh	*Probleme biblischer Theologie. Gerhard von Rad zum 70. Geburtstag*, ed. H. W. Wolff, 1971
RB	*Revue Biblique*
RGG[3]	*Die Religion in Geschichte und Gegenwart*, ed. K. Galling, [3]1957–65
RHPhR	*Revue d'Histoire et de Philosophie Religieuses*
RLA	*Reallexikon der Assyriologie*, ed. E. Ebeling and B. Meissner, 1932ff.
SBT	Studies in Biblical Theology
SThU	*Schweizerische Theologische Umschau*
StudOr	Studia Orientalia, ed. Societas Orientalis Fennica
TDNT	*Theological Dictionary of the New Testament* (ET of *ThWNT*)
ThB	Theologische Bücherei
TheolEx	Theologische Existenz heute
ThHAT	*Theologisches Handwörterbuch zum Alten Testament*, ed. E. Jenni and C. Westermann
ThLZ	*Theologische Literaturzeitung*
ThSt Zürich	Theologische Studien, ed. K. Barth (Zürich)
ThWAT	*Theologisches Wörterbuch zum Alten Testament*, ed. G. Botterweck and H. Ringgren (ET in preparation)
ThWNT	*Theologisches Wörterbuch zum Neuen Testament*, ed. G. Kittel
ThZ	*Theologische Zeitschrift* (Basel)
VR	Kleine Vandenhoeck-Reihe (Vandenhoeck & Ruprecht)
VT	*Vetus Testamentum*
WF	Wege der Forschung
WMANT	Wissenschaftliche Monographien zum Alten und Neuen Testament
WO	Die Welt des Orients, ed. E. Michel, M. Noth and W. von Soden
WuD	*Wort und Dienst* (Jahrbuch der Theologischen Schule Bethel)
ZAW	*Zeitschrift für die alttestamentliche Wissenschaft*
ZdZ	*Zwischen den Zeiten*
ZThK	*Zeitschrift für Theologie und Kirche*

INDEX OF HEBREW WORDS

INDEX OF SUBJECTS

INDEX OF BIBLICAL REFERENCES

(complete for the text, select for the notes)